Loyola University Chicago
Family Business Center
820 North Michigan Avenue
Chicago, IL 60611-2196

UNLEASH THE
ENTREPRENEUR
WITHIN

UNLEASH THE ENTREPRENEUR WITHIN

How to Make *Everyone* an Entrepreneur and *Stay* Efficient

Mitch McCrimmon

PITMAN
PUBLISHING

PITMAN PUBLISHING
128 Long Acre, London WC2E 9AN

A Division of Pearson Professional Limited

First published in Great Britain 1995

British Library Cataloguing in Publication Data
A CIP catalogue record for this book can be obtained
from the British Library.

ISBN 0 273 61456 8

3 5 7 9 10 8 6 4 2

Typeset by Northern Phototypesetting Co. Ltd., Bolton
Printed and bound in Great Britain by
Biddles Ltd, Guildford and King's Lynn

The Publishers' policy is to use paper manufactured
from sustainable forests.

CONTENTS

ACKNOWLEDGEMENTS

I wish to acknowledge with thanks permission granted to include material in a number of chapters which has been published elsewhere:

1. The British Psychological Association. Part of Chapter 3 includes material from 'After Competencies, Then What?' published in *Selection and Development Review*, Volume 11, Number 1, February 1995. Part of Chapter 9 includes material from 'Assessing and Selecting Employees as Suppliers', also published in *Selection and Development Review*, Volume 10, Number 3, June 1994.

2. MCB Press. Part of Chapter 4 includes material from 'Bottom up Leadership', forthcoming in *Executive Development*. Chapter 5 contains material from an article entitled 'What Has Your Organization Learned today?', published in *Leadership and Organization Development Journal*, Volume 16, Number 1, 1995. An article forthcoming in the *Journal of Management Development* entitled 'Teams Without Roles' is included in a modified form in Chapter 11.

3. Martin Leach Publishing. Chapter 11 also includes an article published in *Human Resources*, January 1995, entitled 'Teamwork or Herd Instinct'.

INTRODUCTION

Organizations are under pressure as never before to adapt ever more quickly to markets that threaten to leave behind all but the most fleet of foot. Essentially this means that large businesses need to learn how to operate more like small entrepreneurial firms and less like cumbersome bureaucracies.

At the same time, large organizations need to capture the benefits of efficiency. Bureaucracy does have a positive side to it so long as it is not taken to extremes. The reason efficiency is important is that all organizations have two fundamental and distinct tasks: 1) they need to provide efficient *delivery* of existing products or services, and 2) they need to undertake continuous *self-renewal*. The challenge facing organizations, therefore, is how to retain the culture of efficiency, cost effectiveness and quality while marrying it to a more entrepreneurial culture, however diametrically opposite in character such a partner might be. The bandwagon effect and the inevitably associated hype surrounding the drive to become more entrepreneurial could easily lead us to overlook the more mundane task of keeping today's business ticking over profitably. Full attention must be paid to both tasks. They are equally vital.

> **The bandwagon effect and the inevitably associated hype surrounding the drive to become more entrepreneurial could easily lead us to overlook the more mundane task of keeping today's business ticking over profitably. Full attention must be paid to both tasks. They are equally vital.**

NEW METAPHORS FOR ORGANIZATION DEVELOPMENT

This book explores what it means for a large organization to be simultaneously entrepreneurial and efficient. New metaphors for envisaging organizations are developed to enable us to imagine how such an unlikely combination of disparate traits might live at all congenially under the same roof.

When we say 'welcome on board' to new recruits we are thinking of our firm as a *ship* and so it makes sense to think of it heading in a well-defined, clear direction. This metaphor was workable enough 30 or 40 years ago when the ongoing, efficient delivery of existing products or services was all that was necessary to be successful. We also sometimes think of an organization as a *person* – this metaphor makes sense of the idea of organization development. We are thinking in these terms when we refer to a young entrepreneurial business as *immature* and describe the various stages it must go through to achieve 'adult' maturity.

Sometimes we think of an organization as if it were an evolving *species*, competing with other species in an evolutionary (market) ecology. This metaphor has the advantage of making us think of the firm's external relations with competitive opponents, but it is still not possible immediately to visualize how such an organization can be both efficient and entrepreneurial. Perhaps this is just because the time-scale of species evolution is too long.

A similar metaphor with a shorter time-scale has us visualizing the organization as a *family dynasty*. This metaphor fits the increasing trend toward the corporate body (parent) starting up or acquiring entrepreneurial offspring. It also fits with the move towards greater empowerment of leading-edge knowledge workers (children) to take independent action to develop and introduce new products – hence fuelling self-renewal.

This metaphor also makes it easy to imagine how the corporate body might focus more on the efficient delivery of existing products while letting its entrepreneurial offspring get on with building the new businesses on which tomorrow's prosperity will depend.

DELIVERING TODAY'S BUSINESS WHILE CREATING THE FUTURE

Part of the thesis of this book is that there are two fundamentally distinct organizational tasks: *the efficient delivery of ongoing services or products,* and *self-renewal* (which is an entrepreneurial activity). A second argument offered here is that there is a wide range of industries which differ precisely in terms of the extent to which they need to emphasize delivery versus entrepreneurial self-renewal. This differentiation is a function of the rate of change imposed on them by how rapidly their particular market is evolving. However, rather than portray slower moving industries as being in a static backwater where they can be safely left to muddle along on their own, it is possible to see them as needing to learn from and emulate their faster changing counterparts.

At the leading edge of this continuum are the most rapidly changing industries. They are at the 'leading edge' because the world they will create for us will, over a longer time period, require new services from slower moving industries. For example, the car-rental business may not change as fast as computers and telecommunications, but longer-term, new technologies such as video conferencing, for example, could weaken the market for car-rental firms, or force them into some different business.

Fast changing, leading-edge industries, therefore, will have a long-term impact on slower changing industries. The point of mentioning this hierarchy is that this book is primarily about how to survive in faster changing industries – those industries where your entire product range could become obsolete suddenly so that you are continuously needing to be vigilantly searching for something new to offer – entrepreneurially renewing your offerings.

The ideas presented in this book will certainly be of interest to slower moving industries. Car-rental firms, to continue that example, could begin to launch new entrepreneurial ventures as a hedge against the possibility of their industry dying off – if they had reason to think it might.

SKILLS FOR EFFICIENCY VERSUS THE SKILLS OF CREATIVITY

Focusing then on the entrepreneurial task of large organizations, it is important to explore just how different are the skills required for successful self-renewal versus those necessary for efficient delivery of today's offerings.

Focusing then on the entrepreneurial task of large organizations, it is important to explore just how different are the skills required for successful self-renewal versus those necessary for efficient delivery of today's offerings. Rational managerial skills such as planning, organizing and controlling are more applicable to the delivery function because, like the straightforward task of building a house, we can know in advance and in precise detail what we want to achieve. Conversely, entrepreneurial self-renewal is *open ended*. We cannot know precisely in advance just what new products will or will not sell. We have to be more intuitive and not merely rational. There is a need to take more open-ended, risky and essentially *exploratory* action.

THE DEMISE OF TOP-DOWN LEADERSHIP

It is also critical to develop new conceptions of leadership for the entrepreneurial, self-renewing task of an organization. Top-down leadership is appropriate if you are the captain of a ship and you know precisely where you are going. But the entrepreneurial function needs several independent initiatives to be taken by empowered knowledge workers who are close to the organization's market and at the *leading* edge of their technical speciality. This gives rise to a form of *leadership* that is strictly knowledge based rather than depending on hierarchical position. The upshot of an examination of these different forms of leadership is that the top-down variety may be appropriate for the delivery function while the self-renewal function requires what we might call *bottom-up leadership*.

This argument is simply advancing empowerment one stage further and taking seriously the claim many firms make of being market led. To be fully market led means surely that those inside the organization who are closest to new market developments and to key customers should be seen and developed as *leaders* – not merely as empowered workers.

ORGANIZATIONAL LEARNING AS ENTREPRENEURIAL TRIAL AND ERROR ACTION

Organizational learning is an essential component of entrepreneurial self-renewal. Again, metaphors make a crucial difference to how you think of organizational learning. If you are operating with a picture of a business as a community or other large, somewhat static social group, then you may be led to see organizational learning as knowledge acquisition or personal development on the part of the firm's members. On the other hand, if you are thinking of a dynamic entrepreneurial business interacting with a fast changing environment, then you may be more inclined to envisage organizational learning as being about how the firm adjusts to market feedback.

> **To be fully market led means surely that those inside the organization who are closest to new market developments and to key customers should be seen and developed as *leaders* – not merely as empowered workers.**

On the latter view, learning has to do with introducing new products or modifying existing offerings and adjusting on the basis of feedback – customer reaction to your products. If you see organizational learning in this way, it becomes clear that a firm could adjust rapidly to such feedback by regularly importing new employees who have a fresh perspective. This extreme case shows that such learning on the part of the business as a whole really has nothing necessarily to do with the learning of existing employees. No doubt in practice a combination of employee learning and importing fresh ideas may be ideal, but the fundamental point is that organizational learning is essentially the same process as being entrepreneurial. This is the case because both depend on taking trial and error action in the real world and adjusting on the basis of feedback.

ENTREPRENEURIAL SELF-RENEWAL AS EVOLUTION

At this point we pick up the thread of whether organizational development has anything to learn from evolutionary processes. This theme
also ties in with our earlier discussion of the differing types of skills
that are appropriate for ongoing product/service delivery versus those
which are necessary for self-renewal. The debate over the relevance of
evolutionary processes to understanding how organizations develop
revolves around how much *control* managers can realistically expect to
have over the future of their businesses. The upshot of this discussion
is that control is useful for delivery while managers must learn to
accept the evolutionary force of market *selection* when it comes to the
entrepreneurial self-renewal task.

The only form of control to which managers can aspire over this
aspect of their firm's development is indirect – by understanding the
evolutionary process, they can influence the likely success of their
business in the future. Essentially this means recognizing the critical
role of *variation* as a means of increasing the likelihood that some
products will always be *selected* by the market. Maximum variation,
again, requires multiple independent initiatives on the part of empowered knowledge workers who can show this type of leadership.

At this point we draw together some of the foregoing themes to
argue that being entrepreneurial, cultivating organizational learning
and exploiting the processes of evolutionary variation and selection are
all one and the same process – most simply, trial and error action in the
face of uncertainty. This more open-ended mode of operating is meant
to replace the overly rational practice of planning and deciding – a process that depends on the myth of having precise objectives which are
fully specifiable in advance of acting.

A CULTURE TO STIMULATE ENTREPRENEURIAL
SUCCESS

We then look at the question of what sort of culture should be created
to stimulate entrepreneurial self-renewal. The dangers of so-called
strong cultures are explored – with their tendency to foster uniformity
and sameness of outlook. The desire for a uniform culture is partly a

defensive reaction to uncertainty
in the face of so much business
upheaval of late. It is how any
group behaves in response to a
mortal threat – as, for example,
during a major war. Such a threat
creates a 'we're in this together'
feeling which can be effective in
an immediate crisis but which can

> **The desire for a uniform culture is partly a defensive reaction to uncertainty in the face of so much business upheaval of late.**

also produce a lemming-like degree of group-think which can be
dangerous in the longer term. This is especially true if you accept the
premise that a high level of variation and *diversity* are necessary for
entrepreneurial self-renewal.

As culture seems to take the form of sets of values, we explore the
relationship between values and behaviour to determine what sorts of
value sets might be most conducive to developing a culture that is both
entrepreneurial and efficient.

THE END OF THE CONVENTIONAL EMPLOYMENT RELATIONSHIP

Having discussed issues of organizational dynamics and entrepreneurial processes, we turn to discussing in more detail the human
implications of these projected changes. The role of technical knowledge workers is widely recognized as increasing in importance. It is
essential to look at how their relationships to firms are changing.
Useful metaphors are again explored and the idea of viewing employees as suppliers of services or strategic partners is discussed. Empowerment of leading-edge innovators who increasingly identify with the
role of supplier of services demands a rethink of how such 'employees'
will be 'managed' in the future.

DO SUPPLIERS HAVE CAREERS?

Different conceptions of what it means to have a career are also
explored. The near elimination of the managerial career brings to an
end the exclusive clamouring to ascend the managerial hierarchy. The

advantage of this shift is that knowledge workers can begin to see themselves as having professional careers – much like doctors and lawyers – while the status of managers declines to a level that is not unlike that of hospital administrators. In reality, there will continue to be purely managerial careers for those professionals who specialize in delivery functions such as sales, production, finance or personnel. But they need to make room for non-managerial career streams for their technical colleagues who do not want to feel failures for having spurned a managerial career.

TEAMWORK VERSUS INDIVIDUAL EFFORT

The relative place of individuals and teamwork is looked at with the twin tasks of delivery and self-renewal in mind. Teams can be most useful with respect to delivery due to the obvious need for co-ordinated effort. On the other hand, because of the pressure for conformity which they place on their members, teams may not always be as creative as individuals. What, therefore, is the role of teamwork for entrepreneurial self-renewal? The upshot of this discussion is that both teams and individuals can make entrepreneurial contributions. Teamwork can be most creative, however, if team members circulate widely and frequently.

CREATIVE LEADERSHIP

In light of the foregoing, it can be seen that senior executives have the difficult task of adjusting to a lower status while knowledge workers increase their power to generate the future for their employers/customers. But the best leaders will excel at showing a different kind of leadership – not one of the *content* of future directions. That can only emerge through entrepreneurial trial and error. No, the best leaders will facilitate a massive transfer of power, lay to rest the entrenched power hierarchy and put in place new cultures to support a healthy entrepreneurial enterprise. This will require stronger leadership skills than are shown by the leader who relies on his or her waning technical knowledge to continue to hold on to the myth that top-level executives can provide genuine content direction.

A NOTE ON STYLE

While some of the well-known large corporations that have begun to venture down the entrepreneurial road will be cited as examples, the style of this book is not to overwhelm you with detailed case studies. Nor is it an exercise in hero-worship – as if some businesses had all the answers. There is room to point to what some firms are doing somewhat effectively, but without implying that their managers can walk on water. So, examples are used sparingly. On the whole, even the most admirably entrepreneurial organizations are still in a state of transition. Further, part of what it means to be entrepreneurial is to accept the fact that there is no one best way of achieving this happy state of being. It would be a mistake, from this point of view, therefore, to get too carried away with what any one firm is doing at the moment.

The focus of this book goes beyond exploring possible ways to create a more entrepreneurial organization, it is also an effort to understand *why* organizations are the way they are today and what they must cope with, in human, psychological terms, in order to adapt. Hence each chapter except the last has an aside called 'Psychological slant'. The objective of this approach is to stimulate more in-depth thinking about current trends. Otherwise the sheer pace of events will lead to a greater temptation to jump on every bandwagon or fad that is popular at the moment.

Because the focus of what follows is more on *understanding* than on how to do things, there is a risk of sounding too divorced from practice. To counter this possibility, a balance of theory and practice is sought by including at the end of each chapter – again with the exception of the last – a section entitled 'Practical steps'.

> **The focus of this book goes beyond exploring possible ways to create a more entrepreneurial organization, it is also an effort to understand *why* organizations are the way they are today and what they must cope with, in human, psychological terms, in order to adapt.**

"Overly bureaucratic businesses fail by ignoring the outside world: their managers are too preoccupied internally – with monitoring the slightest deviations from their perfectionist ideals."

"While mature industries tend to compete more on the basis of cost, quality of customer service, it may be precisely the *mature* (read blinkered) mindset of over-familiar managers who are unable to see new product possibilities."

1

RISING ENTREPRENEURIALISM, DYING BUREAUCRACY

All organizations are racing to transform themselves into entrepreneurs. There are few corporate diseases more dreaded today than bureaucracy. Where once bureaucracy stood for efficiency, consistency, reliability and accountability, now it suggests rigidity, lethargy, self-satisfied smugness and the glorification of endless procedures for their own sake, a sort of cancer that can take over any healthy body and destroy it in time.

> **Where once bureaucracy stood for efficiency, consistency, reliability and accountability, now it suggests rigidity, lethargy, self-satisfied smugness and the glorification of endless procedures for their own sake, a sort of cancer that can take over any healthy body and destroy it in time.**

Management theorists of diverse persuasions are grappling with what it means for organizations to become more entrepreneurial, but they are in no doubt that we are in the midst of a profound culture shift. Gifford and Elizabeth Pinchot (1993) have recently devoted a whole book to this theme, *The End of Bureaucracy and the Rise of The Intelligent Organization*. Their well-known and pioneering earlier book, *Intrapreneuring*, advocated stimulating internal entrepreneurs to flourish (Gifford and Elizabeth Pinchot (1985)). In the former, their most recent effort, they rightly point out that 'Bureaucracy demands that reality be divided into neat areas of responsibility, but customer needs and technological possibilities refuse to stay in those divisions, regardless of how cleverly the lines are drawn'.

Despite these valiant efforts, we still have only a vague notion of what it means to be entrepreneurial and whether chasing this holy grail implies that we have to abandon all thought of efficiency and other all-but-forgotten positive attributes of bureaucracy. We know what we like about entrepreneurial businesses. They are exciting places to work. They are dynamic and fast growing. They glorify independence, creativity, improvisation and rebellious opportunism thereby appealing to the child in all of us.

The most successful entrepreneurial firms have a Rambo-like attraction for us with their killer instinct and ability to knock off seemingly invincible goliaths. What greater hero-worship is there in today's business press than the story of an entrepreneurial upstart achieving unheard of growth at the expense of yesterday's heroes? The humiliation of IBM at the hands of Apple Computers and Microsoft is only one of the most recently publicized examples.

> **The most successful entrepreneurial firms have a Rambo-like attraction for us with their killer instinct and ability to knock off seemingly invincible goliaths.**

No sector is immune to today's entrepreneurial trend. Formerly state-owned behemoths are privatized in order to make them more self-reliant. Even public sector bureaucracies are trying to become more responsive to their environment, more adaptable and willing to change. And once worshipped blue-chip heroes are struggling to rediscover their lost growth formula. Unfortunately, many firms seem to start out as small entrepreneurial enterprises only to degenerate into sluggish bureaucracies as they grow and consolidate their hold on their particular market. Thus far it has been very difficult if not impossible to retain the advantages of entrepreneurial smallness with the benefits of size.

It is hard to imagine any organization not claiming it is trying to reduce bureaucracy in order to become more entrepreneurial. To take just one example, the British computer manufacturer, ICL, has been moving in this direction of late, to empower small independent businesses to act more entrepreneurially. Mike Stares (1993), the head of WorkPlace Technologies Ltd., one of ICL's newly devolved businesses, clearly articulates the size of the challenge when he says, 'But how does a large company like ICL, which generated revenue of £2.5 billion in 1992, break free from the shackles of bureaucracy and produce results like a small aggressive company?' ICL has been creating a more entrepreneurial business, according to Stares, by placing 'many of the 14,000 members of staff . . . in subsidiary companies . . . which work under the ICL umbrella but operate at arm's length from the parent company'. Further, 'an entrepreneurial spirit is encouraged and supported by management, who accept that this sometimes involves taking risks. Staff are now rewarded on results not effort'.

Watch out for the bandwagon

But before we all jump on yet another bandwagon, we need to look at the differences between entrepreneurial and bureaucratic organizations. As we shall see, it is critical to avoid losing some of the positive attributes of bureaucratic organizations, i.e. efficiency. The upshot of what follows is that entrepreneurialism and bureaucracy can be seen as two, equally dysfunctional, ends of a continuum: what we really want is a blend of the best aspects of both.

THE ENTREPRENEUR CLASHES WITH THE BUREAUCRAT

From entrepreneurial childhood to adult mature businesses

Because of the typical historical progression from small entrepreneurial business to large bureaucracy, the very meaning of 'entrepreneurial' includes the notion of 'immaturity'. An entrepreneurial firm, in this view, is one that is merely setting out along the road to maturity – much like a child groping towards adulthood. We expect the entrepreneur to be more directionless, creative, unruly and reckless than a mature 'adult' business. The latter is assumed to be orderly, predictable and consistent. Having achieved adulthood, the mature business can settle down, consolidate and maintain a stable adult life.

Just as we like to think of ourselves as immortal, we expect successful businesses to carry on indefinitely 'living happily ever after'.

This comforting picture was shattered when we discovered that mature businesses could decline and die. It has been easy to criticize household name firms such as IBM and General Motors for their inflexibility and bureaucracy but it has been a severe shock to realize that such beacons of seemingly immortal success could not only stumble but even collapse.

The notion of a 'mature' business has, as a result, become something of an anachronism. Maturity in this context now seems to suggest stodginess if not outright senility. The reality is that no business can any longer lose touch with the youthful vigour and creativity that characterize the entrepreneurial business.

Like a child, a young entrepreneurial business is seen as being in a *learning* mode. Now, even mature 'adult' businesses must continue to learn. To stop learning is to develop mental rigor mortis and die.

The jury is still out, however, on whether mature businesses can relearn how to learn and whether those that have already developed arterial sclerosis can somehow rejuvenate themselves.

Part of the reason we are struggling to see just how a mature business can also be forever entrepreneurial is that we have little experience of such an apparent contradiction in terms. We have no comparably familiar metaphors to understand how a mature business could stay in development mode indefinitely. Does this mean never quite growing up? Never achieving any form of stability? Perhaps we need to invent some new metaphors.

On not throwing bureaucracy out with the bath water

In spite of the disrepute the term 'bureaucracy' has fallen into, there is no question that organizations that have some mildly bureaucratic traits are highly successful – just think of McDonald's. It is well organized, dependable and managed cost effectively. It is only when such large businesses become so fixated on procedures as an end in themselves that they overdo these strengths. Paragons of efficiency then become set in their ways and incur too much cost through *excessive* bureaucracy.

Considerable size is unattainable, however, without some structure, some procedures to ensure quality and cost effectiveness. Originally the term 'bureaucracy' simply referred to the positive attributes necessary to manage a large organization efficiently.

As successful as many entrepreneurial firms are, they often fail to reach 'maturity' precisely because they are not bureaucratic enough:

they fail because they are unable to control costs, consolidate advantages and focus their energies on where they can make a profit. Newness pursued for its own sake, regardless of cost or whether customers want the product, can easily become a liability. Many entrepreneurial firms have failed for lack of a minimum of bureaucratic control.

As Rosabeth Moss Kanter (1989) has noted, we need somehow to combine the best of

> As successful as many entrepreneurial firms are, they often fail to reach 'maturity' precisely because they are not bureaucratic enough: they fail because they are unable to control costs, consolidate advantages and focus their energies on where they can make a profit.

entrepreneurialism and bureaucracy while avoiding the chaos of the former and the unresponsiveness of the latter: 'Something new is required, something that marries the entrepreneurial spirit to discipline and teamwork, something that helps loosely managed companies get a little tighter and tightly controlled companies loosen up – a *post-entrepreneurial response.*'

The question is: How do you combine such seemingly irreconcilable cultures? A strong emphasis on efficiency calls for management controls that could drive out all but the most patient entrepreneurial types. Figure 1.1 provides a graphic look at this clash of opposites.

As Figure 1.1 illustrates, a poorly managed entrepreneurial firm can fail by flying out of control, by taking risks that are too poorly thought out and by wasting money unnecessarily. On the other hand, efficiency pursued too religiously and one-sidedly will inevitably strangle initiative and drive the business into a rut. Overly bureaucratic businesses fail by ignoring the outside world: their managers are too preoccupied internally – with monitoring the slightest deviations from their perfectionistic ideals.

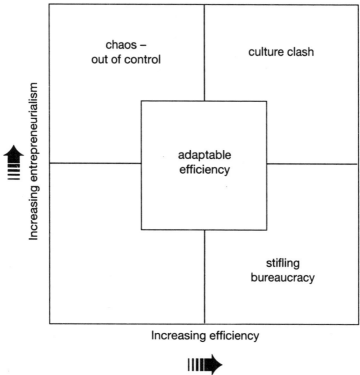

Figure 1.1

A middle way is needed to strike a balance between these two equally fatal extremes – a form of *adaptable efficiency*. What type of organization could mediate between such opposing tendencies? To shed light on this issue, we must examine the two combatants in a bit more detail.

NECESSARY EFFICIENCIES

Routine tasks or operations in slowly changing industries need to be mechanized as much as possible because the survival of such companies generally depends on low cost (among other things). This enables a business to profit from maximum efficiency. Sales organizations are good examples. Although new products may be developed in other parts of the business, the sales team needs to be run efficiently to be cost effective. Selling life insurance and other financial services products, or cosmetics, for example, needs to be managed in a structured manner to minimize cost. There is often very little to differentiate such a firm from its competitors other than cost, service and quality.

Large global sales organizations such as McDonald's and automobile service stations, for instance, thrive on consistency as well as low cost. Part of the definition of quality is the ability to produce the *same* product at all times in all places. Efficient top-down management is required to ensure such consistency. If each McDonald's outlet were allowed to be entrepreneurial, you would not know what to expect from one unit to the next, either in terms of product served or its quality and cost.

Efficiency benefits

- reliability
- cost control
- quality management
- purchasing leverage.
- consistency
- growth manageability
- volume production capability

If you are producing highly engineered components – say, for the aircraft industry – your customer obviously wants them all to be identical within very narrow tolerance limits. High-volume production incurs lower manufacturing costs and you can purchase your materials and sub-components for less by buying in volume.

Taking efficiency to extremes

When we elevate efficiency to an end in itself it dominates the organization too completely. Traits that are otherwise strengths become potentially fatal weaknesses:

- slowness to change
- worker boredom
- excessive procedures
- inflexibility
- unresponsiveness
- stifled innovation.

In his very illuminating book, *The Icarus Paradox*, Danny Miller (1990) showed how organizations can stumble by elevating their strengths to obsessions. He cited, as examples, firms such as Texas Instruments, which were overly cost motivated to the point that they were blind to the need to innovate and be more entrepreneurial. He also illustrated the dangers of being too dominated by an entrepreneurial culture and unable to take advantage of the desirable side of bureaucracy.

CELEBRATING YOUTH AND ENTREPRENEURIALISM

> **Success for larger organizations is now equated with the ability to adapt quickly and improvise.**

Clearly, businesses can no longer content themselves with developing a mature line of products and resting on their laurels. Not so long ago a successful business could, once established, continue to grow by expanding into new markets and making small refinements in existing products. Change is simply too rapid today for any firm to rest content with existing products, no matter how well they may sell in their heyday. This fact of life, however painful, is the prime mover of the drive towards entrepreneurialism.

Driving forces behind the entrepreneurial movement

- Unavoidable evidence that newer firms are overtaking and slaughtering older-established organizations.
- The pace of change in many industries is driven by rapid new product innovation – generally the province of the entrepreneur.
- Success for larger organizations is now equated with the ability to adapt quickly and improvise.
- A growing sense that mere consistency, reliability and efficiency now indicate a lack of imagination rather than permanence or excellence.

The need to become more entrepreneurial is clouded by the fact that many firms are stumbling (in the short term) mainly because of excessive costs and poor quality. The remedy here is simply to produce better products more cost effectively, and this solution is still understandably the most immediate priority of many firms and indeed whole industries.

Much profitability improvement can be achieved by these means, but cost cutting and quality improvement should be seen as just getting in shape for the fight – not as the battle itself. Getting in shape, while a necessary preliminary, is merely a defensive ploy if nothing else is done. The real battle revolves around who can best excite and win new customers with innovative new products. Quality enhancements are deceptive; they yield short-term gains and create a false sense of security. The reality is that no one wants yesterday's product no matter how well built it is or how cheaply it can be purchased.

In faster changing markets, such as those faced by consumer products businesses, it is especially obvious that strong quality and cost competitiveness are hardly even the beginning. Survival in these industries depends on continuous innovation not only to improve existing offerings but to devise wholly new, hitherto undreamed of, products.

In this context, being entrepreneurial is identical with having the ability to create desirable new products which astonish customers and leave competitors flat-footed.

Two examples of firms that are striving to become more entrepreneurial in the sense of increasing the rate of innovation are Hoechst Celanese and Xerox. In the former case, R&D employees are encouraged to develop new product ideas as product champions and to team up with a colleague who has stronger business skills so that entrepreneurialism and efficiency achieve the right balance. This 'initiative, which has been in place for four years, has sparked dozens of new ventures including biodegradable packaging, tools for fibre manufacturing and an employee development programme', according to Tom Kiely (1994). It is also acknowledged by Hoechst Celanese that the approval process it expects budding entrepreneurs to go through may still be too bureaucratic because 'inventors spend an inordinate amount of time drawing up business plans, writing proposals for funding, making presentations and writing memos'.

Xerox began stimulating entrepreneurial new ventures, according to Kiely, in part to stem the loss of employees who had to leave the

> **In this context, being entrepreneurial is identical with having the ability to create desirable new products which astonish customers and leave competitors flat-footed.**

company to start up new ventures. Xerox gives teams of entrepreneurs the freedom to set up new venture companies within the larger corporation.

Rubbermaid is another example of a business that places a very high premium on new product generation. While its products are quite mundane, Rubbermaid is obviously doing a lot right: it has just been named the most admired company in the United States for the second year in a row in Fortune magazine's annual contest. One new product introduced every day, 365 days of the year may be a hard number to beat, but the emphasis can be emulated. Innovation stems from teamwork at Rubbermaid: 'each team is made up of five to seven people (one each from marketing, manufacturing, R&D, finance and other departments).' The culture at Rubbermaid encourages all employees to be on a constant look-out for new product ideas.

While mature industries tend to compete more on the basis of cost, quality of customer service, it may be precisely the *mature* (read blinkered) mindset of over-familiar managers who are unable to see new product possibilities.

> **While mature industries tend to compete more on the basis of cost, quality of customer service, it may be precisely the *mature* (read blinkered) mindset of over-familiar managers who are unable to see new product possibilities.**

The automobile industry illustrates the deceptive benefits of preoccupation with quality and cost control. Competitiveness in this industry revolves around giving customers the level of quality they want at the right price. Innovation in car components may help, as does fashionable styling, but no one has as yet come up with anything so revolutionary as a solar-powered car, or one that can fly. Or some means to whisk us from A to B in a mind-boggling science fiction manner. There is, however, certainly recognition in the car industry that innovation is necessary, but it is taking the form of such things as software applications to improve the driver's control over the journey rather than startling new forms of transportation.

After years of unresponsiveness and decline, General Motors is suddenly raising itself off its death bed, but it is not doing so primarily by being more entrepreneurial. Its new chief executive is heralded as a wonder worker and saviour by reorganizing the business to improve quality, reduce costs and generate better teamwork. In his modest way, however, he acknowledges that this is just to stop the bleeding. It is not yet clear, therefore, just how entrepreneurial General Motors will become in its quest to regain the dominant position it once enjoyed in its industry.

In all likelihood, however, *process* improvements such as those initiated by General Motors are no more than a sort of qualifying school which will merely provide a ticket to compete in the big-league tournament. As difficult as it is to whip an elephant as huge as General Motors into shape, its longer-term competitive success will depend on its ability to be much more innovative in its product offerings – hence entrepreneurial.

What is an entrepreneur anyway?

Just what does it mean to be entrepreneurial? Is it precisely the ability to introduce great selling new products? The conventional one-man band entrepreneur is essentially identified by the willingness to take risks in order to seize a market opportunity. He or she may do so not by introducing a novel product or service but by copying what someone else has succeeded in doing in another location. An example might be opening doughnut shops in one part of the country that has none – after seeing their success elsewhere.

Another example might involve beating potential competitors in seizing an opportunity to supply needed components to a newly opened manufacturing plant nearby. Such an act is more likely to be described as entrepreneurial if it is initiated by a one-man band than if it is simply a repeat performance by a large established organization that already supplies this particular manufacturer with the same component elsewhere.

We don't describe the latter as entrepreneurial because we are not astonished by the big supplier's boldness, its daring risk taking, its creativity or its willingness to lose a large amount of money on what seems to others to be a gamble. So the same act by different sized actors can be perceived as entrepreneurial in one case and merely an extension of existing business in another. Even the doughnut entrepreneur cited above is not likely to generate as much awe as one who introduces a previously unheard of product or service.

But what is wrong with being a copy-cat entrepreneur if the bottom line is highly profitable? There is a widely held view that being both entrepreneurial and a leader in your industry is just too risky and unjustifiable on cost-benefit terms. The argument here is that it is better to let others take the high risks and follow in behind with a product that is just as good, or even better, once the market is seen to be definitely there. This stance conjures up images of vultures waiting for the lions to eat their fill before swooping down for leftovers.

> **A bold entrepreneurial leading firm has charisma. It attracts free advertising in the form of media attention. The interest of potential investors and the brightest employee candidates are also aroused.**

Ultimately, this view is short term. Organizations that depend for their competitive success on their ability to attract the best knowledge workers are taking a bigger risk in not striving for leadership. How stretched will the best knowledge workers be in a copy-cat organization? They will be more motivated by striving to lead, just as any sports person or team does in competitive sport.

This suggests that being entrepreneurial has something to do with showing leadership, that it is not just synonymous with crass opportunism – i.e. making a killing on the stock market. A bold entrepreneurial leading firm has charisma. It attracts free advertising in the form of media attention. The interest of potential investors and the brightest employee candidates is also aroused.

Entrepreneurial characteristics

- Innovation: constant striving to develop new products or services.
- Risk taking: willingness to take risks in as yet unestablished markets.
- Leadership: striving to be the first to introduce the amazingly novel.
- Improvisation: willingness to act without plans worked out to the nth degree in advance and to improvise as necessary.
- Flexibility: the ability to shift direction quickly as circumstances change.

● Learning: the willingness to tolerate mistakes and learn from them.

Advantages of being an entrepreneurial leader

● inspiration and retention of leading-edge knowledge workers
● the capability to occasionally leave copy-cats significantly behind
● the potential to create patentable new products to shut out copy-cats
● speed, in itself, is increasingly becoming a major competitive advantage
● media attention – free advertising.

Your business may do quite well by leading in some areas and following in others, but if you are at least keeping up, chances are you are less bureaucratic than firms such as IBM were when they took so long to get into the PC market. The question remains of how to avoid bureaucracy sufficiently to make it at least to copy-cat entrepreneur status.

The classic example of a business that attributes much of its success to entrepreneurial freedom and new product introduction is, of course, 3M, but even it has recently recognized that it still has further to go. Now it is pushing for the achievement of 30 per cent of sales each year through new products developed within the last four years. The old target of 25 per cent from products introduced in the last five years was deemed to place just not enough emphasis on a high rate of innovation for future business prosperity.

BUREAUCRACY IS NOT INEVITABLE

Danny Miller (1994) has given us a good explanation of why it is so difficult for the same organization to be simultaneously small, flexible and entrepreneurial, while also being big, efficient and cost-effectively managed. The two seemingly opposed cultures tend to be dominated by strong leaders, who, like all other human beings, are good at only one thing or at best a small number of things. Texas Instruments was dominated by engineers who over-valued cost effectiveness. They could understandably not be simultaneously cost focused and risk orientated. It is clearly very difficult for one person to have totally opposite personality traits.

It is also clear that one of the problems of trying to lead a large organization is that unless you have extremely unequivocal views about how things should be done, then you will be unable to get such a large group of people all moving in the same direction. It is like an actor having to perform in a football stadium without a microphone as opposed to acting in a small back-room theatre. In the vast arena you need to shout louder to be heard and to make any kind of impact. Loudness is akin to certainty just as vacillation goes hand in hand with soft-spokeness.

This means that if a large organization, as an hierarchy – read football stadium – is to be led by one person at the top and if it is to pursue a clear, unequivocal direction, then the leader has to very forcefully articulate an exaggerated, single-minded vision in order to get everyone moving in the same direction.

While such an unequivocal one-track direction is not identical with bureaucracy it tends to engender excessive controls to keep everyone on the straight and narrow.

The seductive power of bureaucracy

It is easy to be seduced by small, short-term savings achieved by refining procedures to increase efficiency. The founder of an entrepreneurial business will generally run out of new ideas at some point and have nothing left to expend his abundant energy on unless it is to *refine* what he has already got. *Refinement* of the total organization means greater and greater efficiency to squeeze more and more profit out of the same cash cow.

But why is excessive bureaucracy so apparently unavoidable? What are the factors that lead to bureaucracy?

- size – bigness is harder to manage: once small mistakes become costly
- internal complexity, also a function of size, increases internal focus
- growth means more to protect – hence worry over mistakes or losses
- going public and being run by professional managers means greater accountability to owners and more risk aversion
- bigger firms are more visible – as are their mistakes – hence greater

    vigilance lest those in the limelight appear foolish – a very real fear for hired managers whose careers depend on an owner-boss's whim
- size, again, leads to more errors and greater demands for consistency
- more staff means more stakeholders and slower decision making
- inevitable ageing of founders brings about increased caution
- it is easiest to focus on the immediate, i.e. problems, and to strive to eliminate them permanently – this leads to bureaucracy
- success encourages us to repeat what led to success in the past rather than try something new – we are left with *refining* what we are already good at and refinement can become bureaucracy.

This last point is demonstrated by the now well-known saying, 'nothing breeds failure like success'. So it is a combination of success repeated and refined until it becomes routine and the fact that as we run out of new product ideas we turn our energies to consolidation, to getting more mileage out of what we are already selling. Add to this the pressure of fear of criticism that comes from higher visibility as a business grows and you have a pretty good recipe for creating a bureaucratic organization. (See Psychological slant.)

There are obvious limits to our ability to think young while our age creeps inexorably upwards. The tendency to conserve energy as we age inclines us to seek routine in at least some parts of our lives. No matter how much the older person likes variety and is stimulated by change – the brain is like a computer – at least in so far as it stores and uses the 'software programs' we pick up through experience. Such programs will determine not only how we think but even what we see and what we are blind to.

So, however helpful it may be for older managers to push themselves to stay close to the front line of their business and to take creativity courses – this is only slightly prolonging the inevitable – no matter how unwilling we may be to face it. The more useful solution must be to combine – *in different people* – the advantages of maturity (and all that maturity implies) with the benefits of youthful curiosity, openness and experimentation.

This does not mean that there is no use for the older manager or worker, or even that no older people are creative – it is only that their function should be different, speaking in general terms. It is simply macho pride that prevents ageing managers – especially men – from admitting that certain of their youthful powers are declining.

PSYCHOLOGICAL SLANT

What is the connection between youth – entrepreneurialism and age – and bureaucracy?

The older we get the more we feel threatened by the exuberance of youth – we turn inwards and seem to need to conserve energy – hence we focus on eliminating error. This gives rise to bureaucracy. What we once saw as boldness in our younger days we now see as foolishness. Yet younger organizations are overtaking and defeating their older counterparts. We either have to find a way to continue to think young or form an alliance of sorts with the creativity of youth.

Having your cake and eating it too

So how can an organization be efficiently managed without becoming stodgily bureaucratic, on the one hand, and entrepreneurial but not too reckless and out of control, on the other? There are different ways in which an organization can be entrepreneurial and bureaucratic at the same time:

- the whole organization could, in some sense, simultaneously be both
- different individuals could look after these two functions
- these tasks could be assigned to different parts of the organization
- an organization could swing pendulum-like from one stage to another alternating between loosening up and tightening up over time.

Most advocates of a marriage of entrepreneurialism and efficiency seem to suggest that the *whole* organization could somehow exhibit these opposing traits simultaneously – however counterintuitive this seems, implying dual cultures with no uniform or singular dominating vision. This is almost as hard to visualize as thinking of a person with diametrically opposed personality traits. We have thus far been given little guidance on what such a hybrid or schizophrenic organization might look like.

The next chapter will raise the question: What organizational tasks are the values of efficiency and entrepreneurial adaptability meant to address? We will also explore how these values might be combined and what form of organization might comfortably accommodate them both.

PRACTICAL STEPS

Focusing the strengths of bureaucrats:
- modify the bureaucrat's obsession for *universal* application of rules
- clearly differentiate parts of the business requiring efficiency
- focus procedures on areas of the business where efficiency counts
- re-engineer processes mainly where cost is the major driver
- value the properly applied strengths of efficiency experts
- encourage networking in place of top-down control.

Nourishing entrepreneurs:
- tolerate much looser behaviour in entrepreneurial parts of the firm
- let your entrepreneurs make new product or service decisions
- celebrate mistakes and risk taking in new ventures
- help efficient staff and risk takers work together productively
- encourage external focus – more contact with customers
- stimulate continual experimentation.

"The key is how to achieve a workable union of entrepreneurial vitality, for the sake of tomorrow, while maintaining efficient delivery today."

"As organizations move towards a separation of the delivery task from self-renewal along the lines of the family dynasty metaphor, senior executives should assume a role not unlike that of the venture capitalist."

2

THE SELF-RENEWING ENTREPRENEUR

In the last chapter we explored the challenges facing organizations striving to rise above the risks of the entrepreneurial fast lane without suffering the fate of bureaucratic excess. How can General Motors and IBM, for example, preserve a high degree of profitable efficiency while avoiding stifling bureaucracy, on the one hand, and become more entrepreneurial without risking huge losses, on the other?

SELF-RENEWAL OR DELIVERING TODAY'S BUSINESS?

Some light can be shed on this dilemma by asking what purpose efficiency is intended to serve and why, at the same time, it is so imperative to be entrepreneurial. When we raise the question of what organizations are striving to achieve, it becomes clear that these two modes of operating serve two quite different purposes, as shown in Figure 2.1.

Organizational survival depends on the successful execution of two fundamental tasks:

- delivery of existing products or services
- self-renewal.

Most importantly:

- effective delivery depends on efficiency
- self-renewal is an entrepreneurial activity.

Figure 2.1

This distinction mirrors everyday life: each living thing (plant and animal alike) needs to manage its own daily existence and renew itself by generating offspring.

Both tasks are vital: delivery of existing offerings must be done efficiently for today in order to provide customers with consistency and to make a profit. Self-renewal is essential for tomorrow, to create whole new businesses to meet rapidly changing market demands. This distinction helps us to see that it is not just a matter of becoming more entrepreneurial. The key is how to achieve a workable union of entrepreneurial vitality, for the sake of tomorrow, while maintaining efficient delivery today.

> **The key is how to achieve a workable union of entrepreneurial vitality, for the sake of tomorrow, while maintaining efficient delivery today.**

Unfortunately, the term 'corporate renewal' has become merely another name for any major change programme. Certainly all organizations are struggling for better fitness to face the future, but many of their initiatives are defensive: striving to deliver the *same* services or products more efficiently, more quickly, with better quality or more cheaply.

Such moves amount to running hard to stand still despite unquestionable short-term benefits.

Genuine renewal must produce new offerings and be underpinned by an organization that is fundamentally entrepreneurial in its basic orientation to its particular market.

Only delivery really mattered in the good old days

Twenty or thirty years ago, when change was much slower, organizations could concentrate on the *delivery* of the same products or services indefinitely, gaining advantage by improving efficiency and service, cutting costs, or adding variations on existing themes. Delivery refinement focuses on *process* improvements: changes in the *means* of producing, financing, marketing, and delivering existing services or products.

Self-renewal relates to the *content* of the services or products themselves. Content improvements can be gradual and continuous or sudden and discontinuous. The difficult aspects of self-renewal are deciding what changes to make, especially in volatile markets, and implementing the necessary organizational changes to carry out the intended self-renewal.

Clearly this distinction applies most precisely to fast moving consumer goods industries or to such new service industries as those that provide on-line information, for example.

There is in fact a *continuum* of industries, from those whose market is racing ahead to those where the same products can be happily offered seemingly forever with little change, i.e. property sales, hairdressing, street cleaning, fire fighting, catering and even dentistry. Efficiently selling the same product over time is quite independent of fast growth rate as in the case of mass retailers such as WalMart, Body Shop or McDonald's, which involve relatively straightforward reproductions of identical formulas in new locations. While the technology of such slower product changing industries may improve, the end offering is the same. (See Figure 2.2.)

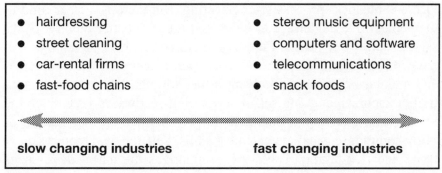

Figure 2.2

Much is made of the need for more dynamic, flexible, entre-preneurial organizations which are fast learners and not too tightly controlled or structured. But this blanket prescription advising all and sundry organizations to jump on the same change bandwagon fails to recognize the distinction between delivery and self-renewal.

The reality is that service and product *delivery* will always be best served by structures and processes which emphasize *efficiency*: consistency, reliability, cost minimization, avoidance of errors and controlled or mechanized production.

A good example is McDonald's (or any similarly structured service business). McDonald's may have to work at keeping people motivated, but its major emphasis is naturally on initiating and maintaining a *machine-like* regularity and predictability at all of its sites across the entire globe.

Even the most fast changing consumer goods organizations need efficient delivery of existing offerings. And some organizational functions such as finance are totally delivery orientated regardless of industry sector. All organizations therefore need to undertake both tasks, but their emphasis will differ depending on the rate of product innovation in their industry. Some industries, such as health services, are undergoing rapid change, but the emphasis is primarily on improving the efficiency of service delivery.

Differences between delivery and self-renewal

Recent popular management initiatives have emphasized delivery enhancement, i.e. total quality management, improving customer service and business process re-engineering. But there is a clear limit to the competitive advantage to be gained through better quality, better service and lower prices. Future gains in competitive advantage will have to come from self-renewal: introducing new products or services and making organizational changes that stimulate the requisite creativity to achieve ongoing self-renewal. Self-renewal is very much the harder task. Delivery refinements largely involve the application of fairly commonsensical management skills. Self-renewal requires creativity and risk-taking. Table 2.1 summarizes the major differences between these two tasks.

The object of delivery is totally *known* at any given point in time. Moreover, it is specifiable in definitive terms. On the other hand, the object of self-renewal can only be specified in very broad terms: *ongoing survival*. The desired future set of new offerings is often completely unknown, which is why its development has to be opportunistic rather than planned.

Effective delivery simply requires good planning and well-structured execution. The more complex the product, the more room there is for waste and inefficiency, hence the need for greater managerial vigilance to determine and maintain the most efficient possible pro-

Table 2.1

	Delivery	Self-renewal
Structure	Hierarchical	Amorphous
Form	Mechanistic	Organic
Main mission	Hold market position	Create new business
Major activity	Raise sales, cut costs	Develop new products
Primary values	Efficiency	Creativity
	Uniformity	Diversity
Change	Static	Dynamic
Tasks	Clear roles	Ambiguous, undefined
Execution	Planned	Opportunistic
Main advantage	Cost control	Knowledge

duction process. No matter how complex the product, however, delivery is still much easier than self-renewal, which partly explains why many organizations are still preoccupied with improving delivery. Very few have seriously or systematically come to grips with what to do about wholesale self-renewal. Or they have done so in a piecemeal fashion, focusing on one or two components of the whole task.

Before we look at self-renewal in more detail and explore how it links up with entrepreneurialism we need to be clear about what it takes for an organization to accommodate both delivery and self-renewal.

So, how can such seemingly disparate tasks be performed effectively by a single organization? How can two seemingly incompatible cultures live under the same roof? What does it mean to be a *single* organization if such diversity is to be encompassed within a single body? And how are we to understand organizational progress and development with these opposing forces apparently pulling in opposite directions?

NEW IMAGES OF ORGANIZATIONS

We need different metaphors to help us visualize new organizational forms – ones that can help us envisage how it might be possible to be entrepreneurial and highly efficient at the same time, with all of the strengths of these two organizational types and none of their weaknesses. We are too limited by thinking of an organization as a singular, uniform entity which is led by one individual in top-down fashion with one single-minded direction.

The way we think about organizations is determined by quite specific metaphors which are not often made explicit. This process is, of course, not unique to thinking about organizations. Metaphors are useful codifying devices which help us understand in simple graphic terms a whole range of human interactions. For example, we often think of the employment relationship as a marriage. Sexual metaphors are frequently used, such as in describing an acquisition or the winning of a major client as a 'conquest'. Another example is referring to hiring a senior executive or engaging a strategic partner as 'jumping into bed with them'.

> One time-honoured metaphor has us seeing a business as a ship – a battleship perhaps, but one that needs to be refitted, refurbished or almost totally rebuilt occasionally.

We cannot easily picture how our organizations might be quite different than they are as long as we hold onto outdated metaphors that do not allow organizations to have significantly different characteristics. For this reason, it is essential to make such metaphors explicit and to explore how we might develop acceptable new metaphors that are consistent with new organizational forms.

The organization as a ship

One time-honoured metaphor has us seeing a business as a ship – a battleship perhaps, but one that needs to be refitted, refurbished or almost totally rebuilt occasionally. This metaphor supports the business process re-engineering bandwagon which can be seen as helping to streamline the ship and making it more efficient and cost effective to run.

In line with this metaphor, we often speak of a new employee as 'coming on board'. The chief executive is said to be 'at the helm' and the finance director may report that the business is 'on course' to achieve record profits. This metaphor has a lot of strength and stability about it which helps us to feel secure and which gives us a comfortable sense of direction.

On the downside, in today's uncertain business environment, the ship metaphor forces us to assume that an organization must have a precise direction, which you can fully plan in advance to achieve. There is no room for diversity of opinion here: every crew member must be pulling in the same direction. Sixteenth-century ships could pursue a wholly exploratory mission where unexpected opportunities could be pursued spontaneously, but today's business ships must, presumably, know where they are going.

The ship metaphor is useful for thinking about organizations with a well-defined product in a relatively stable market (stable in the sense of product or service continuity, despite whatever cost cutting pressures they may experience at any given time). Car-rental firms and the airline industry provide examples. Competition in such industries is based primarily on the value for money of existing services rather than the ability to innovate in order to create something completely different. In such a business, it makes sense to exhort all employees to pull (row?) in the same direction.

This metaphor does not, however, tend to suggest that we should question the ship's direction, the captain's fitness to command or the crew's ability to sail the ship to its destination. Or worse, whether it is possible or even desirable to have such a precise direction.

Compared to more volatile industries where new products, not even imagined by most players, can spring into the market wholly unexpectedly, (the ship's) direction in many service industries is relatively easy to establish. And product change is sufficiently slow that at any given time the agents for change within such organizations are not so radically unlike their conservative counterparts.

The time frame in which change has to occur in fast moving industries is so much shorter and the future is so much more unknown that quite radical creativity and a very intense level of entrepreneurialism need to be fostered. It is, therefore, primarily in such volatile industries that the marriage of creativity and efficiency is such a union of opposites.

The more we are faced by a nearly schizophrenic split between the need to run an efficient operation in order to keep today's business profitable while, at the same time, turning ourselves inside out to invent the as-yet-unimagined, the more unsatisfactory is the ship metaphor.

How can an organization that needs to deliberately foster the requisite diversity expect all employees to be pulling in the same direction? How, in industries such as computers and telecommunications, for example, which could explode in a hundred different directions, can an organization even have a single, uniform direction?

Organization development as evolution

A business could also be seen in evolutionary terms – hence labelling some firms as dinosaurs on the road to extinction. We are operating with this metaphor when we talk of a firm adapting to its environment or learning how to adapt more quickly. An individual firm would be a species, using this metaphor. Over time, a business could evolve into different markets and take quite new shapes in response to environmental pressure and competition from other species. Individuals within the firm may come and go, but the 'species' could continue to evolve and progress.

When we think of an organization as an evolving species it is easier to see how there can be a balance of continuity and diversity. At any given slice of time, there will be a great deal of continuity of vision within an organization. Over a longer period of time, a greater diversity is discernible which is both understandable and acceptable in evolutionary terms.

This metaphor still allows employees to see each other as having a common bond although it is a much more tenuous link than being a member of a ship's crew. Within such a broad group as a species you can have diversity of opinion to the extent of diametric opposition. The greater problem is how there can be sufficient congruence of outlook.

> **When we think of an organization as an evolving species it is easier to see how there can be a balance of continuity and diversity.**

The advantage of this metaphor is that it gives us a credible picture of how a single organization could develop over time in its environment. Unlike the ship metaphor, seeing organizational development as an evolutionary process leads us to think in more dynamic terms and of the interaction between a firm and its environment. If we explore what it means to think of an organization as a species, however, we are immediately led to see that the crucial enabling factor for evolution to occur is *variation* within the organization (species). Environmental change and competition with other species are also driving forces, but what makes the difference between survival and extinction is the ability of the organization to *vary* its responses to its market. Variation may occur over a long time span in which much that is traditional still occurs day by day – hence, again, innovation and conservation living side by side.

This metaphor also helps to make sense of how delivery/efficiency and self-renewal entrepreneurialism could co-exist under the same roof. The role of delivery is to maintain the 'species' on a day-to-day basis in the present (analogous to eating and sleeping) while variation enables the species to adapt to changing environments for the sake of the future evolution of the species.

> Environmental change and competition with other species are also driving forces, but what makes the difference between survival and extinction is the ability of the organization to *vary* its responses to its market.

A disadvantage of this metaphor, at least over short time spans, is that (animal/plant) species do not *appear* to change. It is only over longer spells that the new emerges visibly from the old. Over any given short time period, a species or organization appears to be a single, uniform entity. This is why it is easy for the forces of tradition to win out and stifle change. Another potentially worrying implication of this metaphor is the question of how much control managers can have over the outcome of the organization's evolutionary direction.

The organization as a living, growing – and ageing – person

The idea of organization development or learning is based on the metaphor of organizations as *persons*, which can grow, change, develop and learn. They can also grow old, become disabled, crippled and senile – dying off eventually, in many cases. When we think of organizations this way, we are inclined to search for a corporate fountain of youth to keep the individual fit for as long as possible. We strive to think of how the ageing individual can cast off their crutches, limber up and begin to learn again as they did when they were younger and more curious.

> **The idea of organization development or learning is based on the metaphor of organizations as *persons*, which can grow, change, develop and learn.**

This metaphor underlies the widespread perception of an entrepreneurial firm as an *immature* 'person' and an established business as mature – as if it were a human adult. The stages of an organization's growth from one-man band entrepreneurial ventures to fully mature businesses is described as paralleling the transformation of the human infant through childhood and adolescence to reach adulthood. This provides us with a theory of organization development which, however useful, leads us to make the blanket assumption that all entrepreneurs must be rather childish as people. This metaphor is sufficiently powerful that it is quite likely to cause otherwise conservative would-be entrepreneurs to become more eccentric in order to fit the mould.

The current organizational learning craze fits in nicely with this metaphor. Without much questioning, we simply assume that the process of individual human learning can be applied unaltered to explain how an organization might learn. Of course, we also assume without question that the very idea of learning is something an organization is capable of.

This image has the advantage, over the bureaucratic machine metaphor, of helping us to visualize how an organization can grow, learn and develop, but we still find it very difficult to accept any stage beyond maturity – decline and death.

A problem with this metaphor is that it leads us to expect an organization, like a human person, to be at least capable of having a uniform, consistent personality. It does not immediately provide an image of how diversity might be possible. This is precisely our problem. Operating with this metaphor, how can we imagine a single organization as being both efficient and entrepreneurial with all of the contradictory behaviour patterns that such diversity implies.

The organization-as-person metaphor also strongly reinforces and sustains the notion that business structure must be an hierarchy, in that just as we are governed by our own thinking processes, so is the organization most easily visualized as being led by a brain or head, i.e. top management. The brain does the thinking and the feet do the walking, you might say. So it is not just a matter of top-level executives naturally feeling reluctant to lose any of their power to lower-level employees. They are also constrained by a metaphor that makes them see an organization, like a person, as being governed by a central nervous system.

This metaphor may be an improvement on likening an organization to a ship (which underlies the conventional bureaucracy), but it has in common with the latter a sense of being a uniform or singular entity with its parts all synchronised for movement in a single, well-defined direction – rather than perhaps a loosely-knit federation of diverse sub-communities, for instance.

The organization as social structure or community

When we think of an organization as a community, we gain much needed room for diversity. Too much diversity among a ship's crew amounts to insubordination, or worse, mutiny. But we readily accept that a community can have a range of interests, values and needs. Competing interests, politics and teamwork all make sense when we think of an organization as a community. In comparison with imagining an organization as an individual person, it is less easy to visualize a community all pulling in the same direction or as learning and developing. Nonetheless, communities can grow and pull together, although it is manifestly an easier thing to accomplish in a smaller community than it is in an entire nation.

Competing interests, politics and teamwork all make sense when we think of an organization as a community.

Again, the problem is finding the right balance between unity and diversity. If we narrow the community metaphor too much so that we are left with seeing the organization as a team, we run the risk of expecting too much unity and hence conformity. Move too far in the other direction and it is difficult to see how we can expect much co-operation at all. The best balance may be the image of a small suburban community.

While it can be useful to think of an organization as a community, group or team rather than as an individual, a weakness of this metaphor is that we don't apply the concept of maturity to a group as readily as we do to an individual. While we may be able to imagine what a mature group would be like, it is not as easy to visualize as a mature person. Individual maturity is an *external* phenomenon in that we compare one person's development with another's. Thinking of an organization as a team helps to shed light on the resolution of conflict, but it tends to encourage an internal focus rather than one that is external and dynamic as in the case of individual development or evolution. That is, whenever we think of a group, our immediate image tends to be of relationships *within* the group rather than of its dynamic interaction as a unit in an environment.

Another disadvantage of this metaphor is that teamwork is often used unintentionally as a means to engender uniformity – under the guise of wanting everyone to buy into a single vision. Neither metaphors, however – individual or community – provide obvious images of how an organization could be youthfully entrepreneurial and sagely efficient at the same time.

The organization as family dynasty

Another useful metaphor is the *family dynasty* – a more dynamic, evolving variation on the organization-as-community metaphor. This image allows us to see the established or mature part of the organization as the older generation and to regard newer entrepreneurial parts or divisions as their *offspring*. With this metaphor in mind, we do not have to expect uniform values or a consistent culture throughout the entire firm – at least not across generations. The older generation can carry out the task of maximizing efficiency, where this is appropriate, and the younger generation can be given the freedom to apply their entrepreneurial flair.

With this image in mind, we can say that the organization 'develops' not by wholesale change but by letting old family members and their concerns die off to be replaced by a new generation. The organization, over time, can still be seen as the *same* firm in precisely the way that several generations of a family are still the same family. An acceptable degree of continuity is possible so long as some form of inheritance is passed on to worthy offspring who will carry on something of the family traditions and sustain the family's good name. This metaphor suggests that the firm renews itself by giving birth to new entrepreneurial ventures which are left to operate as independently as possible rather than being stifled by parental control.

With the family dynasty metaphor in mind, it seems natural to let the older generation grow old gracefully rather than struggling to teach old dogs new tricks. We can focus instead on providing the right environment and support to nourish the younger generation so as to facilitate its prosperous growth, thereby ensuring the dynasty's continued survival.

> With this image in mind, we can say that the organization 'develops' not by wholesale change but by letting old family members and their concerns die off to be replaced by a new generation.

The family dynasty metaphor is already commonly applied to executive succession planning in organizations where the business is thought of as some sort of shell or vehicle like a ship that operates independently and simply changes hands over several generations. This limited application of the metaphor is consistent with what really happens in family-owned businesses. The only difference with publicly-owned corporations is that, in these firms, top management's favoured successors are less likely to be their genetic offspring.

This metaphor becomes even more thought provoking when it is applied to the business as a whole, where the entire organization is thought of as the ageing parent nourishing offspring in the form of new ventures operated as autonomous divisions. The advantage of this application of the metaphor is that it provides a means of seeing how an organization could have a stable, efficient part and one that is, at the same time, entrepreneurial. On this view, the corporate body of the organization could focus on those aspects of the business that require efficiency and consistency while entrepreneurial offspring are nourished to become the organization of the future.

One counter-intuitive element of this metaphor is that human family dynasties can take 50 or 60 years to change hands – witness the British Royal Family. The metaphor is still useful, however, so long as we think of the process operating in hyper fast-forward in the context of dynamic business markets.

> **This metaphor becomes even more thought provoking when it is applied to the business as a whole, where the entire organization is thought of as the ageing parent nourishing offspring in the form of new ventures operated as autonomous divisions.**

An advantage of the family dynasty metaphor, however, is that it makes it easy to see entrepreneurial offspring developing new products, maturing, milking their cash cow of ongoing popular products for a while and eventually dying off as their product lines become obsolete, but in turn surviving through their own offspring.

A large family dynasty is also a community of sorts, but one with a stronger identity, a greater sense of itself as a distinct entity or individual. This metaphor accounts for the stronger political infighting you find in organizations than you might see in a typical neighbourhood community and especially the keener interest in succession. Also it makes more sense to think of a family dynasty as having economic interests that are in competition with those of other families, whereas a community is mainly concerned with services for itself and with caring for its own members.

Most essentially, however, the family dynasty metaphor spotlights cross generational relationships and links in nicely the image of entrepreneurial firms as being youthful while mature businesses are more adult-like. This image makes it easier to see how the mature part of the firm could focus on the more conservative task of delivering today's offerings efficiently while youthful newcomers usher in new products thereby renewing the dynasty.

There is no reason why we have to restrict ourselves to just one metaphor in our efforts to make better sense of organizational dynamics. While we may like to think of the organization from the inside as a family dynasty, it can be seen as an individual person from an external perspective. We can therefore use different metaphors for different purposes. The point is not to be limited to out-of-date or restrictive metaphors such as the ship image. But even this metaphor is still applicable to the delivery function which will always have clear goals and will always value efficiency as it strives to reach its destination.

> **As organizations move towards a separation of the delivery task from self-renewal along the lines of the family dynasty metaphor, senior executives should assume a role not unlike that of the venture capitalist.**

The organization as venture capitalist

A final metaphor worth looking at has us seeing the organization as a venture capitalist – an investor in promising new enterprises. The important feature of this metaphor is that most venture capitalists – unless they take an equity stake in their investments – have an arm's length relationship with their ventures. Their role is to evaluate, monitor and provide funds in accordance with results and promised returns. As organizations move towards a separation of the delivery task from self-renewal along the lines of the family dynasty metaphor, senior executives should assume a role not unlike that of the venture capitalist. New ventures that are either developed organically or acquired should be managed in a similar arm's length fashion. One of the reasons why many such acquisitions fail is because senior executives meddle in businesses they know little about. This applies to new directions in the organization's familiar industry as well as to industry dissimilar acquisitions.

This metaphor, therefore, helps us to envisage a new role for senior executives and, in addition, provides a way of seeing how two metaphors can be usefully combined. If we were to rely on the family dynasty metaphor alone, we might be tempted to accept the fact that senior executives should play a very hands-on role in all parts of the business just as does the family patriarch or matriarch. But this heavy involvement is precisely what stifles a youthful entrepreneurial spirit, which is best guided and financed but not too closely managed.

LINKING SELF-RENEWAL AND ENTREPRENEURIALISM

So, thinking of business evolution along the lines of a changing family dynasty reinforces the prevailing identification of entrepreneurial offspring with youth. Indeed, to date, the best examples of successful entrepreneurial businesses are smaller firms such as Apple Computer and Microsoft when they first started to present a serious challenge to IBM. Apple and Microsoft were founded and run by younger people. Most successful entrepreneurial ventures within larger organizations are smaller, discrete business units. One of the most celebrated examples is 3M where so-called 'skunk works' are like *nurseries* for the development of new ventures. Other organizations try the acquisition short cut – with varying degrees of success. An example of such 'adopted' entrepreneurial 'children' would be McCaw Cellular, the American entrepreneurial mobile telephone company recently acquired by AT&T.

In slower changing industries the ship metaphor is satisfactory even for the purpose of envisaging change – any ship can be rebuilt – at sea if necessary. The point is that such change is incremental and does not entail a radical departure from what has gone before – at least not in terms of the actual content of what the organization produces. A tugboat can be refitted and modernized but not transformed into a hovercraft.

In fast changing businesses, top management is often too busy with delivery matters – keeping costs down and improving quality to think about what to do next, creating something that is completely new. In addition, future market direction is so uncertain that the process of creativity and renewal is best separated to some extent from ongoing delivery. Self-renewal in this context is therefore best achieved by setting up relatively independent entrepreneurial ventures operated as discrete divisions – as 3M does for instance. And this use of new ventures to create the future for an organization is most easily envisaged along the lines of the metaphor of a family dynasty where the existing delivery-orien-tated corporate body – the elder family group – nourishes distinct off-spring in the form of new ventures.

Organizing for effective self renewal

The straightforward connection between self-renewal and the need to be more entrepreneurial is that self-renewal is likely best achieved by a continuous effort to give birth to new ventures that are, as much as possible, allowed to be self-managing.

What would such an organization look like? At any given time there should be a range of organizational units which vary in accordance with the amount of emphasis they place on delivering an existing service/product versus creating new offerings. Conventional manage-ment, conceived as the application of delivery skills, should accordingly be devoted to the delivery process, leaving those with entrepreneurial inclinations to start new ventures. Senior executives should devote more time to the delivery function and to operating as venture capital-ists if they are managerially orientated.

The European-based firm Asea Brown Boveri (ABB) is much lauded of late as an example of a business that has gone to great lengths to orga-nize itself around multiple, highly independent units. Not satisfied with creating some 1,300 independent businesses, it has further subdivided these businesses into about 5,000 autonomous profit centres. The next stage is to create cells consisting of cross-functional teams made up of 10 employees each. While each unit, of whatever size, is expected to be innovative, there is no doubt that some business units will be in more mature sectors, and therefore needing to focus on cost minimiza-tion, quality and good customer service to a greater extent than cre-ating new products as a means of sustaining profitability.

> **While some employees and organizational functions may enjoy focusing primarily on the delivery side of the business, you should encourage entrepreneurial thinking from all employees.**

While it may be illuminating to distinguish between the separate tasks of delivery and self-renewal – it does not follow that you would be well advised to overly *compartmentalize* these tasks, despite how discrete they may be on paper. This would be to advocate an old-fashioned and narrowly structure-based approach to the issue. A multi-unit business like Asea Brown Boveri needs to place discrete emphasis on both of these tasks but it would be a mistake to restrict some units to delivery only work while allowing others to be totally entrepreneurial and unconcerned with the delivery side of the new products they create.

While some employees and organizational functions may enjoy focusing primarily on the delivery side of the business, you should encourage entrepreneurial thinking from all employees. This approach is in itself entrepreneurial as it suggests being open to opportunity wherever it might arise within your firm and from whomever might come up with fresh product or service ideas. There is no inconsistency in encouraging entrepreneurial thinking from every employee, on the one hand, and still investing strategically, on the other hand, in those ventures and people that seem to show most promise of generating winning new product lines. (See Psychological slant.)

PSYCHOLOGICAL SLANT

It would be politically correct to advocate greater creativity and entrepreneurialism on the part of each and every employee and at all levels. This is fine as far as it goes, but if you think about this issue strategically, it is wise to invest most of your efforts where the greatest payoff is most likely. And, psychologically, the truth of the matter is that younger people and those mature employees who come to the organization from different industries and fresh perspectives are likely to be the most creative. As we age and stay in familiar situations for prolonged periods, the more ingrained are our thought patterns, habits and ways of looking at the world.

Where are we now?

The connection between entrepreneurialism and self-renewal is clear: *Self-renewal is the goal, entrepreneurialism is the means.*

Enough is being said elsewhere about improving organizational delivery: all of the literature on total quality management and business process re-engineering, for example.

What follows will therefore focus on what is necessary to develop a self-renewing organization based on using entrepreneurialism as the engine. Several sub-components make up the complete vehicle (see Figure 2.6), the sum total of which are mutually supporting and essential to reach the goal of on-going self-renewal.

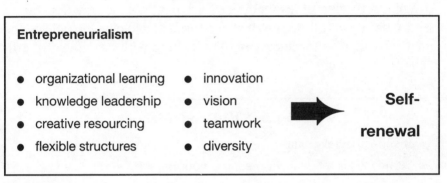

Entrepreneurialism

- organizational learning
- knowledge leadership
- creative resourcing
- flexible structures

- innovation
- vision
- teamwork
- diversity

Self-renewal

Figure 2.6

We have some understanding of what it takes for an individual to be an entrepreneur, but the issue is much more complex for large organizations, especially if they have reached an overly bureaucratic stage of development. All of the components indicated in Figure 2.6 are important and will be discussed in due course. Organizational learning is a particularly critical element. Such learning seems to come naturally to the individual entrepreneur. For the inward looking bureaucracy, relearning how to learn may prove to be a major undertaking.

Knowledge leadership is perhaps not an intuitively obvious part of what it takes to make a large organization more entrepreneurial, but as we shall see, it is also critical.

> Briefly, knowledge leadership is the explicit recognition that many businesses are now 'knowledge-driven' and this means that so-called knowledge workers must be more than empowered to make decisions, they must be encouraged to provide *renewal leadership.*

Briefly, knowledge leadership is the explicit recognition that many businesses are now 'knowledge-driven' and this means that so-called knowledge workers must be more than empowered to make decisions, they must be encouraged to provide *renewal leadership*. This component will be one of the most difficult for large organizations to embrace wholeheartedly because it requires some relinquishing of authority on the part of senior executives – who are already feeling threatened by the amount of power they have lost thus far.

While self-renewal and entrepreneurialism will occupy the bulk of the discussion to follow, it will also be essential to develop images and practical solutions for integrating this culture with the culture of efficiency and delivery.

PRACTICAL STEPS

Set self-renewal goals:
- clarify what self-renewal means in your organization
- identify what groups and individuals are best placed to offer most in the way of achieving the required rate of self-renewal
- set challenging targets for the amount of revenue you want to generate each year from new products or services.

Implement support components:
- empower new ventures to take their own risks and tolerate failure
- create new organizational structures to enhance flexibility
- institute an organizational learning initiative to help the business learn from mistakes
- develop new product teams which include customers
- elevate the status of key knowledge workers and encourage them to lead
- create professional/technical career streams for knowledge

"While *everyone* in the organization should be encouraged to be more entrepreneurial, in practical terms it will be more effective to initiate some separation of the tasks of delivery and self-renewal."

"While management skills are essential to *exploit* entrepreneurial opportunities profitably, they will be best applied to the *delivery* process whereby existing products and services are efficiently produced."

3

WHEN YOU CAN'T PLAN, IMPROVISE

There are two ways in which organizations can be entrepreneurial:

- over the longer term: by eliminating excess bureaucracy, while striving to make the *total* organization more entrepreneurial
- in the shorter term: by creating entrepreneurial units that operate independently of the 'mother ship'.

The latter approach is most conducive to self-renewal in fast changing industries because there may *be* no long-term future unless fast action is taken. While *everyone* in the organization should be encouraged to be more entrepreneurial, in practical terms it will be more effective to initiate some separation of the tasks of delivery and self-renewal. The larger, more stable, part of the organization can then focus on the delivery of existing services while new entrepreneurial units can lead the self-renewal effort.

> While *everyone* in the organization should be encouraged to be more entrepreneurial, in practical terms it will be more effective to initiate some separation of the tasks of delivery and self-renewal

The short-term strategy of creating entrepreneurial units is likely also to be the best long-term self-renewal strategy. Urging the whole organization to be more entrepreneurial will take longer and it will at best serve only to complement the initiative to generate renewal through entrepreneurial offspring.

ARE THERE DISTINCTIVE ENTREPRENEURIAL SKILLS?

While many established organizations recognize that they need to become less bureaucratic and more entrepreneurial, there appears to be little awareness of how different are the skills involved in managing efficiently from those that are required to achieve entrepreneurial success. Although many companies are attempting to empower more employees, there appears to be little acknowledgement of the extent to which conventional management skills, i.e. planning, organizing and controlling, are not appropriate in an entrepreneurial culture.

What we need to sort out now is just what skills should prospective entrepreneurial employees have and how should you develop them?

Can a manager be an entrepreneur?

The question: 'How do you become more entrepreneurial?' needs to be answered at a number of levels. We have looked at the organizational level and concluded that there is merit in creating entrepreneurial units first, while encouraging a broader organizational change effort over the longer term. At the level of individual employees, the required skills and behaviours need to be identified which will enable them to be more entrepreneurial. A third level, to be explored later, relates to what changes need to be made to the organization's culture to support an entrepreneurial orientation.

> **At the level of individual employees, the required skills and behaviours need to be identified which will enable them to be more entrepreneurial.**

There seems little doubt that managerial competencies are totally different from entrepreneurial skills. They seem to be at starkly opposite ends of the spectrum. Just as there is a continuum of organizations – from the highly bureaucratic to the excessively risk orientated, the same range of behaviour patterns can be found in individual people. The nearer you are to the managerial end of the continuum, the more likely you are to *over* manage and generate bureaucracy. The nearer you are to the other end of the spectrum, the more likely you are to fail because of wanton disregard for costs and poor use of time and other resources.

The interesting question is whether it is possible for one person to be *wisely* entrepreneurial: enough of a risk taker, innovator and improviser to recognize and create new opportunities, while still able to employ enough managerial skill to exploit them profitably. The short answer is that some people will indeed combine the best of both skill sets, while, in many other cases, it will be necessary to create teams of people where managerial types are employed to complement those with a more entrepreneurial bent. (See Figure 3.1.)

- The *manager manipulates what is*: people, things and information to produce a result that is clearly specifiable in advance.

- The *entrepreneur tries to create what isn't*: by a lot of guesswork, improvisation and learning from mistakes.

Figure 3.1

While management skills are essential to *exploit* entrepreneurial opportunities profitably, they will be best applied to the *delivery* process whereby existing products and services are efficiently produced. The delivery function can be compared to a vacuum cleaner which follows behind the entrepreneur to sweep up the opportunities he or she creates – as if he or she were an unmanageable cat running across the floor leaving dirty paw prints all over your new carpet!

> While management skills are essential to *exploit* entrepreneurial opportunities profitably, they will be best applied to the *delivery* process whereby existing products and services are efficiently produced.

3M recognises the opposition between planning and entrepreneurial action. In the words of Roland A. Mitsch, Senior Vice President of Research and Development at 3M, 'The question is, how do we balance priority setting with a climate of freedom? Prioritizing and providing freedom to innovate cannot be trade-offs; both are needed.' While it is certainly true that both are needed, we are only fooling ourselves if we think that no trade-offs are involved. Prioritizing can only be used in an entrepreneurial culture if its role is strictly limited to an extent never contemplated in more command-driven businesses or economies.

On resisting the temptation to 'manage' the entrepreneurial process

Senior executives in most organizations learned their management skills in the context of the *delivery* function – the day-to-day effort to keep the existing business operating profitably. This means they have learned how to cut costs, improve quality and increase sales – mainly of existing product lines or services.

Entrepreneurial behaviour is much more intuitive and responsive to external stimulation. Such open-ended and partially undirected behaviour allows the entre-preneur, operating in *exploratory mode*, to recognize what to do on the spur of the moment and in the face of uncertainty. Unlike cut-and-dried management problems,

> **It is only through trial and error that the entrepreneur can determine what will be successful and what will not.**

there can be no precise objective to plan to achieve if you are develop-ing a new product for a market that is just emerging. It is only through trial and error that the entrepreneur can determine what will be suc-cessful and what will not.

Managing in the good old days

The conventional management skills of planning, organizing and con-trolling served well enough 30 to 40 years ago, when the delivery of existing products and services was all that was necessary for business success. These skills were adequate simply because the primary value of the organizational task of delivery is *efficiency* (as it always has been). An efficient result is easiest to achieve the more precisely it can be known and defined. Managerial skills are *rational tools* in which we use our thought processes to analyse situations and decide which skills/tools to use. Planning, for example, is a tool that helps us to set out the specific steps we should take to achieve a clearly identified objective.

If you want to build a house, for instance, and you have exact specifications down to the last detail, including location and completion time, and if you have adequate resources, then there is no excuse for not getting it right. It is simply a matter of good planning and then of controlling all variables *en route* to completing the project.

Every business has established products or services which need to be delivered in precisely the same structured way in which you would tackle the building of a house. Because organizations have not yet fully thought through how different is the entrepreneurial task, we have failed to develop the new skills and attitudes necessary for success in organizational self-renewal.

There is also the very fundamental problem that conventional managerial skills, because they are based on *reason*, allow us to exercise *control* over outcomes to a degree that is impossible in dynamic fast changing markets where only an entrepreneurial approach will work. Psychologically, most managers find it very disturbing to contemplate letting go of such control. It is so undeniably *reasonable* to plan what you are going to do. How else (you think) can you expect to get where you want to go? How else can you use your scarce resources most efficiently? Unfortunately, the rapid pace of change creates more uncertainty which leads to more fear, which in turn leads us to want to exert more control – a vicious circle. (See Figure 3.2.)

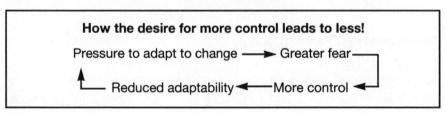

How the desire for more control leads to less!

Pressure to adapt to change ⟶ Greater fear

Reduced adaptability ◀ More control ◀

Figure 3.2

We can only control what we know, but the future is inherently unknowable. What is worse is that the future is coming at us faster and from many more directions than ever before. Efforts to exert more control only succeed in narrowing our focus to a limited, comfortable territory and this isolates us from those areas that are changing most rapidly. More importantly, we then over emphasize *static* managerial skills which deal with static data, people and things. This limited approach causes us to avoid developing the open-ended, *interactive* skills of continuous external monitoring, risk taking, learning from mistakes and improvising in order to change direction quickly. (See Psychological slant.)

PSYCHOLOGICAL SLANT

Top-down control stifles entrepreneurial initiative but it is generally so subtle as to be unrecognized. Flattening the hierarchy and preaching empowerment just deals with the visible tip of the iceberg and thus may get you only half way there, such is the fear of non-conformity, of disagreeing with the boss.

Just as more diversity is ever more vital, many organizations are moving in the opposite direction: they are unwittingly imposing more control in the form of so-called strong cultures and teamwork. Employees who are too creative can be labelled as poor team players – a fatal disease if you are currently on the teamwork bandwagon.

Recent research has shown how powerful are the forces that cultivate 'yes' men and women in organizations. Even in peer groups, there is a centripetal force towards conformity of opinion that can stifle creativity. Most startlingly in our age of teamwork, this research suggests that individuals, for this reason, are likely to be more creative than teams!

Managerial skills as rational tools

The entrepreneur may be good at recognizing an opportunity and he may quite deliberately and rationally immerse himself in new technologies, markets and customer problems. As a result, he may find that new product ideas spontaneously occur to him. This may be a *skill* of sorts which others do not possess, but it is not a *rational* skill in the sense of something we can simply *apply* at will whenever we wish to produce a new product idea.

From this point of view, our conventional set of managerial skills is simply a tool kit which requires quite straightforward application. Such skills only seem esoteric because of the complexity of the problems they are sometimes applied to.

What makes planning a *rational* tool, for example, is that, like a hammer, you can pick it up and apply it at will to execute a well-defined task – like pounding a nail into a board. Planning can only be applied when you know precisely what you want to achieve. While you can certainly plan to set up an entrepreneurial unit in your business or to revamp your R&D department, the hoped for *output* can only be vaguely indicated. The

> **The precise new products to be developed can only *emerge* with a combination of loose planning, a great deal of trial and error, intuition and luck.**

precise new products to be developed can only *emerge* with a combination of loose planning, a great deal of trial and error, intuition and luck.

Planning in an ivory tower

The difference between planning and entrepreneurial idea generation is that you can fully control and manipulate planning, but you can only *arrange the circumstances* deemed appropriate to stimulate the generation of new ideas and hope they emerge. The rational side of the entrepreneurial process is limited to the planning to mix people, technology and customers together and shake them up. What comes out is based on uncontrollable intuition, guesswork, luck and a certain amount of

> **You can plan to be more entrepreneurial – just as you can plan to be a better planner, but planning can only be applied to the achievement of precisely known and controllable outcomes, it will not work where *responsiveness* is the key to success.**

stubbornness to forge ahead in the face of so much uncertainty. You can plan to be more entrepreneurial – just as you can plan to be a better planner, but planning can only be applied to the achievement of precisely known and controllable outcomes, it will not work where *responsiveness* is the key to success.

Once you know what you want to achieve you can sit in your ivory tower and plan your action steps. By contrast, entrepreneurial behaviour is *interactive*. One of the technological waves of the immediate future is interactive television, where the viewer, like the entrepreneur, can browse with no goal in mind but respond to 'opportunities' that look interesting as they arise.

While planning is a relatively passive process, the entrepreneur can only succeed by constantly *interacting* with his environment. He needs to be constantly trying new things and getting immediate feedback in order to know how best to improvise. The entrepreneur is like the blind man feeling his way with his cane, where the planner can clearly see the door he is heading towards.

Responsiveness is essentially the opposite of planning. It is not enough to simply build responsive flexibility into new product development plans, the whole process must resemble a *search* rather than a *journey*.

> **Responsiveness is essentially the opposite of planning. It is not enough to simply build responsive flexibility into new product development plans, the whole process must resemble a *search* rather than a *journey*.**

Similar comments apply to strategic planning for well-defined, shorter-term, business goals. Suppose McDonald's objective is to achieve world-wide dominance in the fast-food industry by the end of the decade. Its strategy may be to open a certain number of new restaurants a month around the globe. Because each restaurant is built to a standard recipe, the only problems the company might encounter are purely operational and can be minimized through effective planning and other conventional management skills.

McDonald's senior executives can be very rational and deliberate in planning this expansion – but this is not innovative as far as products are concerned. They do not have to race ahead in a market where there is great uncertainty about how the market will evolve. No doubt someone will eventually come up with a new and exciting fast-food concept that could unseat McDonald's dominance in its industry, but the possibilities are not as limitless as they are in other industries. For this reason, McDonald's managers can exercise more control over the company's future.

If we look again at the distinction between delivery and self-renewal (as represented in Table 3.1, which we used in the last chapter to separate out these two fundamentally different tasks), we can now see also that totally different skills are required for success in these two tasks.

Table 3.1

	Delivery	Self-renewal
Structure	Hierarchical	Amorphous
Form	Mechanistic	Organic
Main mission	Hold market position	Create new business
Major activity	Raise sales, cut costs	Develop new products
Primary values	Efficiency	Creativity
	Uniformity	Diversity
Change	Static	Dynamic
Tasks	Clear roles	Ambiguous, undefined
Execution	Planned	Opportunistic
Main advantage	Cost control	Knowledge

It is clear that effective delivery of existing products or services requires managerial skills, while self-renewal depends on entrepreneurial talents.

So who's got entrepreneurial skills in big companies?

There are some intuitively obvious skills that you should have if you are to make your mark as an entrepreneur, either in your own business or, more importantly for our purposes, in large organizations. Responsiveness, for example, is clearly more important than planning provided you are not so far down the continuum of these opposites that you do no planning at all.

What other skills are necessary? It seems sensible at this point to look at how 'competency profiling' can help us understand and facilitate the development of more entrepreneurialism in organizations?

WHAT GOOD IS COMPETENCY PROFILING?

The competency profiling bandwagon has been rolling for over 10 years now. Organizations are jumping on board with growing enthusiasm. There is now even a journal devoted to the subject, called – you guessed it – *Competency*. There are, however, rumblings of discontent emerging, albeit quiet rumblings so far.

The upshot of what follows is simply that competencies may be useful for precisely defined jobs with clear objectives, but entrepreneurial, empowered employees are better left to figure out for themselves what they need to do to be effective.

The point is also about the value of letting people learn from their mistakes as opposed to telling them what to do – which is partly what competency profiling does. Any proactive management of an entrepreneurial knowledge worker's input flies in the face of the market-led imperatives that fast changing businesses need to adopt today if they are to be sufficiently innovative to survive.

The only way to make a persuasive case for subduing competency mania is to present a viable alternative. This entails questioning some deeply held and generally unquestioned assumptions about what an organization needs to do to be effective in today's fast changing and competitive environment.

What purpose were competencies intended to serve?

> **Any proactive management of an entrepreneurial knowledge worker's input flies in the face of the market-led imperatives that fast changing businesses need to adopt today if they are to be sufficiently innovative to survive.**

One of the more important assumptions underlying the use of competencies is the idea that an organization needs not only to *have* the right person in the right job, but also to have as much *control* over such placement as possible. At one time, personality traits were deemed to be a good means of matching people to jobs, that is, until some nit-picker noticed that the same output could be achieved by two people with quite different personalities. Although the same problem crops up all over again with competencies, we have probably turned a blind eye to this fact simply because no one has any better idea.

Having the right person in the right job has obvious benefits (assuming you know what you want to achieve). You would hardly want a plumber working on your teeth!

The catch is: do you *know* what you want to achieve? In the good old days of slow change, organizations could forecast well in advance and in precise detail every output they intended to generate. Unfortunately there is a lot more uncertainty around now and it will get worse before it gets any better (if it ever does). (See Figure 3.3.)

THE BIG ISSUE

The real issue here is the extent to which a *rational* and hence mechanical approach to thinking, deciding and organizing is achievable and even desirable rather than a more reactive, opportunistic and entrepreneurial style.

Figure 3.3

It is easy to manage in industries where you can see ahead and where very little changes. But fast changing businesses must let themselves be *led* by their markets, they cannot plan and control their output to the same degree and this means less applicability for competency profiling.

Here again it helps to think of a continuum of industries, from the slow moving with relatively little product change (barber shops, flower stalls, house sales), through consumer goods industries where new products are born and die as fast as fruit flies. The forces underlying managerial decisions in the slower changing industries are largely *rational* (recall McDonald's). You can think through alternatives, knowing full well their various consequences, make your decision and then act: all in a logical, rational sequence. (It helps if your firm has a monopoly.) Faster moving industries are governed to a greater extent by *evolutionary* forces, where often the best you can do is introduce as much product *variation* as you can dream of and hope that something gets *selected*. The rational model of thinking and deciding breaks down in this environment.

> The essence of entrepreneurial action is that you have to *act first* and then reflect on what does and does not work. Too much detailed prior thought spells paralysis.

The essence of entrepreneurial action is that you have to *act first* and then reflect on what does and does not work. Too much detailed prior thought spells paralysis. Not enough is known in advance about the likely consequences of various alternatives. Entrepreneurial action is essentially *exploratory* or experimental. It is *drawn* or led by a fast changing environment rather than *pushed* by rational thinking and deciding. Competency profiling has to do with thinking through in advance what needs to be done as opposed to simply improvising. The point is comparable to the distinction now being made between old-fashioned a priori strategic planning and the view that strategies have to *emerge* on the basis of what works and what does not in trial and error action. The notion of being 'market led' also reinforces this theme.

So the problem with competency profiling is that it is best suited to jobs and business contexts where everything is highly predictable and stable.

What are competencies?

Competencies are essentially *process* skills in the sense that they are about *how* the job is done; they are not about the *content* of the job. Another nit-picker might argue against this view as follows: 'Although the content or output of entrepreneurial activity is unpredictable, we can still identify the process skills necessary to be entrepreneurial. You have just specified one of them – act in an exploratory, improvisory manner rather than a sequential, rational way.'

There is research, however, which shows that quite different people can be successful entrepreneurs. But this is not the most important point. It is not that organizations are happy to merely *have* the right person in the right job, the whole essence of human resource planning is the desire to identify, place and manage the right person in the right job. This control motivation is also a fundamental feature of a strongly rational view of organizational functioning.

The conclusion to be drawn from seeing competencies as process skills is that they are most applicable in contexts where knowledge or content is not the issue, where what is important is the efficient use of very standardized, routinized knowledge.

We need to think more about content in situations where knowledge creation is the issue of importance. Knowledge *creation* is not the sort of thing you can manage quite so neatly as you can its routine application.

It might be argued that entrepreneurs with different styles or personalities (process skills) could be equally successful, but they do need appropriate content knowledge about the technological field in which they wish to innovate. But even this claim is not true. A marketing person or an end user might just as well see an opportunity and recruit the necessary technical skills to realize his entrepreneurial vision. So there is no specific skill set or knowledge necessary to be an entrepreneur in any particular field.

When to control and when to roll

Efficient delivery depends on smooth, cost-effective co-ordination of all the moving parts of the organizational machine. As much as the machine metaphor has been derided of late, it is nevertheless irreplaceable in some form wherever maximum efficiency is essential. For this type of organizational purpose, it is relatively easy to specify what everyone needs to do. The competency approach is in its glory in this context.

This case is not so easily made with regard to the task of organizational self-renewal. Suppose we could specify the process skills (with a reasonable degree of accuracy) which are needed by today's highly specialized knowledge workers to be sufficiently entrepreneurial to continually generate new business offerings. It is still not obvious that they should be *managed* in this controlling way (and what other reason is there to want to define them).

> So there is no specific skill set or knowledge necessary to be an entrepreneur in any particular field.

It is arguable that you need a diversity of people with diverse content and process skills to ensure a wide enough range of variation in offerings to be truly successful. The *delivery* values of efficiency and having well-defined slots for people will likely stifle creativity in an entrepreneurial context. Empowerment of knowledge workers means that people should be left to their own devices, within reason, if they are to have any hope of developing their own brand of entrepreneurial flair.

Would we still not want to hire them and move them here and there on the basis of some idea of what they are good at and not so good at?

It is important to keep in mind that there is no question that you do want to *have* the right person in the right place. The only issue is whether we should be using competency-based management tools to achieve this end *no matter what the organizational context.*

Here again the distinction between delivery and self-renewal may be helpful.

In the past, when all industry changed slowly, every organization could focus mainly on delivery. Although such organizations may have been too multi-layered and inward looking, their objective of efficient delivery was well enough served by an hierarchical, machine-like structure. This mindset still infects our thinking about organizations today, unfortunately. While such machine-like organizations needed *content* skills (technical knowledge) at lower levels, the managerial role was seen as a pure *process* undertaking. Hence the alleged trans-ferability of 'general' managers across industries.

Even though we are starting to recognize the extent to which fast moving industries are knowledge driven, we still overly exalt process skills and the managerial role and hierarchy. The distinction between delivery and self-renewal shows how managerial or process skills are much more important for delivery, while knowledge and technical con-tent skills are more critical for self-renewal.

So far, all that this means is that we should start paying more atten-tion to technical competencies as well as to process skills in deciding who to hire and who to move.

In day-to-day practice, this is what happens now. When pulling together an important project team, we identify the best functional or commercial people for the job and just hope that, among them, they have the process skills to make effective use of their knowledge. Of course, some projects fail for lack of such process skills, but the point is that too much rational analysis (profiling of process skills and assess-ment) prior to action can be detrimental in an entrepreneurial context.

A SUBSTITUTE FOR COMPETENCY-BASED MANAGEMENT

Facilitating output versus controlling input

An important feature of process skills is that they have to do with *input*. Content skills have more to do with *output*. In the latter case, for example, if you are an accountant, your output will be statements about costs and benefits, whereas if you are a dentist, your output will be healthy teeth. In both professions the process skill of attention to detail is useful. Similar process skills are useful for both of these kinds of work because they have to do with *how* the job is done, not what is done.

If your goal is efficiency (doing things right as opposed to doing the right things) you do want to control input. It is not enough that the job is done, you also care about how it is done. How else are you to minimize waste, inefficiency and hence cost?

The problem with taking a similar approach to nourishing entrepreneurs is not so much that you do not care how the result is achieved but that you do not know precisely what the output will be or how it might be attained and further, control stifles creativity and initiative.

It is clear that to achieve delivery efficiencies we need to focus our managerial attention on individuals. (I don't mean individuals as opposed to teams, but individuals as opposed to their environment.) The idea is to strive to fit individuals into the right slots for the sake of efficient delivery.

> **Your entrepreneurial organization is more likely to flourish if you focus on the design of a stimulating environment rather than directly on skills.**

Turn them loose and get out of the way

Your entrepreneurial organization is more likely to flourish if you focus on the design of a stimulating environment rather than directly on skills. It is a matter of then turning loose a variety of people with strong technical skills and letting them figure out the process bits for themselves. (Note that the popular theme today of basing corporate strategy on organizational core competencies is about having technical know-how that differentiates you from your competitors, it is not about having excellent managerial/process skills.)

Abandon theories that do not work

Theories that are not working have anomalies they cannot explain. In the case of the overly rational model of organizational functioning, of which the competency approach is but one component, at least two anomalies spring to mind:

1) Why is it that, at least sometimes, quite different people can do the same job equally well?
2) Why do people stubbornly persist in learning the hard way and reinventing the wheel when it would be so much more *efficient* if they would only listen and do what they are told?

The truth here is that people learn best by doing and by making their own mistakes. While you cannot tolerate much error if you want to achieve maximum delivery efficiency, you actually need to encourage more error-prone learning-by-doing if you seriously hope to develop a fully entrepreneurial organization. And it is in this context that competency profiling and slot filling just get in the way at best and, at worst, kill what you actually want to achieve.

> **Management by results never really worked in old-fashioned delivery-dominated organizations because they were too internally focused and process-fixated to pay much attention to the sort of results and technical skills that generated new product offerings.**

How then do you manage this messy self-renewal process if not by controlling inputs: surely by rewarding people for their results (output). Interestingly, bad theories also tend to be perverse or absurd when extrapolated to their logical conclusions. One such perversity popular today is rewarding people for developing managerial or process skills instead of for their achievements.

Management by results never really worked in old-fashioned

delivery-dominated organizations because they were too internally focused and process-fixated to pay much attention to the sort of results and technical skills that generated new product offerings. Further, such organizations were too punitive in their approach to managing by results, i.e. no mistakes or else! This type of culture only encouraged game-playing to fudge results and avoid punishment. Hence the real reason for the (actually regressive) move to controlling input (competencies) is to exert more control, ultimately over output, but by getting a tighter grip on input.

So what is the option to competency-based management and when do you use it?

Manage the culture and leave people alone

To achieve entrepreneurial outputs, it is more effective to manage the environment in which people work than to manage people directly – this is the fundamental difference. Competency profiling is about managing people directly.

The alternative approach suggested here also involves treating employees as if they were *suppliers*, as if they were in their own business. This is far more empowering than managing how people do things – which is essentially what the competency approach is all about. Telling people what competencies they need to do a job properly is very 'theory X' (people are too stupid and lazy to figure out for themselves how to do a job), as opposed to the more empowering 'theory Y' (people are sufficiently intelligent and responsible to think for themselves).

Every organization will have a delivery task as well as a self-renewal one – only the degree of emphasis will vary. At this point it would be easy to fall into the bad habit of thinking about delivery and self-renewal *roles* for people, but an essential thrust of this argument is that the concept of *role* is more appropriate to the delivery task than it is to self-renewal. For the sake of simplicity, let us suppose that everyone can contribute to both delivery and self-renewal.

When to manage people on the basis of competencies

- In entry level recruitment where you have no track record to go on.
- When filling jobs that are wholly delivery orientated and have clearly identifiable process skill requirements, i.e. so you get a diligent, detail conscious accountant rather than a careless one.
- When promoting people to general management positions where the priority is not *content* but co-ordination and process skills – managers are primarily co-ordinators so far as delivery is concerned.

When recruiting graduates, a knowledge-driven organization will want to emphasize technical specialization to a greater extent than process skills. The latter will be more important in jobs such as those that mainly require the processing of information or taking customer orders over the telephone, for example.

It is important to keep in mind (again) that there is no objection to the idea that you need the right person in the right place. The issue is rather how to manage such placement. As teams and individuals become more self-managing and identify the right people to work with on projects by networking at their own initiative and by selling proposals to their superiors, the manager will have less involvement in having to make such placements in the old-fashioned, rational, a priori manner.

Practically speaking, how should you decide who to put in a particular new product development team? This will vary depending on what end of the delivery/self-renewal continuum you are at. Suppose you are in an industry that needs to innovate fast just to survive. As your highly skilled and potentially innovative knowledge workers increasingly come to be regarded as *suppliers* of services, whether internal or external, they should come to you with proposals for new products. Your decision making should back off from staff placement to deciding what ideas to invest in – much as does a customer or venture capitalist.

The bottom-up alternative

Proposals will arise (bottom-up) by knowledge workers networking with each other and with customers. It will then naturally emerge who should work on the project team if the proposal is accepted. It will not be a matter of some manager two levels up the hierarchy sitting in his office poring over competency profiles. As such projects develop, he can then decide which ones to continue to support, based on results, and which to let wither.

This conception of the manager's emerging role fits in with our criticism of the overly rational theory of organizational functioning. Rather than rationally analysing job requirements, deciding who to place where and then acting, the manager of tomorrow will have to be more responsive to the bottom-up flow of decision making.

The holistic angle

In complete harmony with the overly rational view of organizational functioning, competency profiling is essentially *reductionistic*. Our need for control inclines us to want to break everything down into its underlying elements or atoms. Modern organizations need increasingly to view human behaviour in *holistic* terms. What an individual does is very much the result of an interaction between individual competencies, complex motivations and situational factors – both in the culture of the organization and in his or her personal life. One such important motivating factor is the extent to which one is told what to do versus thinking for oneself. This is especially true of entrepreneurial behaviour because it is virtually defined in terms of interaction with, and feedback from, the environment (market).

> **Rather than rationally analysing job requirements, deciding who to place where and then acting, the manager of tomorrow will have to be more responsive to the bottom-up flow of decision making.**

The upshot of all of this is that organizations that want to be truly creative will have to re-examine the rational model of thinking, deciding, acting and organizational functioning in all of its easily overlooked manifestations.

So, when we speak of entrepreneurial skills or attributes, the idea is to see these as organizational *values*, which you should use to encourage employees to behave accordingly, rather than as competencies that you might be tempted to use to put individuals into entrepreneurial slots.

THE ENTREPRENEUR AT HEART

Creating the future

Creativity is at the core of entrepreneurial activity. This is not the creativity of the artist sitting in isolation in a studio, but rather the creativity that arises from dynamic interaction with a fast changing environment. Once a new idea is conceived, its implementation and exploitation require good management, but in the early stages of bringing new product ideas to fruition – the end product shape is too unknown to be as precisely planned as the building of a house. For entrepreneurial activity to be comparable to house building you would have to imagine house builders who have never built or even seen a house and, to make matters worse, have to guess what sort of house the customer might be inclined to buy once it is finished.

This form of creativity only works if the person or team involved can recognize an opportunity when they see one. Bill Gates, the founder of Microsoft, made much of his fortune from the software operating system called DOS. But he only knew that he wanted to create computer languages. A bit of luck was involved as well when IBM asked him to develop an operating system for their PC and he just happened to know of someone who had one.

Gates apparently told IBM where to get the DOS operating system, but IBM wanted someone else to take responsibility for this part of the PC so they could focus on building the hardware. As a result, Gates stumbled into a fortune. The difference between Gates and IBM was his willingness to think creatively and to recognize and act on an opportunity. Even he, however, did not see it initially and had to be prompted by IBM. So it is by no means easy to see the future.

You need to be creative in order to see possibilities where no one else does, but entrepreneurial creativity is not just limited to creative responding to a market that seemingly creates itself. The most creative entrepreneurial organizations will create whole new markets through their hunches about the direction in which existing markets are moving. These leading entrepreneurs will also create new opportunities for others who are quickest to see the implications of the leader's innovations for a particular market.

Let go of control and embrace the unexpected

The frightening aspect of launching entrepreneurial ventures, if you are a senior executive schooled in conventional management skills, is the loss of control entailed. It is not just that too much control stifles creativity – as it would do if you restricted an artist to designing a known type of commercially viable art – but that the market's evolution is so uncertain.

> **The most creative entrepreneurial organizations will create whole new markets through their hunches about the direction in which existing markets are moving.**

This means that entrepreneurial creativity is essentially an exploratory, almost playful activity. It entails an active search for opportunities by networking with other market leaders and customers. The search for new products is worse than looking for a needle in a haystack, because in this case, you don't know which haystack to look under and you don't know what the needle looks like.

Customer feedback

If I am in a customer contact job, should the organization tell me what competencies I need to do a good job? Is this not the outdated approach of the staff function dictating to the line and, far worse, telling the customer what is best for him? Clearly, I would be better advised to ask my customers. One customer might value speed, another might prefer a friendly relationship, another's first priority might be regularity and reliability, still another might have quality at the top of his list. A highly technical customer might value a chat about the latest technical developments and so on. Even if I distilled a core set of such process requirements from my experience to decide what *most* of my customers wanted, that still wouldn't tell me how to treat individual customers.

Non-managerial career paths

This will be a hard one for many managers to swallow because it means (especially in fast changing industries) having to admit that climbing the traditional hierarchical ladder is less important now it is moving away from the core organizational competence that will drive the organization into the future.

Where are we now?

We started this chapter by asking what sorts of skills characterize the entrepreneur in large organizations and concluded that too narrow a focus on individual skills is part and parcel of a decidedly anti-entrepreneurial way to proceed. The upshot of this is to look instead at how to change the organization so that entrepreneurial behaviour will flourish. Leaving open the question of just what skills people will need to be successfully entrepreneurial is itself an entrepreneurial approach to the question we started this chapter with.

More discussion is needed of the cultural changes you will have to make if you want to stimulate extensive entrepreneurial behaviour. This will be reserved for a later chapter, along with more on non-managerial career paths.

One of the most fundamental organizational changes you will need to consider in order to stimulate more entrepreneurial behaviour in your business is to re-conceptualize *leadership* and it is to a discussion of how to do this that we now turn.

PRACTICAL STEPS

- advocate process values instead of process competencies, that is focus on the cultural environment you want to develop rather than directly on people themselves: cultivate values about how employees should treat customers and each other, teamwork, etc

- reward people on the basis of outputs or results

- let people manage their own performance by soliciting their own feedback from their own customers – internal or external

- try people out on short projects, let them prove themselves on bits of jobs (cross-functional projects for example) rather than assessing them against an alleged entrepreneurial competency profile

- develop non-managerial, professional career schemes that foster contribution to organizational self-renewal.

"Anyone who takes any initiative that has a significant impact on an organization's direction or how it does its business, can be said to be showing leadership."

"The fundamental point here is that leadership should not be restricted, on a long-term basis, to one individual who happens to be entrenched in a formal, hierarchical position."

4

DRIVING TO SELF-RENEWAL –
KNOWLEDGE LEADERSHIP

If there are indeed two distinct and quite different organizational tasks – 1) ongoing delivery of existing products, and 2) self-renewal – might there not also be different kinds of leadership required to achieve these objectives?

In the last chapter we looked at the issue of whether it is advisable to focus on the likely skills an entrepreneurial employee should have and we concluded that it is more appropriate to focus on building a supportive culture rather than trying to identify entrepreneurial candidates and fit them into new venture slots. Individual entrepreneurs should simply emerge if the cultural environment is appropriately stimulating and supportive. The more successful among them will be *leaders* despite having no positional authority. The question in need of addressing now is: What does it mean to show such leadership and how should you encourage it?

BOTTOM-UP LEADERSHIP

There is now a widely recognized distinction between management and leadership (or between transactional and transformational leadership). The idea is that managers or transactional leaders focus on the straightforward implementation of decisions and monitor progress towards clear-cut goals while leaders, particularly the transformational variety, help to create new directions. What these types of leadership have in common is that they are both top-down and conceived as applying to leaders who are also in positions of formal authority. Entrepreneurial leadership may be transformational, but it is not necessarily top-down. The purpose of top-down leadership is to get every-one pulling in the same direction – vital to achieve the efficient co-ordination necessary for the cost effective delivery of existing services or products.

Entrepreneurial leadership essentially needs to turn aside from what the mainstream organization is doing. It is a matter of starting over with a new venture albeit under a broad corporate umbrella. Corporate entrepreneurs are likely to be those employees who are:

- immersed in new market trends and product/service possibilities
- technical/knowledge leaders with no *status quo* to manage or protect
- able to command respect and to provide direction based on expertise
- close to the bottom of the organizational hierarchy
- passionate about novel ideas whatever their background.

So what is leadership, really?

> **Entrepreneurial leadership essentially needs to turn aside from what the mainstream organization is doing. It is a matter of starting over with a new venture albeit under a broad corporate umbrella.**

We know intuitively that the ability to lead has something to do with providing direction. As business becomes more knowledge intensive, market direction and the development of new products and services depend increasingly on leadership from so-called knowledge workers. Knowledge has long been recognised as a source of power and as it shifts to workers who are at the 'leading' edge of their technical field and/or close to the customer, the knowledge possessed by managers can become obsolete overnight, fuelling their anxiety and identity crisis.

Search for new sources of leadership

To pin down the changing meaning of leadership, it is useful to explore the ways in which it is shifting away from the positional hierarchy to other sources.

We speak loosely of 'market leaders', and 'thought leaders' (ideas people). Organizations are warned to be market led or die. The notion of 'consumer led' economic recovery stems from the felt powerlessness of both business and political leaders to lead us out of recession, suggesting, at a macro level, the need to develop some conception of *bottom-up* leadership. The virtue of being market led is seen as indisputable today, but if the market 'leads' the organization from just outside its boundaries, then leadership on the inside must come from those who are closest to the market – not necessarily from executives at the top of the pyramid.

Business leadership, in its most general connotation, can come from anywhere within or outside organizational boundaries. Anyone who takes any initiative that has a significant impact on an organization's direction or how it does its business, can be said to be showing leadership. Such leadership does not have to be provided only by those who are in positions of formal authority.

Unfortunately, mainstream organizational leadership theory is not readily able to deal with such anomalous forms of leadership. Historically, theorising about leadership has always operated with an hierarchical organization in mind where leadership is conceived exclusively as a top-down direction. The question that leadership theorists posed themselves was: What is the best means of influencing people *over whom one has formal authority*? Traditional theories of leadership acknowledged the existence of *informal influence*, but their main interest was how to characterize the leadership of those with the power of position and formal authority.

It is increasingly apparent that this whole tradition of leadership theory is severely limited if not completely bankrupt. Formal authority has been eroding for decades. The thin end of the wedge, back in the seventies, was the recognition that better educated workers respond more positively to 'enriched' job responsibilities and involvement in significant decision making, effectively rendering management a shared enterprise. Now, formal authority is nearly obsolete as a cornerstone of leadership.

Hierarchy is not inevitable

As leadership shifts from the organizational hierarchy to leading-edge knowledge workers and budding entrepreneurs who are close to the market, the inevitable question is: Why has hierarchy remained so powerful for so long? Why has so much effort been expended to define the characteristics of the *formal* leader? And why do we seem to want to follow a *single individual*, someone who has, in some sense, a complete set of whatever attributes it takes to be a leader?

According to Abraham Zaleznik (1989), hierarchy is a brute fact of human nature:

> 'Despite experiments with the equalization of power, the fact of hierarchy persists … Ranging from the animal kingdom to human groups, relationships form into an hierarchy.' In support of his defence of hierarchy, Zaleznik argues that, 'In study after study of group formations in work and "natural" groups, leaders and followers align themselves into a remarkably predictable relationship with few at the top and many at the bottom of the power pyramid.'

This claim seems intuitively correct. In any informal group of workers who have never met before, someone will be more knowledgeable about the subject under discussion and/or more personally persuasive than the others, thereby ending up exerting more influence, hence assuming a position at the top of an hierarchy, however transient it may be.

But *transient* is precisely the point! First of all, it is debatable whether such a pecking order is indeed inevitable. Knowledge workers and organizations increasingly see each other as strategic partners rather than as superiors or subordinates.

The fundamental point here is that leadership should not be restricted, on a long-term basis, to one individual who happens to be entrenched in a formal, hierarchical position.

But, more importantly, even if one person is inevitably more influential in any human group discussion, it does not follow that such an hierarchy should be elevated to the status of a formal organization. In network organizations, groups and teams will be much more transient. Projects come and go quickly and team members network with a wide range of contacts outside their immediate team to a far greater extent than in the past. The person who is most influential in one group may be least influential in another and leadership will be constantly shifting. The point is that influence will increasingly gravitate to the person with the most market/technical knowledge at any given moment, quickly shifting relative to a million-and-one different subjects.

The fundamental point here is that leadership should not be restricted, on a long-term basis, to one individual who happens to be entrenched in a formal, hierarchical position.

Zaleznik goes on to argue that hierarchical status must be clearly established, otherwise people feel anxious: 'If groups are unsuccessful in alleviating status anxiety, ever more regressive defences will appear, including hostile projections of malevolence onto various group members.'

But surely such anxiety is to a great extent a function of expectations. If workers are accustomed to being thoroughly unempowered and having to rely on direction from above, we should expect them to feel anxious when faced with the sudden loss of clear hierarchical leadership. Such anxiety is common when a group that is used to an autocratic manager gets a new boss whose style is markedly more democratic. The new style is experienced relative to the old and feels like an absence of leadership. As knowledge workers become ever more empowered and confident, most of this status anxiety should dissipate.

A certain increase in anxiety is unavoidable in organizations today anyway. It is becoming virtually impossible for those at the top to articulate a single clear direction (applicable to an entire, diverse organization) – except in nebulous terms. Multiple directions are pursued simultaneously, led by a wide range of diverse knowledge workers. It is only those who are dependent on the security of total organizational unity and uniformity who will feel a debilitating degree of anxiety in these altered circumstances.

THE DEATH OF HIERARCHY

Is hierarchy finally on the way out then? Or does it have an unassailable staying power? Zaleznik's point about the universality of hierarchy throughout the animal kingdom reminds us just how primitive it is to want to follow one specific individual. Until very recently, rising to the top of an organization was not only a function of perceived leadership qualities. Age and experience (presumably including wisdom) were also vital along with a natural human desire for some form of personal progress. (See Psychological slant.)

PSYCHOLOGICAL SLANT

Very primitive and historically unchallenged factors are among the many and complex reasons why we are motivated to preserve the status quo of organizational hierarchy

- *we need to think that we are making progress as we age to avoid facing the feelings of decline and death – career progress means promotion*

- *historically (and primitively) we associate leadership with age*

- *power helps us to feel indestructible and to a degree immortal*

- *at a primitive level we seem to need to look up to someone*

- *our feeling of achievement is dependent on an admiring audience, so executives need to encourage others to follow in their footsteps*

- *the biological drive to pass on our genes to an eldest son underlies the need in top executives to foster internal succession*

- *internal succession policies maintain an explosive mixture of subservience and aggression towards the top, powerfully sustaining the status quo*

- *at a primitive level, a single clear direction is anxiety reducing.*

The destructive side of hierarchy

However deeply and unconsciously entrenched, we are surely witnessing the disintegration of hierarchy. It will soon go the way of the Berlin Wall. The market will force it to accept the leadership of leading-edge knowledge workers. An alternative conception of leadership is now beginning to take shape. Unfortunately, entrenched paradigms are notoriously difficult to criticize; their omnipresence makes it impossible to imagine any other way of looking at things. Now that hierarchy is receding in the face of market pressure, it is easier to look critically at the negative side of hierarchy:

- Excessive dependency – career success is too dependent on the whim of a powerful few and this inhibits creativity in organizations – jokes about 'career limiting' moves are all too serious, hence avoidance of risk.

- Disempowerment – lack of initiative because leadership is expected exclusively from the top, hence abdication of personal responsibility.
- Excessive fear caused by a concentration of power leads to blaming, defensiveness, an unwillingness to admit errors, poor communication and inability to learn from mistakes.
- 'Theory X' behaviour – the behaviour of lazy or poorly motivated workers is likely *caused* in large part by their recognition of their powerlessness – a naturally dispiriting and depressing state of mind.
- Executives notice subordinates avoiding responsibility but fail to correct the situation by attacking the root cause. Instead they impose greater control thereby making the problem worse.
- Blockage of creativity at the top of the pyramid due to the preoccupation with preserving power rather than focusing on what is best for the organization – attention is diverted to internal process and politics – away from the market.
- A ruinously expensive obsession with advancement to managerial roles to the detriment of market-valued skills that could enhance an organization's core competence and improve its competitive advantage.

This last, vitally important, point needs elaboration. A classic dilemma in organizations is whether to promote the best technical person to the role of manager. Merit seems to demand it, but the too often tragic consequence is that the organization gains a poor manager and loses its best technician. The culture of hierarchy forces everyone to strive for hierarchical advancement. Failure is the only option. A mind-boggling amount of talent, direction and energy is thereby squandered.

> **The culture of hierarchy forces everyone to strive for hierarchical advancement. Failure is the only option. A mind-boggling amount of talent, direction and energy is thereby squandered.**

The solution is surely to elevate the status of knowledge workers who exert informal influence through their performance, and reward them accordingly while not burdening them with too much unnecessary managerial baggage.

A fully market-led organization should require such individuals to continually prove themselves through their performance in any case, not allow them to rest on their laurels by giving them the tenure and status of position.

ENTREPRENEURIAL KNOWLEDGE WORKERS AS LEADERS

Knowledge workers are notorious for respecting competence and good ideas while scoffing at influence attempts based solely on position. Leadership to them must take the form of indicating substantive possible scenarios deemed worth working towards, not necessarily something as grandiose as a vision, but simply a better idea, however small, which knowledge workers feel they can bring to fruition through their efforts. Such scenarios will often take the form of technical 'what if' possibilities which excite the imagination of the knowledge worker and which seem achievable, however challenging to bring about. Such novel possibilities are exciting because they arouse feelings of conquest and a competitive desire to be first, like being the first person to climb a challenging mountain. This is a form of leadership to which everyone at the forefront of his or her professional field can aspire.

More importantly, this is a form of leadership completely divorced from the formal authority of position. An example of such a leader might be someone who is regularly coming up with new product ideas. How does this form of leadership compare with positional leadership? There is the impact of such leadership on select groups of individuals to consider, but this is not the same as leading an entire organization. Part of the answer to the latter question is that the 'whole' organization is no longer the only meaningful unit of analysis – especially those that are loosely held together federations of distinct businesses.

> **But as today's knowledge workers are increasingly empowered to risk testing their ideas in the marketplace, the market itself will determine which of such leadership initiatives the organization will follow.**

Immediate colleagues tend to see such a technical leader as a role model to emulate and learn from. Traditional leadership theorists would argue that they have always recognized this knowledge-as-power type of informal influence. What is not so readily acknowledged is how rapidly and comprehensively the most critical source of leadership is shifting in this direction in contemporary leading-edge organizations.

Innovative firms like 3M have long had such entrepreneurial, knowledge worker leaders who have struggled to exercise a leadership impact on the broader organization. Without positional power or personal charisma, many fail to have any broader impact. When they do succeed (as with 3M's famous Post-it notes) it is only through persistence, rebelliousness, behind the scenes networking and recruitment of support champions. But as today's knowledge workers are increasingly empowered to risk testing their ideas in the market-place, the market itself will determine which of such leadership initiatives the organization will follow.

WHITHER CONVENTIONAL TOP-DOWN LEADERSHIP?

Not all organizations are so driven by technological change nor so dependent on knowledge workers. Service industries, for example, compete through high-quality service delivered cost effectively. Knowledge workers are not fundamental to the core business of McDonald's, for instance. Even within fast moving consumer goods and high-tech industries, many functions, including finance, sales and production need to concentrate on efficiency, cost and quality rather than the wholesale creation of new products and totally new businesses from nothing.

Leadership within a delivery-orientated organization

As we have seen, organizations have two distinct tasks: delivery of ongoing products/services and self-renewal. The latter depends on knowledge-led entrepreneurship, while the former requires traditional managerial skills.

It is interesting to note that leadership in knowledge-driven industries must revolve essentially around the *content* of the proposed new direction (hence knowledge-based leadership), whereas delivery leadership is fundamentally *process* or relationship orientated. This explains why most traditional leadership theory portrays leadership in terms of superior-subordinate *relationships* and strives to characterize the ideal influence *process* – because prior to today's higher pressure to innovate, the primary competitive differentiator was low-cost, efficient delivery of existing offerings.

Traditional leadership theory is also based on the assumption that leadership is not industry specific. (Situational leadership deals only with variations in relationships and specific task situations – across all industries.) Even those theorists (such as Abraham Zaleznik, 1989) who have drawn a distinction between managers and leaders on the basis of concern for process versus concern for content have supposed their prescriptions to be universally applicable.

Leadership in a delivery dominated organization is primarily concerned with motivation, such as in cosmetic sales firms like Mary Kay or Avon. Charisma is a useful leadership trait in such a context to extract the extra effort needed to meet and exceed sales targets. This is the sort of leadership that cheer-leaders provide to a football team. Charisma is less important in a knowledge-based firm and can be seen as phoney by knowledge workers who are suspicious of any form of influence other than that based on technical competence.

So-called transformational leadership fails to make the distinction between content and process and is really just a hyped up version of older conceptions of leadership. In fact it is only possible to develop a theory of transformational leadership by painting a straw man picture of leaders labelled as transactional. The theory of transformational leadership can be seen as a last-ditch attempt to salvage fast eroding hierarchical leadership. It is based essentially on the observation that leadership was not working, that organizations were stagnating or evolving in chaotic fashion. Excellent top-down transformational leadership is clearly useful to motivate workers engaged in the delivery of existing products or services, but it does not apply so readily to knowledge-based functions and industries.

Leadership in the renewal-orientated, knowledge-driven organization

Leadership skill in an entrepreneurial part of an organization is the ability to influence others to work towards the realization of a concept or idea. Such leadership skill will not necessarily depend on position, charisma or brilliant interpersonal skills. Knowledge workers are most likely to be influenced by the logic of the possibility presented, their desire to achieve and natural competitive feelings. Being more empowered than their organizational ancestors, they will not need to wait for the 'boss' to tell them what direction to follow. Opportunistic knowledge workers who

> **So-called transformational leadership fails to make the distinction between content and process and is really just a hyped up version of older conceptions of leadership.**

are themselves actively searching for new ideas will be quick to jump onto an obvious gem (provided it does not violate their own pet notions too radically – a significant cause of resistance to change in anyone, knowledge worker or not).

Irrespective of whether they have any formal authority, it is very tempting to say that *only* those knowledge workers who have a bit of charisma in addition to good ideas could be described as *real* leaders. Only they could both develop substantive new directions *and* influence (lead) the larger organization to change. But this is to fall into the trap of seeing leadership primitively as pertaining to the behaviour of a single individual. The need to equate leadership with the action of one person is bound up with our primitive need for hierarchy.

A fundamental shift in our conception of leadership is now demanded by growing market, business and technical complexity. The revolutionary effect of these changes is one of completely *dispersing* leadership across a wide range of diverse individuals, some of whom will not even be within the organization. Such dispersed leadership is not just spread across more individuals, but more importantly, broken down into components that allow everyone to show some aspect of leadership, however small. This suggests that we should stop characterizing leadership solely in terms of the personality or behavioural attributes of individuals and start thinking about *leadership acts*.

Leadership acts

It is immediately clear that this is a very empowering notion. Individuals no longer need to pass or fail with regard to whether they have the requisite attributes in sufficient quantity to be considered *a* leader. Anyone can show the occasional leadership act defined as any initiative that influences how an organization does its business.

This conception of leadership gets around the absurdity of saying that an innovator who is technically excellent, who has no formal authority and whose ideas have fundamentally changed the direction of the organization, but who has zero charisma, is not a leader. He may not be a leader as traditionally conceived but his initiatives are definitely leadership acts which clearly lead the organization.

Rather than struggling to formulate an exhaustive list of traits with which to characterize the ideal leader, we can classify leadership acts. Instead of referring to task- and people-orientated behaviours of *the* leader, we can refer to leadership acts that have an impact on task direction, and leadership acts that influence how people work together. It does not really matter how many different people it takes to generate a particular leadership impact.

Dispersed, multi-directional versus individual, top-down leadership

Anxiety caused by uncertainty induces us to want clear leadership, preferably from one strong individual. Certainty is rightly valued in service businesses that need efficient delivery, but high technology, fast moving consumer goods firms need to pursue several directions at once. They need to back possible losers due to the unpredictability of what customers will buy. For example, Sony needs to continue to sell CD players (delivery) while developing high-risk new formats such as its mini-disk, and researching (perhaps several) other possibilities.

There is great confusion over the issue of whether clear, unequivocal direction is necessary. This misunderstanding revolves around lumping together individual and organizational needs. Clearly an individual can only concentrate on one thing at a time in order to do it well, but an organization, which is little more than a federation of discrete businesses, hardly needs to be pulling in a single direction. In the latter, diversity is a strength. It is only a liability in excessively top-down controlled firms where too few try to know too much about unrelated businesses.

In multi-product businesses, leadership is dispersed across those individuals who are closest to their own product markets. More importantly, the components of leadership will increasingly be spread across more individuals as well. In any given team, each member might exhibit technical leadership acts on different projects. If each team member has reasonably effective interpersonal skills, he or she may display people leadership acts from time to time. In self-managing teams, no one person needs to be designated as *the* leader.

NEW FUNCTIONS FOR SENIOR EXECUTIVES

What becomes of senior executives in entrepreneurial, less structured, network organizations? The first answer is that there will be fewer of them. Most of an organization's members will be in small, floating, cross-functional teams staying close to market and technological changes.

Being a senior executive and retaining one's technical and market edge is almost a contradiction in terms in today's fast moving markets. But it is equally hard to be a generalist and maintain an accurate overview if you are too far removed from current developments. Much substantive leadership will come from leading-edge knowledge workers, but senior executives can show leadership in a number of ways by:

- networking outside the organization and pulling together groups with likely synergies, even if there is no obvious product in mind
- recognizing and developing leadership in others, encouraging them to focus on the development of core business competence, rather than internal status and position
- personal mentoring, internal consulting and troubleshooting
- creating and maintaining environments that stimulate learning and innovation
- encouraging risk-taking ventures and sponsoring new idea leaders
- helping the organization to balance its need to retain its unique and discrete identity against the need to have open boundaries for the active exchange of ideas with outsiders

- keeping delivery of existing offerings on the rails efficiently and profitably.

It is useful to think of leadership *functions* (as well as leadership *acts*) in place of old-fashioned talk of *roles* which is bound up with structure, hierarchy and an excessive focus on individuals. Clearly several people can fulfil a function. Any organization needs to fulfil a variety of leadership functions. Most leadership acts will fall into one or more leadership categories, i.e. developing new products, enhancing quality, convincing people to contribute to a counter-intuitive plan, etc.

Some of these categories should be formalized as leadership functions that would be seen as essential for competitive success. Such functions can be fulfilled by a variety of senior executives so long as you do not regress to thinking that any one individual needs to be the super exemplar of all or most of these functions. Senior executives can exhibit leadership by ensuring that all critical leadership functions are fulfilled by someone, and by as many people as possible.

Formal authority

As customer

The formal authority of senior executives in entrepreneurial organizations is that of the customer. 'Subordinates' will increasingly be regarded as suppliers of services. Senior executives are charged with the trust of the shareholders to manage the financial resources of the company. It is up to them to 'buy' the best combination of products and services to sell on to the organization's customers.

Senior executives can exercise leadership with respect to 'employees' much as they are beginning to with conventional suppliers and strategic partners. However, influence will flow in both directions in equal measure. Suppliers (knowledge workers) will often exert more leadership than they receive in return.

As venture capitalist

Senior executives can be compared to venture capitalists in this context. They have a pool of capital to invest in product lines that are run as virtually separate businesses. The authority of the senior executive as venture capitalist is also that of the customer rather than that of the traditional boss.

As broker

While knowledge workers liaise directly with existing customers, senior executives can search further afield for new customers, new markets and strategic partners. They can fulfil the function of broker by looking for synergies between the offerings of their business and the needs of potential customers and partners.

Growing older but still better

In the good old days, there was a close parallel between growing older and climbing the hierarchical ladder, getting away from the firing line or coal face as it was called. As the ranks of senior executives become depleted and they begin to take on the function of broker/venture capitalist, anxiety about career progression is bound to increase.

Career progress in organizations will simply have to be redefined. One can progress in one's career just as does any professional such as a doctor or lawyer – by gaining in prestige despite lack of hierarchical progression. This entails staying closer to one's technical profession throughout one's career.

There is a commonly held belief that innovation is the province of younger people. But creativity in older managers may be largely stifled by preoccupation with gaining and preserving position.

Delivery functions and organizations need less creativity and can be managed hierarchically. Indeed, there is an hierarchy of organizations along a continuum from fast moving, highly knowledge-based industries, i.e. computers, to relatively more slowly changing service industries. An alternative source of traditional career progression would be to move from fast changing businesses to slower paced organizations where commercial skills can contribute to improving the profitability of delivering relatively stable services.

Senior executives today have new ways of using their authority (other than in the role of traditional bosses) – as customers, brokers, venture capitalists, etc. – as well as new ways to show leadership. The recognition and cultivation of leadership in knowledge workers does not necessarily mean that senior executives are less important. At the moment they are in a position to display leadership by adapting and working out for themselves new ways of showing leadership.

Where are we now?

Entrepreneurial organizations cannot neglect the day-to-day delivery of existing products and services if they are to exploit new ventures generated by risk taking. They also need to cultivate entrepreneurial skills in their employees and while it may help to champion and recognize a defined set of entrepreneurial behaviours it is essential not to be too prescriptive and bureaucratic about the way you identify and develop the right people. This 'human resource' process should, in itself, be as entrepreneurial as possible.

A specific skill that it is most important to recognize is entrepreneurial leadership. But recognizing such skill is only half the battle. You also need to change your culture sufficiently to allow room for such leadership to live side by side with more conventional leadership of the top-down variety. This means elevating the status of the former at the expense of the latter and this will be no easy task. It calls for a unique form of self-sacrificing leadership on the part of those already in power.

We need now to turn away from looking at entrepreneurial skills and explore one of the essential processes by which organizations can create and sustain an entrepreneurial culture: *organizational learning*.

PRACTICAL STEPS

- while remaining entrepreneurially open to variations, define as clearly as possible a range of leadership behaviours you would like to encourage among budding entrepreneurial employees

- implement support systems to encourage and cultivate leadership acts at all levels. This will entail major culture change in many firms

- actively help those with positional power to adapt to a radically new culture and to avoid inappropriate use of their authority

- develop a high-profile recognition system to reinforce leadership acts in order to identify and reward role models

- invest time and resources in risk takers who show new product or service leadership to help them further their development.

"The relationship between such individual learning-as-knowledge-acquisition and organizational learning-as-getting-fast-feedback needs to be made as close as possible."

"Individuals need to be encouraged to learn in the same manner as the entrepreneurial organization does – by taking risks, experimenting and adjusting their behaviour on the basis of what succeeds and what does not work (not just on the basis of mistakes)."

5

WHAT HAS YOUR ORGANIZATION LEARNED TODAY

The key to an entrepreneurial future or just another fad?

'Organizational learning' is one of the hottest buzz words of the moment. Just when you thought you were coming to grips with such (ancient) ideas as total quality management you are told that organizational learning is even more crucial for the survival of your business. Many claim that it is the only source of sustainable competitive advantage for the future – a sort of organizational fountain of youth.

> **Organizational learning is undoubtedly a good idea if only we could figure out what it is and how to do it. Unfortunately, its perceived importance is leading every human resource guru of any persuasion to claim it as his own.**

Organizational learning is undoubtedly a good idea if only we could figure out what it is and how to do it. Unfortunately, its perceived importance is leading every human resource guru of any persuasion to claim it as his own. We are told that anything at all to do with employee involvement, all forms of employee training and even creating a quality organization, contributes to being a learning organization. In consequence, the concept is in danger of becoming so diffuse as to render it meaningless or too all encompassing to provide useful guidance to practising managers.

We are thus left with more questions than answers. For example, what is the difference (or link) between individual and organizational learning? Does such learning involve the development of new attitudes and new skills or is it primarily about the acquisition of esoteric, market leading, high-tech knowledge, that is the sort of knowledge that builds up an organization's core competence? Can a one-man band, entrepreneurial organization in a low-tech industry learn? Or does the concept just apply to fast moving, knowledge-driven companies?

Most important for our purposes in this chapter is the question: What is the connection between being an entrepreneurial organization and being one that learns?

LEARNING IN THE SMALL ENTREPRENEURIAL FIRM

Never too small to learn

How we think about organizational learning is partly governed by whether we focus on large, perhaps rather bureaucratic, organizations which need to learn faster, or whether we look at smaller entrepreneurial firms. If an entrepreneurial firm is highly successful you could say either that it does not need to learn or that it is already very good at it. You would be inclined towards the former view if you saw organizational learning as being predominantly about undoing bad habits.

If we focus on large blue-chip firms, which perhaps need to learn faster, it is an obvious next step to look at the people who make up the organization and ask what is blocking their learning. This leads us to look at the organization as a system with deep-set ways of doing things which can inhibit learning.

If we start by asking what characterizes the learning of a smaller, successful entrepreneurial business, we tend to be drawn more to the interaction between the business and its environment instead of look-ing inside the company at its employees. What seems to characterize entrepreneurial learning in the smaller firm is trial and error action and quick adjustment based on market feedback.

The simplest example of this type of organizational learning would be a sole proprietor of a market stall, who, instead of obliviously ped-dling the same wares year in, year out, watches customers carefully to see what they buy from other stalls, and who regularly displays new wares to see what will attract customers. He quickly drops what is not selling and tries something else. He *is* the organization and this is surely pure organizational learning.

An advantage of this example is that it shows that organizational learning is not restricted to knowledge-intensive high-tech businesses. It also draws our attention to the *essential* feature of organizational learning. (See Figure 5.1.)

ESSENCE OF ORGANIZATIONAL LEARNING

Organizational learning is not fundamentally the acquisition of esoteric high-tech knowledge by leading-edge knowledge workers, or the introspective breaking down of mental blocks which get in the way of our seeing the world in a new light. It is simply trial and error action leading to organizational adjustments based on market feedback.

Figure 5.1

This simpler picture of organizational learning is obscured if we think first of large bureaucratic organizations. Many large firms are so averse to risk taking and so paralysed that they need to do some mental gymnastics before they can even begin to take the sort of entrepreneurial action necessary to generate real world feedback. And it is in this context that organizational and individual learning get muddled in together.

> **Many large firms are so averse to risk taking and so paralysed that they need to do some mental gymnastics before they can even begin to take the sort of entrepreneurial action necessary to generate real world feedback.**

Individual employee learning will definitely involve knowledge acquisition which is often of a very technical, highly specialized nature. However vital this form of learning may be, it should not be confused with organizational learning.

IS LEARNING RATIONAL OR ENTREPRENEURIAL?

Organizational versus individual learning

When we focus on the organization–environment interaction, we can view the organization itself as being an individual rather than just a short-hand way of referring to a collection of employees. The organization-as-individual in its environment is merely one among many other individuals: customers, suppliers and competitors.

Only the individual organization as a whole can act in its environment. Only the organization as a whole can introduce a new product, see the error of its ways – thereby learning – and modify the product. No department, small group or subset of the total organization, however they act, can call themselves *the* organization. (See Figure 5.2.)

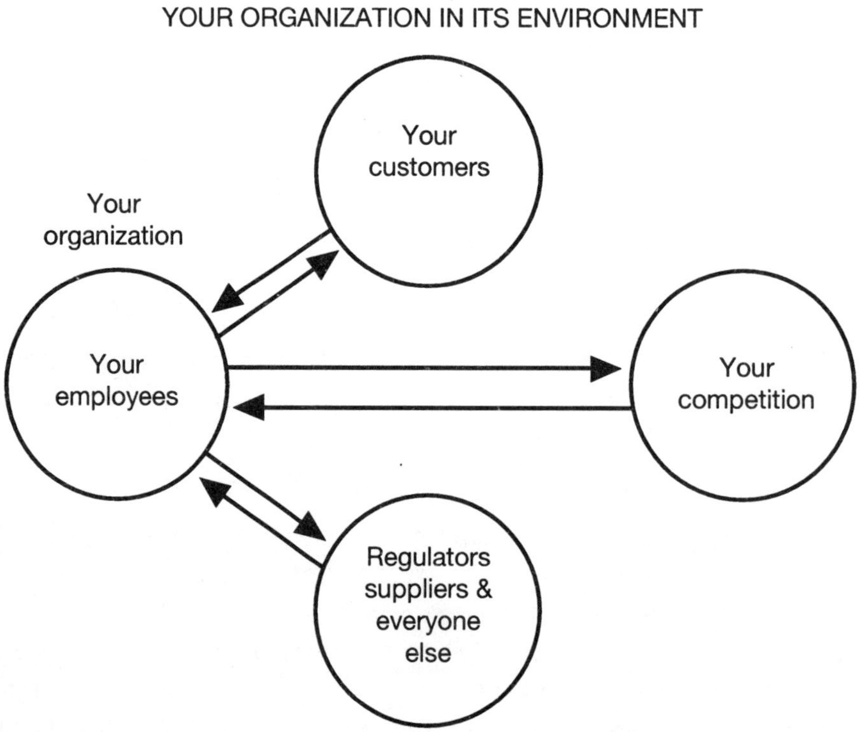

YOUR ORGANIZATION IN ITS ENVIRONMENT

Figure 5.2

Avoiding the internal focus trap

'Why should we look at our own organization from the "outside" in this manner?' you might object. Interestingly, we see ourselves personally from the inside and everyone else from the outside. So we do the same with our organization and others in its environment. And this is at least one major reason why we tend to view organizational learning as being a matter of employee learning – they are inside. But this is the slippery slope that leads to too much internal focus and, in extremis, to

> **Entrepreneurial organizations do not suffer from analysis-paralysis. They act quickly without thinking through alternatives to the nth degree.**

isolation from reality. It is precisely because we are in fact inescapably trapped inside ourselves that we have to make a special effort to see ourselves and our organizations from a third-person perspective, difficult as this may be.

There is no denying the importance of employee learning, but however much they may need to learn, the subject of organizational learning is only of interest with regard to understanding organizational effectiveness if the organization itself can be seen as having the capability of doing something different in its environment as a result of learning.

Small organizations have 'smaller insides' to get trapped in

Entrepreneurial organizations do not suffer from analysis-paralysis. They act quickly without thinking through alternatives to the nth degree. They take risks and are willing to learn from their mistakes. The learning of individual people *in* the entrepreneurial organization seems therefore to depend on the organization's learning. This is a very important point because if we start our investigation of organizational learning by thinking about larger, slower moving corporations, we seem to be led to the opposite conclusion – that organizational learning is based on the prior learning of its members.

The idea that organizational learning is more basic than that of its individual members makes a crucial difference to how you might go about implementing organizational learning. If you focus on your organization-in-its-environment, you will be led to look at ways to make it more entrepreneurial. If on the other hand, you focus on the learning of your organization's human members, you may strive to boost any manner of individual training and development programmes, the building of a library and efforts to break down outmoded thought patterns – all in a very unfocused way.

It is important to be perfectly clear that organizational and individual learning are quite independent and different. An example may serve to show how an organization might learn without much, if any, learning on the part of the people in it. Consider an instance of product failure – individual employees in the organization may begrudgingly contribute to modifying the failed product until it sells but stubbornly try the failed idea in another form – thinking that customers are stupid – hence failing to learn from this particular product failure. But the organization learns by introducing product modifications or new products and seeing what sells. Equally, other employees may really see the light, based on the organization's success with the modified product. Individual learning is, in both cases, clearly derivative rather than a prior condition of organizational learning.

When a product fails (or succeeds), it is the organization's product. It does not belong to any one person or group of persons in the organization. It is therefore the organization which gets feedback in the first instance. While this may seem like a mere semantic quibble, it is actually extremely vital. The reason this is so is that if we focus on enabling the organization to get feedback on its actions then we are led to concentrate on how *it* behaves in its environment with respect to its competitors. This approach helps to encourage an external focus rather than an internal one.

Conversely, individual employees can learn without the organization learning anything. Imagine an R&D organization staffed by leading-edge specialists who are forever learning in order to stay at the forefront of their field. But the organization as a whole could be very bureaucratic and slow to act. It could persist in offering products that no one wants – seeing itself losing market share but not knowing what to do about it except, defensively, to cut costs. Hence, individuals are learning, but the organization is not. Brilliant product innovations may be created but the organization may simply dither too long in introducing them to its market until the opportunity has passed. This suggests that an organization has to take risks to learn. In essence, *it* has to *act* and make mistakes. *It* has to vary its responses (product introductions or modifications) to maximize the range of feedback it gets – so that, thereby learning, it can modify its behaviour in accordance with the demands of its environment.

So why is there so much emphasis on employee learning?

At the root of the confusion over employee versus organizational learning is what might be called the *rational* theory of thinking, deciding, acting and organizational functioning. This theory is simply that people think-decide-act all in a unidirectional, logical sequence and, somewhat incidentally, get feedback on their actions. I say 'somewhat incidentally' because, however much value the rational model puts on feedback, the most emphasis is placed upon the think-decide stage. This theory can also be called the 'inside-out' theory of human action because it sees behaviour as resulting primarily from what goes on inside our heads. (See Figure 5.3.)

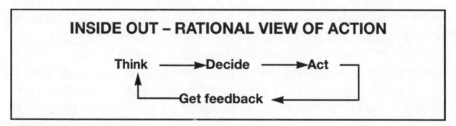

Figure 5.3

While it would be absurd to claim that action can occur without *any* prior thinking and deciding, the rational model overly emphasizes the causal value of the thinking stage. It is this over emphasis that leads to paralysis, an overly analytical approach to strategy formulation, too much inward focus and too little willingness to take risks and learn from mistakes. This model causes us to put too much effort into getting the decision right before acting.

The behavioural, entrepreneurial view recognizes that we often act without fully thinking through the implications. It is simply a different

> **The behavioural, entrepreneurial view recognizes that we often act without fully thinking through the implications.**

emphasis. In this view, the more important links are between action and feedback. For the sake of learning, thinking becomes a matter of reflection on feedback rather than something we do fully in advance of acting.

A good example of the overly rational outlook can be found in a new book by one of the leading organizational learning theorists, Peter Senge (1994). His *The Fifth Discipline Fieldbook* contains contributions from several other writers, one of which goes as follows:

> '... the premise that organizations are the product of our thinking and interacting is powerful and liberating ... Once we start to become conscious of how we think and interact, and begin developing capacities to think and interact differently, we will already have begun to change our organizations for the better.'

The product of our thinking? What about the impact of our competitors, our customers, our own mistakes and 101 other environmental forces?

For example, if a relatively successful firm suddenly and rapidly starts losing market share and slips into the red for the first time in its history, a once cozy culture can suddenly become very oppressive. Panic leads to pressure, haste, blaming, paranoia and all sorts of other anxiety-driven negative behaviours. Here, it is the competitive environment that causes irrational and defensive behaviour patterns. In this light, the above statement by a contributor to Senge's *Fieldbook* is just naïve at best.

The important point of all of this it that it explains why some commentators tend to see organizational learning as based upon the learning of individual employees. It is as if the organization were a person, with employees serving as its brain or mind. The inside-out theory forces us to see the learning of employees as being of first priority because the organization can, presumably, only act differently if its employees first learn to think and behave differently. Just as individual thinking and deciding are seen as preceding an individual's actions – in a sequence from inside the mind of a person to outside behaviour – so organizational learning is often seen as being based on individual learning – in a similar inside-out direction.

Staying close to the real world

Too much introspection and not enough real-world feedback is the root cause of self-doubt and defensiveness. Hence contrary to most theorists, such as Peter Senge in his *The Fifth Discipline*, I don't think that the most important cure for the problem of blocked learning is more introspection. What is needed is what Tom Peters (1987) calls a bias for action. It is only through risky action that real learning can take place. Such action must include an element of risk – otherwise nothing new can be learned.

Learning the behavioural way

We all have had the experience of finding it difficult to adjust to a new environment. We start out by complaining about how stupid the new ideas are and how the change was introduced, while extolling the virtues of our tried and true approach. But as we grumble our way through adjusting to such a significantly changed environment, we often start to find that we actually quite like the new way of doing things. Sometimes we then

> **Too much introspection and not enough real-world feedback is the root cause of self-doubt and defensiveness.**

become the most enthusiastic of advocates of the new approach. It is common to then experience a guilty sense of disbelief that we could have been so blind in the first place.

What this example shows is that, in many such instances, no amount of prior mental gymnastics or persuasion would likely have any impact on our attitude toward such a major change. What has to happen is that we need to put our brains on hold and *act*. It is only through trying something new and getting feedback (seeing how it works for ourselves) that we come to change our attitude (if we are to do so at all) – thereby learning.

The morale of this story is that the rational theory of thinking, deciding, acting and learning has put the cart before the horse. Certainly, at any given moment, we must think and decide *something* in order to act at all, but the major form of learning, which depends on prior *unlearn-*

ing, is often best achieved behaviourally by experimenting with new ways of doing things and seeing what works. This brings up a favourite analogy: the rational model expects us to decide whether we like an unfamiliar kind of food without first tasting it!

The entrepreneur learns behaviourally

Entrepreneurs and others who advocate a more market-led approach to business recognize that the important link in the causal chain that leads us to behave the way we do and adjust as necessary is as follows: *action-feedback*. The still necessary, but less important, link is think-decide.

It may help to think of the relationship between thinking, deciding, acting and feedback as lying on a continuum that varies in terms of the degree of emphasis placed on thought prior to action versus action with less definitive prior thought:

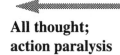

All thought;   **Manic action;**
action paralysis   **no thought**

What I am saying is essentially that the overly rational view of thought and action leads us to be too far down the left-hand side of this continuum, not that we want to move to the other extreme. Even moving to the middle would entail a lot more willingness to act and take risks, without having every possible feedback outcome anticipated to the *n*th degree in advance.

Another manifestation of being too far down the left side of this continuum is that top managers do the thinking and deciding and workers do the implementing. Such top managers see themselves as comprising the brain of the organization.

A related implication of this overly rational view is that if you really want to sort anything out you need to progress your thinking in the direction of ever increasing levels of depth or abstraction to the most fundamental visions, values and philosophies of life. These 'first' principles are useful from the point of view of *appreciation* of what one does *after the fact*. They can be thought of as codifications of what works in practice – the point being that we should ultimately be guided by what works in practice, i.e. feedback – this keeps us close to reality – the customer or whatever reality gives you real-world feedback on your actions. If high-level values and principles are thought of as codifications of best current practice, then such allegedly deeper principles are seen as logically derivative rather than logically more fundamental.

The rational model goes hand in hand with the centuries-old worldview to the effect that the earth is at the centre of the universe and everything revolves around *us*.

Taken to the extreme, this view starts from the innocent observation that our attitudes determine how we view the world around us and then moves disastrously to the conclusion that there is no external reality so that whatever we think goes. This is the basis of totalitarianism and all of the I-know-best attitudes that permeate so many organizations. A more behavioural theory argues against this view, saying instead that there is no *centre* or simple one-way causal direction – everything is in dynamic interaction.

IMPLEMENTING ORGANIZATIONAL LEARNING

The organization must therefore act and take risks to learn. Again, this does not mean that *no* prior thought is required. Of course it is. But such prior thought should be only the *minimum necessary to take exploratory, experimental action*. The idea is to start generating real-world feedback on organizational actions as soon, and as frequently, as possible. Such entrepreneurial thinking should be dispersed around the organization and concentrated on the initial identification of a range of likely possible actions (product or service revisions).

This approach to organizational learning implies that it is not necessary for every employee to become a better learner. Some writers on the topic of organizational learning convey, in euphoric terms, a utopian ideal of an organization as a big happy learning community. The reality is that some people learn faster than others and some will learn very little if anything. A further reality is that, however many older people are fast learners, it is younger people who are most likely to break with tradition and create new futures.

When we concentrate on the need to create a more entrepreneurial organization instead of on unfocused or generalized employee development, it becomes clear that you can strategically invest in those employees who are most likely to make your organization act more entrepreneurially.

It follows that the focus of organizational learning should be on those individuals who are most closely involved with the introduction of new services or products. This does not mean more training courses or mind games, but rather, empowering leading-edge knowledge workers to act on behalf of the organization. Younger people are the best learners. They have fewer entrenched thought patterns and views of what has worked in the past, along with a more healthy disrespect for authority – something that should be celebrated (albeit channelled) rather than suppressed in the interest of 'teamwork'. (See Figure 5.4.)

SURPRISING, BUT TRUE . . .

For an organization to learn, existing employees do *not need to learn at all!* The organization could adapt, on an ongoing basis, solely by the regular infusion of new employees with fresh ideas.

Figure 5.4

The fundamental point that an organization could learn solely by importing new perspectives from outside is meant only to drive home the argument that too much preoccupation with the other extreme – how to help existing employees learn better – is surely pursuing the wrong direction altogether. This backward approach is a symptom of confused thinking on the nature of learning and is caused by our total absorption in an old-fashioned rational model of human behaviour. This point is not intended to advocate churning out existing employees at a high rate or that you should ignore their need to learn.

Ideally, the best learning organizations will strive to learn by a combined approach, such as the following:

- developing an exploratory, market-action-orientated culture
- hiring people with widely different perspectives and backgrounds
- exposing existing employees to new people and ideas
- encouraging active networking and collaboration with outsiders.

A good way to encourage organizational learning is to empower your best learners among your existing employees, in addition to regularly bringing in new younger people or contractors/consultants if necessary to create a critical mass in favour of change. Openly reward healthy rule-breaking and defiance of policy – create visible role models of such people.

Creating the conditions for a learning organization

The inside-out, overly rational theory of thought and action encourages us to focus on individuals and to try to get them to think differently. The first step, in this view, is to get people to examine their preconceptions so that they can begin to look at the world afresh.

A more experiental theory encourages us instead to look at the environmental or cultural blocks that might be getting in the way of learning. The solution is to introduce people to new environments, suddenly if the organization needs to learn quickly, but gradually over the longer term. Ideally, all employees should change as much of their circumstances as often as it is reasonable to do so in order to foster the ongoing learning that is best facilitated by experiential exposure to the unfamiliar.

In this view, behavioural feedback or reinforcement is the key, so we are led to ask what behaviour we are now reinforcing and how we can start reinforcing the behaviour we want.

By thus changing the environment, those already inclined to break loose from what they regard as stifling bureaucracy will do so quickly. And rather than playing mind games with more inhibited or mentally blocked employees, it is likely that they will learn *vicariously* by observing the behaviour of role models and, most importantly, the positive reinforcement that follows their behaviour – this is why it is vital to reward risk taking visibly, to celebrate it.

The link between individual and organizational learning

While you might agree that action and feedback are more important for learning than excessive introspection, there are some organizations whose entrepreneurial action depends on highly technical knowledge acquisition, research and creative thinking. So what is the relationship between such antecedent mental activity and the sort of feedback-generating behaviour you want to encourage? It is simply a matter, surely, of getting the balance right, as appropriate for your industry, between the extremes of excessive thought and overly hasty action.

To take an example, organizations vary to the extent that they are knowledge driven and to the extent to which they are in fast changing industries. Computers would be an example of both – knowledge driven and fast changing. Fashion would be an example of a less knowledge-intensive, less high-tech business but one that is equally fast changing. In terms of learning, they both have to adapt fast, but in the case of fashion, learning reduces to its purest form because it involves extensive and continuous interaction with its market, customers and competition. A fashion company learns by trying new lines and seeing what sells.

A more knowledge-driven business needs to emulate this purer form of learning as much as possible. This is not as easy for it, however, because much of its interaction with its market is based on learning by the acquisition or creation of an esoteric form of knowledge, i.e. core competence. The relationship between such individual learning-as-knowledge-acquisition and organizational-learning-as-getting-fast-feedback needs to be made as close as possible. This means encouraging knowledge acquirers to test their ideas in the market-place at the earliest possible stage rather than staying too long in the ivory tower that knowledge acquisition too easily becomes.

> **The relationship between such individual learning-as-knowledge-acquisition and organizational-learning-as-getting-fast-feedback needs to be made as close as possible.**

Helping individual employees to learn

Individuals are often encouraged to learn by trying to understand the perspectives of their more adaptive peers – generally peers working for faster moving competitors. The analogy of learning about the culture of a foreign country is sometimes used. We are advised that if we want to fully understand the culture of our own country, we really must go and live in – not just visit – another culture, preferably one that is as foreign as possible relative to our own. The organizational counterpart to this advice might be to arrange an exchange programme where you work for several months in a supplier organization, customer or strategic partner firm that is notably more entrepreneurial than yours. A similar learning experience could be obtained by exposing employees, with less adaptive behaviour patterns, to internal project teams composed of the organization's most highly entrepreneurial staff. Such exposure is likely to be more effective in generating learning than emphasising introspection to break down mental blocks.

> **Individuals need to be encouraged to learn in the same manner as the entrepreneurial organization does – by taking risks, experimenting and adjusting their behaviour on the basis of what succeeds and what does not work (not just on the basis of mistakes).**

Individuals need to be encouraged to learn in the same manner as the entrepreneurial organization does – by taking risks, experimenting and adjusting their behaviour on the basis of what succeeds and what does not work (not just on the basis of mistakes).

A marriage of organizational and individual learning

So, just what is the relative place of organizational and individual learning? In Figure 5.5 the implication is that we want to stimulate learning that encourages both employees and the organization as a whole to behave sufficiently differently that some market feedback is thereby generated.

Both the organization and individual employees can learn in ways that are either entrepreneurial or not. Both can learn by imitating others and both can learn by striking off into uncharted waters, thereby taking risks and learning in an entrepreneurial fashion. The latter would occur when both are focused on novel product introduction. This is represented in Figure 5.5 as the intersection of the two circles. Maximum entrepreneurial learning would occur when individuals work with the organization to generate new product or service offerings quickly.

It is quite possible to get the integration of individual and organizational learning wrong. As discussed earlier, the organization can learn, change or adapt by importing people with fresh perspectives even if

INTEGRATING INDIVIDUAL AND ORGANIZATIONAL LEARNING

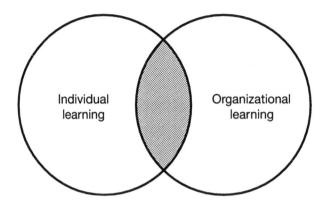

Figure 5.5

there is no learning on the part of existing employees. Similarly, employees can acquire all sorts of otherwise valuable knowledge without the organization implementing it or doing anything differently as a result. Your organization could, therefore, founder despite an active effort on the part of individual employees to learn continuously.

Advocating an excessively high rate of turnover among employees would be to get carried away to the other extreme. Continuity helps to avoid the unnecessary repeating of avoidable mistakes.

Ideally, the best means of facilitating organizational learning is to invest most of your effort into what is likely to yield the greatest return. This means rewarding the fastest learners with more opportunities to learn. Learning for individuals and the organization alike should be focused on taking action that is by nature entrepreneurial.This implies encouraging risk taking at all levels: individuals, teams, profit centres, divisions and at the level of the entire organization. We then have a single definition of what best facilitates learning at all levels: *All action must lead as directly as possible to market feedback.*

A fully entrepreneurial organization obviously cannot be prescriptive about what learning is useful and what is not. Being prescriptive is simply not being entrepreneurial. A great range of *variation* must indeed be fostered. Nevertheless, it is not inconsistent to strategically invest most heavily in learning what is yielding immediate results and to move such employees more proactively and regularly who are clearly fast learners and whose learning most directly contributes to organizational learning.

What about employees who are set in their ways?

There is no doubt that the longer we pursue a single or narrow career track and the older we get the more likely we are to develop fixed ways of seeing the world – which makes it increasingly hard for us to learn anything radically new. The rational approach to this problem, as advocated by Peter Senge (1994) and others, is to encourage an exercise in navel gazing, that is to advocate an introspective analysis of why we hold onto the views we take as natural and comfortable. The behavioural, entrepreneurial stance is that individuals stuck in old routines should be encouraged to expose themselves to new approaches and suspend judgement until they have behaved differently and reflected upon the feedback (results) of their new behaviours. A behavioural theory of learning knows full well that we often experiment without knowing what we are doing or whether we might prefer a new course of action and learning then consists in our after-the-fact reflection on the consequences of our new actions and how we feel about them.

An example . . .

Out of work executives are often trapped by the inclination to spend too much time in reflection prior to acting. They seem to think that they can definitively decide what the next stage of their career should be without actively exploring various job markets. The analogy of buying a house is illuminating in this context. You may start looking at houses with a set of rough criteria in mind of what you want, but you may see features you like which you hadn't thought of in advance. This could lead you, perhaps completely, to revise your criteria. The more that out of work executives ponder prior to acting, the more self-doubt creeps in (a vicious circle) and, conversely, the more

> **Finding a new direction is thus a process of *discovery*; it is a search, rather than an introspection-based decision.**

they interact with their environment and get feedback the more confident of their direction they become. Finding a new direction is thus a process of *discovery*; it is a search, rather than an introspection-based decision. (See Psychological slant.)

PSYCHOLOGICAL SLANT

While we can continue to learn as we age, it is easy to fool ourselves into thinking that we are learning more than we really are. However much new material we digest, it is all interpreted in the light of our past experience. All of our experience provides us with filters which take the form of sunglasses fixed in place over our eyes. We cannot erase our past experience. We can never see something familiar as freshly as it is seen by a newcomer. We may think we are doing well because we are finally learning all about computers, but this type of learning is not necessarily causing us to give up many of our most cherished beliefs or values. The best we can do to maximize our ability to see things freshly is to be newcomers often by shifting our positions as radically as we can and often during our careers. In practical terms this means such things as working abroad in significantly different cultures and working in as many different organizations/functions as possible. This prescription isn't a very comforting one, but it is realistic.

THE PLACE OF KNOWLEDGE ACQUISITION

It has been essential thus far to focus on only one type of learning, that which occurs by *doing*. This narrowing of the subject has been necessary in order to underline the importance of entrepreneurial or exploratory action as the foundation of all learning. It is now time to round out the picture by discussing the role of knowledge acquisition, knowledge creation and the sharing of knowledge throughout the organization.

Different forms of learning

Clearly knowledge acquisition must be considered a form of learning and this includes knowledge that you may never apply, such as some esoteric bit of history. However, if learning is to lead to improved organizational effectiveness, the greatest emphasis must be placed on knowledge acquisition which quickly generates changed organizational action. Because there are many types of learning, therefore, it is necessary to distinguish them quite explicitly. From a results-orientated point of view we are really only interested in learning that leads to changed behaviour.

Entrepreneurial learning at the organizational level

It is worth repeating that, when we speak of organizational learning, it is important to visualize the organization as an *individual* acting in its market environment. An organization can change its behaviour for different reasons as well as exhibit different types of learning. Policy revisions or changes in management may produce new organizational actions but these changes are not necessarily the result of learning – at least not on the part of the total organization.

Similarly, an organization may cut costs or introduce better quality products in response to what its competition is doing. And these behavioural changes are clearly the result of learning, even though it is of the imitative variety.

Entrepreneurial learning, however, must take the form of introducing products or services that do not as yet exist. This type of learning does not amount to imitation of someone else or the application of knowledge gleaned through past experience. It is learning through *trying something new* – not in a laboratory or as a prototype – but in the organization's environment of real-world customers and unforgiving feedback. Trying something new in an R&D lab could constitute vital employee learning which must no doubt proceed the introduction of a new product. But once the product is in the market-place and begins to go through a process of revision over a period of several months in light of customer feedback, then it is true to say that both the organization and some of its employees are learning and that they are doing so in an entrepreneurial manner.

Knowledge creation versus knowledge acquisition

An organization can create new knowledge when it introduces a new product and learns to modify it beyond recognition on the basis of its successes and failures in the market-place. Individuals can only be said to be creating new knowledge *within* or independently of the organization. R&D staff create new knowledge in this way all of the time, but unless the organization acts upon these new ideas in its environment and modifies them in accordance with feedback, then, in such a case, the *organization* is not creating knowledge.

Organizations with a record of frequently leading in the introduction of novel products are model entrepreneurs. They take risks to lead in their market and they create knowledge that other organizations can, by definition, only *acquire* by watching them.

An hierarchy of knowledge acquisition

Some types of knowledge acquisition are more useful than others. If a secretary in the personnel department learns to use a new word processing package, this may have some remote impact, however slight, on the organization's ability to introduce new products and modify them faster. At the other extreme is knowledge acquisition of the sort that contributes towards refining what Hamel and Prahalad (1994) call an organization's core competence. Canon, to use one of their favourite examples, has a core competence in imaging technology which they apply in a wide variety of products.

Such core knowledge may be acquired by leading-edge technical workers in labs just as readily as it might be through failed product launches. Any product is made up of countless components and processes, each of which can be tested in its own environment – that of the lab – before it reaches the environment of the end customer. In high-tech companies, technical knowledge can reside in the heads of a few individuals, or if it is widely understood throughout the firm, the organization could be said to possess this knowledge. Much employee learning in such companies must necessarily precede the type of organizational learning that takes place only after the initial version of the product is in the hands of customers.

Hamel and Prahalad's emphasis on core competence, however, obscures the fact that many organizations in lower-tech industries can act much more quickly and independently of such esoteric knowledge or its laborious acquisition. This is an important point because it is all too easy to forget the vital relevance of *action* as the foundation of learning.

In between the two extremes of the secretary learning a new word processing package and R&D workers enhancing the company's core competence, a great deal of learning goes on. Some of this knowledge acquisition will be more directly related to new product introduction than others. An entrepreneurial organization can invest more in knowledge acquisition that is more closely related to core competence enhancement and the introduction of new products without being so prescriptive as to become bureaucratic.

Some knowledge acquisition will take the form of reading a book, taking a course or understudying an expert. Benchmarking would be the organizational equivalent of the latter. Some of it could be classed as learning by doing rather than simply being passive knowledge acquisition. This active learning would occur when individual employees try new approaches to old problems.

Here again there is a distinction to be made between knowledge acquisition and creation. One employee may learn by doing, but what is learnt may be already well known by more experienced employees. In another case, an employee may create new knowledge by discovering a completely new approach to an old problem.

At the risk of belabouring the issue, it is worth repeating that the main value of distinguishing between organizational and individual learning in this way is to ensure a high degree of emphasis on entrepreneurial action on the part of the organization as a whole so as to avoid an undue degree of internal focus. Ideally, this approach to organizational learning will encourage organizations to keep their eye on the ball: learning entrepreneurially by taking fast action to introduce and revise new products or services.

Organizational learning versus supporting employee learning

Some commentators on these issues have confused organizational learning with an organization's having a learning culture that explicitly supports individual employee learning. Thus many firms consider themselves to be learning organizations simply because they very actively promote learning on the part of their employees.

Organizations with technologically complex products certainly do need to acquire new knowledge at a high rate, but our discussion makes it clear that this could be achieved, in principle, by outsourcing R&D or by a continuous influx of people with new ideas – all with very little learning on the part of existing employees. The best organizational learners will mix the two approaches: they will support a wide range of employee learning initiatives and bring ideas in from outside at a high rate.

Revising a conventional approach to organizational learning

David Garvin's article (1993) in the *Harvard Business Review*, 'Building a Learning Organization' appears to be highly regarded. He offers us the following definition:

> A learning organization is an organization skilled at creating, acquiring, and transferring knowledge, and at modifying its behaviour to reflect new knowledge and insights.

> **The best organizational learners will mix the two approaches: they will support a wide range of employee learning initiatives and bring ideas in from outside at a high rate.**

The problem with this definition is one of emphasis. It seems to suggest that modifying the organizations's behaviour is something only done after an unspecified amount of knowledge is acquired or created. It could be taken to prescribe too much knowledge acquisition independently and prior to the organization's taking risky, exploratory action.

Garvin outlines five main ways in which organizations learn, in his view:

- systematic problem solving
- experimentation with new approaches
- learning from their own experiences and past history
- learning from the experiences and best practices of others
- transferring knowledge quickly and efficiently throughout the organization.

Garvin cites Xerox, among other firms, as a good example of the first principle. However useful it may be to have all of your managers take a course on systematic problem solving, such a step is quite far removed from entrepreneurial action at the organizational level. Initiatives such as these could easily become bureaucratic simply by making a more intuitive, off the wall or individual approach to problem solving seem to be bad practice.

More importantly, this suggestion is part and parcel of what is already too great an internal focus, which is the very reason why many organizations are poor learners.

On the whole there can be no quarrel with the value of these techniques, so long as they are seen as less fundamental than entrepreneurial action on the part of the organization as a whole, action that is *exploratory, intuitive and responsive* rather than quite as systematic and scientific as Garvin advocates.

Sharing knowledge across the organization

Transferring or sharing knowledge is of course important but, as a practice, it can easily become too bureaucratic. Many multi-divisional organizations are bending over backwards to engender more synergy and sharing of ideas across divisions. Paternalistic pressure is placed on managers to share knowledge with their sister divisions.

A more entrepreneurial approach would be to create an electronic bulletin board similar to those offered by computer online services such as CompuServe. An electronic bulletin board is organized into various 'forums' on a wide range of topics and any user can attach notices or questions for others to answer. Keen users will 'browse' through such forums to pick up bits and pieces of information and to offer their own advice to others. Users must see such sharing of ideas as being in their own interest if they are genuinely to use computerized forums as a tool for sharing knowledge. Sharing cannot be forced or legislated.

Where are we now?

We have painted a picture of organizational learning as an evolutionary process in which firms interact with their market/environment. Some product initiatives are successful (get selected) and others fail.

The organization learns in order to *adapt* more effectively to a changing environment. The focus of this chapter has been narrow so that we could become as clear as possible about the nature of organizational learning. Much more needs to be said about the sort of culture that it is necessary to foster if this type of entrepreneurial learning is to become a way of life in your business.

Before we can look at the culture issue directly, we need to explore the notion of organizational dynamics. This is important because concepts such as culture are actually quite static as they are discussed by most commentators. Company cultures are generally described as if someone's personality were being discussed – something quite fixed and unchanging. Rather than describe how an entrepreneurial culture should *be*, what *traits* the ideal culture should have, it is more essential, therefore, to look at how cultures evolve and can be helped to grow and change.

Before we can discuss organizational culture, then, we need to look at the culture in which we discuss such concepts. This means examining in more depth what we have called the rational model of thinking, deciding and acting.

PRACTICAL STEPS

- identify strategic learning areas of your business – where new product innovations will yield your quickest and greatest payoff – invest most of your resources for learning in these areas
- unleash the entrepreneurial spirit of key knowledge workers by empowering them to take risks in your market-place
- begin rotating employees into different functions and do some swaps with sister divisions, customers or suppliers
- initiate a balanced approach to importing fresh ideas versus support for the learning of existing employees
- benchmark your culture against entrepreneurial firms
- set up a computerized knowledge network/electronic bulletin board
- celebrate attempts to learn by employees who take market risks initiate fast, real-world, feedback mechanisms.

"Changing the culture of your organization is a major means of having an indirect impact on the direction in which your firm is then likely to evolve."

"The key to ongoing entrepreneurial success is to maintain a high rate of continuous variation even across successful product lines."

6

EVOLVING INTO A FUTURE YOU CANNOT PLAN FOR

In the last chapter we discussed organizational learning by contrasting the need to improvise, explore and be responsive with the common preference to think that you can always make definitive decisions on a wholly rational basis prior to taking any exploratory action. We concluded that you can use rational managerial tools such as planning when you are engaged in a clear-cut project with a well-defined objective and concrete parameters – such as building a house, for example.

When you are operating in an open, responsive mode, you are prepared to let things happen to a certain extent. You are acknowledging that so much is unexpected that you cannot plan for it as precisely as you would like. You are accepting the fact, however reluctantly, that you must instead become more of an opportunist. This entails learning how to be more responsive and to worry less about being in control of all of the variables that might have an impact on your firm. The alternative to centralized planning and control is to encourage entrepreneurial action on a broad front on the part of all of your employees.

If business needs to be more responsive, with strategic direction *emerging*, as some writers on corporate strategy now argue, then significant questions arise as to the whole dynamics of organization development, change and evolution. There is a heated debate raging in academic circles about the relative roles of planning and evolution in organizational dynamics. The planners maintain that managers can have a significant impact on the direction of their organization, while the ecologists counter with the claim that the forces of markets and competition have the greater part to play.

The rational approach to organization development assumes that growth can be directed from the top of the firm. The evolutionary view is that you must unleash your potentially most innovative employees to take risks on your behalf in order to provide the selection forces in your market sufficient variation on which to operate.

Where will this discussion take us?

The role of evolutionary forces in organizational change will be examined in this chapter with a view to identifying just what the practising manager can do to have a greater impact on the direction of his business. This discussion will make it clearer why it is necessary to develop 'bottom-up' conceptions of leadership as discussed earlier. It will also further clarify the place of learning in organizations and help to specify more precisely what form such learning should take. A clearer picture should also emerge of the importance of an entrepreneurial approach to business.

IMPROVISING AND RESPONDING VERSUS PLANNING

All of these themes have in common a recognition of the need to place more emphasis on responsiveness and improvisation at the expense of wholly rational planning and decision making, where 'rational' in this context refers to dealing with variables that are fully within one's control. This look at evolutionary processes will also set the stage for an exploration of the meaning and role of organizational culture in the next chapter. We need to see just what sort of culture you should aim to foster in order to take full advantage of your knowledge of evolutionary forces.

Letting it happen without complete loss of control

We naturally experience a degree of fear at the thought of an evolutionary explanation of organizational change with its implied loss of control. But understanding such processes might actually give managers *more* control over the future than they now have in today's climate of uncertainty and ambiguity. It may be that managers need to focus less on concrete objectives when they plan and more on the *processes* that

underlie organizational dynamics. This may mean giving up one level
of control in favour of another, albeit one with less definitively man-
ageable outcomes. Control in this sense would be more indirect.

An ecological analogy might clarify this point. Suppose you wanted
to alter the population of a particular species in a certain ecology or
habitat, and instead of focusing on
the species directly you changed
the water levels in its environment. You would be basing your
action on an understanding of the
ecological *dynamics* of the situation thereby creating an indirect
impact on the species in question.
This is still a form of control –
however limited. The species may

> **Changing the culture of your organization is a major means of having an indirect impact on the direction in which your firm is then likely to evolve.**

adapt and alter in unintended ways and there may be other unexpected
side effects – at least until we learn a lot more about such ecological
dynamics. But if the only alternative is no control at all, then it would
be a course of action worth trying.

The first step in coming to grips with how managers might gain more
of this sort of control over the direction of their businesses is to understand in greater detail what the evolutionists are saying. It is because
this type of control is more indirect that it is necessary to discuss its
underlying processes before exploring the subject of corporate culture
(next chapter). Changing the culture of your organization is a major
means of having an indirect impact on the direction in which your firm
is then likely to evolve.

Evolutionary processes in an organizational ecology

It is important to be clear what is not being claimed by the evolutionist
camp. There is no suggestion that organizations evolve in accordance
with a fixed pattern that has been set years ago and which is unalter-
able. It is recognized that, even in the natural world, there are many
chance interactions which dramatically alter the course of evolution. It
is more a matter of understanding how *selection processes* work. Just
as analyzing such processes in the natural world will give scientists a
degree of control, in principle at least, over the future course of evolu-

tion, so we should expect business managers to be able to acquire a similar sort of control within their own dynamic business ecologies as they learn more about selection processes.

Selection processes in business are really no mystery to practising managers. They are simply the market's reaction to the new products you introduce – where the term 'market' refers to all players in a particular market – competitors, suppliers, environmentalists, consumer groups, government regulators and the general public, not just your customers. It is clear that some products are 'selected' by the market and others are not. Writers on corporate strategy have long worked out creative approaches to planning in volatile markets. There is no suggestion that you should do any less strategic planning. The only question is the relative role of strategy and some sort of evolutionary selection process.

Even when not in doubt, do something different!

It is also well known that *variation* is an important evolutionary mechanism. In business, variation takes the form of introducing a range of similar products in the face of market uncertainty, or of diverse product types just in case none of one particular product grouping does very well. The cliché about not having all of your eggs in one basket reflects this uncertainty as does the need to have significant product *variation* in the hope that something you are offering will be *selected*.

In the good old days, you could introduce new products on a 'take it or leave it' basis. When competition was less intense, your customers simply had to accept the product you were offering in spite of any deficiencies it might have had. While you certainly wouldn't produce more of a particular product than you could sell, you may have had a near monopoly on certain markets or at least over a relatively unvarying share of a market. Control was largely in your hands and you could flourish with the use of quite straightforward rational managerial skills.

Selection and variation clearly work hand in hand. While you are likely to have a pretty good hunch about what product might be selected, you recognize that, in today's hyper-competitive and fickle markets, you really need to vary your offerings in order to ensure that enough gets selected that you will make a profit on balance across your entire range. Such variation could be *concurrent* – that is, different products introduced simultaneously or *sequentially* – in which case you would be lightning fast in varying the make-up of an existing product as soon as you saw that it was not selling as well as you expected.

A potential selection pitfall

One of the obvious difficulties we all experience when a response gets selected (or, in more common-sense terms, when something *works*) is that we tend to want to do the same thing again. The downside of this tendency is that we then narrow our focus, hence limiting the amount of variation we are inclined to exhibit. It is this pattern that has given rise to the new cliché to the effect that nothing fails like success. If you have all of the success you want, you naturally question why you should vary the formula. We are only motivated to vary what we are doing if we are faced with some sort of insurmountable obstacle.

> **The challenge, therefore, is to force ourselves to sustain a relatively high rate of variation at all times if we are serious about creating and maintaining a truly entrepreneurial business.**

When we vary our responses in the face of an obstacle, we are essentially exploring alternatives in order to find a solution to a problem. Once we find a solution, variation stops and we are back on a single track. Continuous, ongoing variation is inefficient, a waste of time ... or so we normally tend to think. The challenge, therefore, is to force ourselves to sustain a relatively high rate of variation at all times if we are serious about creating and maintaining a truly entrepreneurial business.

In favour of continuous variation

By now it is perhaps clear that the distinction between variation and no variation parallels the distinction between organizational *renewal* and service/product *delivery*. It is fine to limit variation and apply a known formula if you are concentrating on the *delivery* of existing products or services that are achieving the degree of success in their markets which you want. When it comes to how you go about stimulating renewal, however, you want to foster continuous variation. For the sake of renewal, you want to be operating in exploratory mode all of the time. You can only induce market selection forces to work in your favour if you give your markets new choices (variation) on a regular, frequent basis. Clearly, it is not incompatible to limit variation with one set of products and increase it with another set.

If you are in an industry that is fast changing, you need to decide what product ranges or features to vary (renewal) and what to maintain (delivery). The difficulty is that success is a misleading guide. You would be naturally inclined to maintain your most successful lines and not vary a good thing. Accordingly, less successful lines would be varied. The difficulty is that not varying your successful lines may end up leaving you in an evolutionary cul-de-sac. Hence the really hard decision is to invest in changing/improving your best selling products so that they stay

> **Hence the really hard decision is to invest in changing/improving your best selling products so that they stay ahead of your competition rather than just keep up or fall behind.**

ahead of your competition rather than just keep up or fall behind.

If you are in a much slower changing industry from the point of view of product innovation, you still have the luxury of hanging onto a successful formula. To use McDonald's again as an example, why should it change much of its formula? In the short term, there is no reason at all why it should. Its industry is not changing as fast as computers and telecoms. In the longer term, however, it is quite possible that they could be caught short if someone comes up with a radically new fast-food concept and if McDonald's are unable to adapt quickly enough . . .

So how does selection work?

It is not a simple matter of survival of the fittest in a static unchanging environment. The environment for your business is the total market, encompassing any stakeholder who has an interest in what you are doing. This includes competitors, suppliers, consumer groups, environmentalists, government regulators and the general public, in addition to customers. What makes such an environment *dynamic* is that the actions of any sufficiently influential group of these parties could totally alter the environment in which you are struggling to survive and prosper. Selection in the natural world is just as dynamic, with competition causing opposing species to adapt as each side develops new strategies to gain an advantage.

If it were a simple matter of dealing with a static environment, such as learning how to predict and perhaps control the weather, the problem would not be so difficult. The challenge in a dynamic environment is that there are active *agents* as well as passive variables and you cannot predict how agents will act either in response to your moves or independently of what you are doing. Just as you are replying to their latest idea, they may have moved well beyond that level to an entirely new and unexpected innovation.

Whenever you take any initiative to enhance your competitive position in your market-place, selection mechanisms will come into effect. Selection in this context is simply the fortuitous combination of events which determine the success you achieve. Your initiative may succeed because of timing. For example, just as you are about to launch a new product – say, to do with limiting car pollution – favourable legislation is passed that enhances your product's appeal. You know that selection has operated in your favour if your new product meets or exceeds your sales forecast. What might not be selected today may be an overwhelming success tomorrow because the environmental (market) factors that determine what gets selected at any given moment are constantly changing. Just as with a natural ecology, our market initiatives not only *occur* in an environment (market), they also *change* it, both for others (customers, competitors, etc.) in that environment and for ourselves.

So far this seems all rather obvious. Yes, the *events* described above may be familiar enough, but it is their explanation in evolutionary terms that is novel. The manager's role is limited, in the evolutionary scheme of things, to introducing a suitable range of variation. It is no longer possible to decide precisely in advance of acting what products you will back. Only luck and arrogance can sustain the myth of rational control.

IN SEARCH OF NEW FORMS OF CONTROL

How does selection differ from strategic planning?

You may be thinking that you are already strategically staying close to your market, monitoring everyone else's moves, and responding quickly and opportunistically to sudden changes in the 'environment'. The question is: 'What does thinking in evolutionary terms add to the picture, practically speaking, of what you are already doing?'

The essential difference is the degree to which you can predict and control what will be selected. If your strategy is to expand a straightforward but highly successful service operation, such as a restaurant chain, to different parts of the same country, there are relatively few unknowns compared to launching a new high-tech hi-fi product such as the digital audio tape (DAT) recorder or mini disk. When you are formulating your strategic plans in a service industry where you can either control or predict all of the relevant variables then you can proceed in the conventional manner of handing over the planning activity to your planning department or restricting it to top management.

The more unknowns you face the more important it is to disperse initiatives across a wide range of individuals, teams and functions throughout the organization, thereby creating greater variation. The greatest number of unknowns will occur in industries which are fastest changing, such as computers and telecommunications. Being wholly entrepreneurial as an organization means allowing diverse initiatives to be tried with little or no centralized strategic planning.

So, it is most appropriate to use conventional strategic planning in contexts with less environmental uncertainty and when you are dealing with well proven products or services. In contrast, when you are operating in a highly uncertain environment (market) and introducing totally unproven products, then you need to rely on less controllable variation and trust in the luck of market selection forces. This dichotomy is depicted in Figure 6.1.

Changing the meaning of strategic planning

In fast changing environments where you have to rely on variation and selection, it is not a matter of abandoning strategic planning. You can clearly have an explicit strategy to engage in a high rate of variation in certain product markets and to hold the line in others. But once you have decided, in general terms, how much variation to invest in and which product groups to focus on, you then have to step back and let nature take its course. This means empowering employees who are technically and in other respects closest to your customers to take risks with the introduction of new products and with the modification of existing ones.

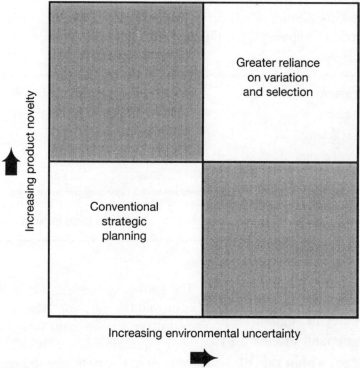

Increasing environmental uncertainty

Figure 6.1

Strategic planning is a deliberate, rational, top-down decision-making process. It is change driven from the centre of the organizational circle. When you let nature take its course, you are letting change be driven from the circumference of that circle – by those employees who are in closest contact with your customers and with the technical leading edge of your products.

In simpler times, you could formulate a strategic plan that specified down to the last detail precisely what you had to do to achieve definitive corporate objectives. Today, you can plan this precisely only to a certain point, after which a more exploratory, open-ended search mode must be adopted. As you experiment with different products, and codify what seems to work, you will note that a particular strategy may *emerge* in the form of learned practices that are leading to success. Such strategies may then be applied in other markets, but again, only up to a certain point – which cannot be specified in advance. The appropriate balance of a priori strategic planning and exploratory, entrepreneurial action can only be determined by your own organization acting entrepreneurially.

There is a continuum of industries from slower to faster changing – as discussed in Chapter 2. (See Figure 6.2.)

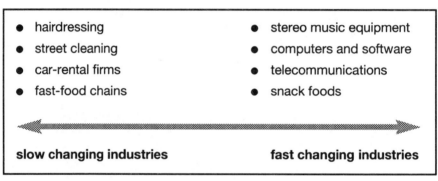

- hairdressing
- street cleaning
- car-rental firms
- fast-food chains

- stereo music equipment
- computers and software
- telecommunications
- snack foods

slow changing industries   **fast changing industries**

Figure 6.2

> **The key to ongoing entrepreneurial success is to maintain a high rate of continuous variation even across successful product lines.**

The further to the left side of this continuum you are, the more definitively you can formulate your strategic plans. The further you are to the right, the more you have to find a balance between strategic planning and exploratory, entrepreneurial action. Industries to the right end of this continuum are most unable to predict or control what specific products will sell. In these circumstances, managers must strive to maximize variation and rely on selection to determine what to emphasize and what to drop. The key to ongoing entrepreneurial success is to maintain a high rate of continuous variation even across successful product lines.

New forms of control for an evolving market

While you cannot focus narrowly on a single product, you can decide to focus on a range of variation around a particular theme. You can exercise control by keeping on top of what variation is on offer in a particular market across all of your competitors and by watching closely what customers seem to like. This vigilance can help you to maintain a narrower range of variation in your own offerings. Too much variation can backfire and actually confuse customers. There is clearly too much choice in many product ranges, such as computers and software, for example. Apple Computer, Inc has recently dropped some of its models for this reason. But still it currently has two very similarly priced colour ink-jet printers on the market and customers are unsure which one to buy. The very real danger in many markets is that customers may not be able to keep up with the bewildering variety on offer.

Every firm needs to move from offering too much variation to consolidation or rationalization and back again to greater variation – like a thermostat adjusting to changes in room temperature. When you offer two products that are nearly identical, customers can see this as indecision or a lack of confidence. There is no question that many firms do lack confidence in their choice of models and features, but this is a fact of life in markets ruled by selection forces rather than rational thought. The important thing is to have the confidence to take a risk even if you cannot have confidence in particular products.

Other firms rush to market quickly with immature products which they then have to quickly retract and modify. Many of the Japanese home electronics firms introduce products in just this exploratory manner. Such firms risk being seen as not knowing what they are doing. They are most likely to be disparaged by those who are still stuck in the rather constipated 'right first time' mindset. The fact of the matter is that customers would rather have a poorly conceived product if it excites their imagination than none at all. The ill-planned product helps the company learn and gains it market visibility which is often an advantage when the second version is introduced.

So what can you control? Here are some suggestions:

- what range of products to focus on
- how much variation to introduce at any given time

- how quickly to introduce new products
- how quickly you will modify existing products
- how quickly you will vary successful product lines
- the extent to which you will allow the introduction of new products that are superior to your own best sellers.

> **The greater the extent of market unknowns, the more important it is to have many minds taking independent initiatives.**

There is evidence to suggest that the most successful entrepreneurial firms will 'cannibalize' their own product lines by introducing better products even when their existing lines are still selling well. IBM's refusal to do this in the eighties often led to competitors leaving it behind with innovations it had deliberately chosen to delay. Because product managers are held responsible for sales revenue in the short term, they are naturally reluctant to introduce new products that, in the short run, could undermine the sales of existing best sellers. This practice is a recipe for obsolescence and long-term decline.

Organizational evolution and entrepreneurial action

At its core, what essentially defines an organization as entrepreneurial is its willingness to take risks with the introduction of unproven products. What differentiates an organization that happens to be run by an entrepreneur from one that is more thoroughly entrepreneurial is that, in the latter case, such risks can come from a multitude of independent sources within the organization. By allowing risk to be so dispersed, the organization seems to be taking a bigger risk than the one with more centralized decision making. But the reality is that when decisions about what variation to introduce are too central, the risk of failure to keep up in the organizational renewal race is even greater. The greater the extent of market unknowns, the more important it is to have many minds taking independent initiatives.

Empowered employees acting independently will lead to more creative variation than if ideas are pooled for consensus and the lowest common denominator is chosen. Whenever novel ideas must be fed into the centre for widespread discussion and review, conservative

forces will inevitably force a
watering down of any idea that is
too novel. This was how IBM
operated throughout the eighties
as it lost ground in the personal
computer arena. Its process for
evaluating new ideas was just too
extensive and hence bureaucratic.
Entrepreneurial initiatives arising
from individual employees died a
slow death in IBM's centralized
approval maze.

> **Empowered employees acting
> independently will lead to
> more creative variation than
> if ideas are pooled for
> consensus and the lowest
> common denominator
> is chosen.**

Clearly, entrepreneurial action is well suited to a business context
that is volatile and governed more by the forces of evolution than by
rational, strategic control. Entrepreneurial action and selection/varia-
tion mechanisms are really two sides of the same coin. The former is
demanded by the latter and only those organizations able to act in an
entrepreneurial manner can expect to thrive in such a dynamic context.
So, it is this evolutionary nature of modern organizational dynamics
that is making it essential for organizations to behave more
entrepreneurially and hence to the greater empowerment of all employees to be individual entrepreneurs.

Clarifying the need for bottom-up leadership

An entrepreneurial organization is characterized by an inability to
know in advance precisely what to do. It recognizes that it must *discover* its direction through real-world action that generates a lot of
feedback. Product variation represents a range of *tentative feelers*
launched into the dark in the hope of obtaining a positive response
from customers.

In Chapter 4 on leadership, it was argued that employees must be
empowered to take such exploratory action on behalf of the organization. Employees who are in the strongest position to make educated
guesses about what might sell are likely to be so-called knowledge
workers who are at the leading edge of their technical field and close to
the customer.

If an organization operating in such an exploratory mode is searching for direction, it will ultimately get it only from selection forces at work in its market. But direction on what variations to offer, however tentatively, must come from leading-edge technical workers, those in whom an organization's core competence most precisely resides. An organization that likes to think of itself as market driven, cannot in reality be so if it relies exclusively on leadership from those who are most distant from the market. In most organizations, it is unlikely that top management will be able to stay close to all of the firm's markets in both of the important senses of what it means to be close to a market – close to customers – and up to date with the technical leading edge of their products.

Top-level leaders can provide broad direction in terms of fundamental values and what parameters to emphasize in making product variation decisions, but they would be foolish to try to make such product decisions themselves. These decisions must be made by leading-edge technical workers and this is precisely the type of leadership that organizations need to cultivate from the bottom up. This is really just taking empowerment one step further and recognizing that those in whom your core competence resides need to be encouraged to go beyond making empowered decisions – they need to be made to see that their knowledge is a vital source of power which can be used to provide the organization with essential renewal leadership. Such leadership consists in devising completely new variation ideas to offer the market, and in leading by example – taking empowered risks to offer product variation to the market. Leadership of this sort may also take the form of convincing appropriate sponsors in the organization to provide the necessary investment to launch a new product.

> **An entrepreneurial organization is essentially made up of numerous individual entrepreneurs who are willing and able to show such leadership.**

An entrepreneurial organization is essentially made up of numerous individual entrepreneurs who are willing and able to show such leadership. The action of these individual entrepreneurs constitutes leadership only if they are successful in redirecting a significant portion of the organization's resources to back a new product venture. Any such action that successfully redirects the organization, to whatever degree, is clearly an important form of leadership.

Organizational learning as evolution

When vital knowledge held by a few is disseminated throughout the organization, this can be called a form of organizational learning. When experienced employees update their skills in an area of organizational core competence, their development is also related to organizational learning. However, these forms of learning miss the most essential features of organizational learning – features that become immediately clear when the notion of such learning is linked to the impact of evolutionary forces on organizational development.

As the organization adjusts its market offerings on the basis of what variations are selected, it could be said to be *evolving* naturally through the action of market selection. *Such natural evolution and organizational learning are one and the same process.* As the organization monitors feedback across the range of its offerings, it learns what to modify. Learning is induced by trial and error action plus ensuing feedback. This is fundamentally what learning is all about, and it is the identical process that we are calling organizational evolution. Dissemination of such learning throughout the organization really amounts to *consolidation* of what is learned. The core learning itself is the initial feedback-induced behaviour modification that takes the form of new product variations.

> **Learning that coincides with organizational evolution is also characterized by the *creation of new knowledge.***

Learning that coincides with organizational evolution is also characterized by the *creation of new knowledge.* When knowledge is disseminated or when you are taught new skills by someone else, nothing new is created. What is already known is simply shared. The entrepreneur who introduces a new product variation and *discovers* that the market likes it has learned something but, more importantly, he has also created a new piece of knowledge. This type of organizational learning is fundamentally *creative* in just this sense. Organizational evolution essentially creates the future. By introducing novel products, whole new markets are often thereby created and this creativity generally also alters the everyday environment in which we live, and we change and hence evolve accordingly as well.

It all fits together

So there is a clear link between all of these concepts:

- entrepreneurship
- organizational learning
- organizational evolution
- bottom-up leadership

Organizational evolution points to the environment–organization dynamics that underlie how organizations adapt and change. Organizational learning is the same process simply focused on how any one organization interacts with its market/environment. Entrepreneurship is the engine that creates sufficiently new and frequent variations to ensure that something among a range of offerings gets selected. And bottom-up leadership is simply the impact on the broader organization which such entrepreneurs must have if their organization is to capitalize on the learning their trial and error actions generate. (See Psychological slant.)

Mastering the unknown

Leading entrepreneurial firms literally create the future. The further they can stay ahead of their competitors the greater will be their economic rewards and sense of achievement. Individual entrepreneurs reduce their fear of the unknown by developing a track record in which they experience more success than failure. Or, at least they achieve enough notable successes to compensate for mistakes even if the mistakes are more numerous than the successes. They establish this track record by ensuring that they initiate numerous tries – enough product launches that some are eventually successful. The more successful they are in using their intuition to guess what will sell, the less fear they are likely to have of the unknown.

An organization that wants to become more entrepreneurial, essentially has to create a culture in which it is safe for employees to develop such a track record of success for themselves. And this is the topic of the next chapter.

PSYCHOLOGICAL SLANT

Reason is everyone's primary control mechanism. It allows us to control others, to rationalize away our concerns, to figure out how to get something we want and to avoid what we don't want. But reason can only work with what it knows. And this is why we are so afraid of the unknown. Generally we use our reason self-defeatingly in the face of the unknown, to deny it or rationalize it away. Unfortunately, reason is not sufficiently powerful on its own to help us get something we want in situations that are fast changing and where we are in competition with others for the same thing. In these situations we have to use our intuition in combination with reason.

A successful entrepreneur knows how to apply reason to the process of interacting with a market while using intuition or hunches to decide what specific products might succeed. Psychologically, the entrepreneur manages to see the unknown as exciting rather than as something to be feared. He knows that the rewards that come with taking a risk that works are far greater than those that follow the straightforward application of a formula where the output is precisely specifiable and controllable in advance.

Risks are easier to take if we take them often and if mistakes are not severely punished.

PRACTICAL STEPS

- empower leading-edge knowledge workers to take more risks
- set targets for the number of new products you will introduce
- celebrate bold entrepreneurial efforts even if they fail
- encourage learning by taking risky action in the real-world market-place
- let employees learn for themselves – the hard way
- get rid of the 'right first time' slogan
- get rid of the stigma that is attached to 'reinventing the wheel'
- celebrate the value of intuition
- stop ridiculing everything that is not based on reason and hard facts
- stop expecting watertight proof to back up new venture ideas
- elevate the status of action over certainty and efficiency
- curtail the immobilizing power of critical reason.

"An entrepreneurial culture is one in which the push for diversity and variation is paramount."

"Despite the natural creativity of some individuals, everyone can be encouraged to think more creatively by a culture that explicitly and continously challenges and rewards employees to come up with something new."

7

CREATING AN ENTREPRENEURIAL CULTURE

An entrepreneurial culture is one in which all employees think and act like entrepreneurs. An organization does not have an entrepreneurial culture if all of the new product ideas and decisions are made by the founder who happens to be an entrepreneur. The culture of such an organization could be very oppressive and bureaucratic if the founder/entrepreneur institutes strict procedures for the implementation of only his own ideas.

Many large and successful entrepreneurial businesses are in fact founded by entrepreneurs, but their long-term success is clearly at risk if they are the sole source of new initiatives. This is why there is a need for organizational renewal. Some successful organizations are functionally structured, quite conventional in many respects, but they have an effective R&D department. Could such an organization not be considered entrepreneurial? The difficulty here is that there is a continuum of organizations which are only relatively more entrepreneurial than others. There is no watertight definition which will include just the organizations we want to consider as entrepreneurial and exclude others. The clearest we can be is to specify those characteristics likely to be associated with organizations that are maximally entrepreneurial and encourage others to use such organizations as role models.

In this chapter, therefore, we need to see just what culture is and how it governs the behaviour of employees. We also need to get a clear idea of what features a culture should have if the organization is to be as entrepreneurial as it can be. Finally, we need to look at ways of managing the transition to a more entrepreneurial culture.

WHAT IS ORGANIZATIONAL CULTURE?

Any workable definition of culture must say something about how the behaviour of the majority of employees is governed. There does not need to be any implication that everyone in the organization behaves in the same way or that there are no subcultures in the firm. One organization's culture may be very different from another's or quite similar. Deal and Kennedy (1982), in their popular book on organizational culture, point to the differences between the cultures of General Electric and Xerox. In GE, employees are thoughtful and deliberate. They are analytical, as you would expect in a culture populated by engineers. Xerox, according to Deal and Kennedy, is dominated more by the behaviour of sales people and so fast action seems to be valued. Despite such dramatic differences, each of these firms could be said to have distinctive cultures even if they each had quite different subcultures within their organizations.

Many writers on organizational culture present culture as a unifying force. A culture is supposed to be what leads employees to act the same in similar situations. There seems to be a need to see culture as uniform so that it can help to minimize employee anxiety in the face of uncertainty. The need for anything that is anxiety reducing is indeed a powerful force. Uniformity is also self-serving from the point of view of those in power in an organization because a large part of their agenda is how to get everyone agreeing with their vision of the firm's future. However, many other writers argue that organizational structure and culture should closely mirror the market in which they operate. From this point of view it is arguable that much more diversity is required if innovation is to flourish rather than conformity.

Organizational culture is a bit like an individual's personality. Despite any personal inconsistencies a person may display, what we want to know about an individual is what traits *differentiate* him or her from someone else. This differentiation carries no implication of the strength of the distinguishing traits. It is only necessary that there is something distinctive about a person if we are to say that he is different from others.

Accordingly:

An organization's culture is the set of factors that lead employees to behave differently on a long-term basis from the employees in another organization.

Long-term versus short-term characteristics

This definition distinguishes culture from *climate*. There is a lot of confusion over these two terms. Culture is like an individual's personality – it is long lasting. Climate is more like an individual's temporary *mood*. If an organization experiences losses for the first time and must go through a period of large-scale redundancies, the climate may be temporarily one of fear and insecurity. But this is a short-term set of factors which is causing some short-term behaviour patterns. Another short-term climate-affecting factor might be the introduction of a new chief executive whose style is markedly different from that of his predecessor. His style may be so different that he does not last more than a year. Before he is able to change the culture of the organization permanently, he is dismissed. During his short tenure only the climate of the organization was affected. People behaved differently on the surface but adhered to their old ways behind the scenes. The fundamental values and ideals of the employees were unaffected by the temporary change in climate.

The set of factors that govern behaviour

Our definition of culture does not focus merely on the description of how people happen to behave in a particular firm but on the underlying factors that govern that behaviour. Such factors are generally *values* of one sort or another – however much difference there may be between values that are merely espoused versus those that are really acted upon. Rituals and stories about corporate heroes also undoubtedly influence the behaviour of new recruits but such factors are influential only because they exemplify the company's core values. There is no comparable celebration of counter-cultural, deviant or aberrant behaviour. So it is core values that are demonstrated in rituals, celebrations and stories about heroes.

Strong versus weak cultures

By focusing on what factors minimally differentiate one organization's culture from another's, the issue of how strong a culture needs to be is left open. Our definition allows for weak cultures that have only a few differentiating factors and have strong competing subcultures. Deal and Kennedy (1982) maintain that organizations with quite strong cultures are more successful than those with weak cultures because the former creates such a strong degree of identification with the organization among its employees.

In organizations with allegedly strong cultures, employees are acutely aware of what makes their organization different. Deal and Kennedy hold up the Tandem Corporation as an ideal of a strong culture that seems to be associated with clear business success. Informality, fun and togetherness are encouraged at Tandem. Employees are thereby stimulated to identify with the organization as they would with their own family. Strong identification is maintained through rituals and celebrations where heroic actions on the part of individual employees are publicly recognized. What appears to make this culture strong is that all employees identify with the company's mission so thoroughly that they are prepared to exert extra effort on its behalf. Being part of such a culture is seen as an exciting privilege by employees. Selection processes at Tandem are unusually thorough and this conveys the feeling to new recruits that Tandem is a special place to work, a place where you must clearly be able to fit into if you are to be accepted.

> **Strong cultures can be dangerous because their high level of togetherness can stimulate conformity.**

However, a culture that merely encourages a high level of dedication is not necessarily an entrepreneurial one. Moreover, a level of identification that fosters similar behaviour on the part of all employees is not necessarily very conducive to a high level of variation or diversity. An entrepreneurial culture needs, among other things, a large proportion of renegades – individuals who are prepared and encouraged to challenge the *status quo*. Such a culture can take on the form of a religious cult where existing values, practices and processes simply cannot be challenged.

Strong cultures may be appropriate in a sales organization such as Mary Kay Cosmetics or Amway, but counterproductive in firms where diversity is a necessary strength. Self-renewing firms need to adopt an exploratory attitude if the new is always to be sought above the familiar. Sales organizations such as Mary Kay depend on very strong motivation to pursue one single purpose. They have no need for diversity or creative thinking. Most such sales organizations will strive to develop a uniform culture, one in which its values are imbued with near religious significance. In reality most organizations have a range of subcultures – the problem is that they do not necessarily see this diversity as a source of strength.

Before we look at how different types of firms develop different cultures based on different sets of values, we need to explore the nature of values in a bit more detail.

What are values and how do they work?

Values say something about how people are expected to behave. This behavioural aspect of values is critically important. For example, if your organization values the environment very strongly, then employees are expected to exhibit behaviour that avoids harming the environment, if at all possible. The behavioural dimension of values is easily forgotten when we speak of values in wholly abstract terms and describe them as inviolable principles. If we say that we place a high value on treating employees or customers in a certain way, then we are saying that only a quite specific set of behaviours is encouraged – or perhaps even allowed – with respect to employees or customers.

Another implicit but critical feature of values is the unstated implication that appropriate behaviour will be *rewarded* while behaviour that violates a value will be punished. It is worth exploring this behavioural dimension of values in some detail because the topic of corporate culture is really only interesting if there is in fact a definite link between culture and how employees behave.

Reward for conforming to organizational values may be quite tacit – simply acceptance. Reward does not have to be something tangible like a pat on the back or a salary increase. Reward for behaviour that exemplifies an important value can range from mere acceptance to public celebration and elevation to hero status. Similarly, punishment can range from ignoring the offender through reprimand and firing.

Values are stronger than practices or habits, but like the latter, values refer to patterns of behaviour that are either rewarded or punished. There is no sharp line between a practice and a value. One part of the organization may have a practice of preparing reports in a certain way.

It is not an important enough practice to be organization wide or to be considered a value. Still, in one part of the organization, a quite specific set of behaviours is expected in certain (report writing) circumstances. Habits are behaviour patterns that are generally more individual and more neutral as far as the group as a whole is concerned. The reward for a particular habit may be quite implicit and mundane – a habit could be a behaviour pattern that simply works in achieving some routine objective – such as the route you take to drive to work, for instance.

Deal and Kennedy (1982) see culture as 'a system of informal rules that spells out how people are to behave most of the time'. Rules make explicit what behaviour is appropriate in certain circumstances. Rules differ from practices in being more explicit and carrying with them a stronger expectation of conformity. We have rules to codify even routine practices. Values are simply rules that we feel have some intrinsic and usually strong worth in their own right. Rules, on the other hand, have a slightly negative connotation as they imply that we might not want to behave accordingly but that, if we do not, some form of punishment may be forthcoming.

Values differ from rules or practices in being elevated in status (by a group of which you are a member) to strongly enforced behaviour patterns. Values and rules are essentially what the psychologist BF Skinner called *contingencies of reinforcement*. Like a value, a reinforcement contingency is a relationship between: 1) a specific type of behaviour, 2) a specific context, and 3) a reinforcing or punishing outcome of the behaviour. Whether a certain reinforcement works for a particular individual depends on the extent to which the person desires that reinforcement. For example, most cultures depend on the reinforcing power of *acceptance* to control behaviour in accordance with its values.

Rituals, celebrations and hero-worship implicitly convey the message that this is a highly desirable group to belong to and that if you want to be accepted as a member of it, then you will behave in accordance with its values. The purpose of rituals and celebration is primarily to continually recharge the reinforcing power of belonging to this group. Obviously, if it is your behaviour being celebrated you feel reinforced according to the extent that you value being a member of this group. You would not get so excited by the same recognition from a group you despise.

Acceptance, however, is a powerful reinforcer with which to control behaviour only for those individuals who have strong needs to *belong*. The need to belong and to be accepted by others must be stronger than the need for independence. People who tend to be quite independent often need to demonstrate their independence precisely by rebelling against prevailing group values. And the stronger the pressure to conform, the stronger is their felt need to rebel. On the other hand, the need for acceptance is so powerful for most people that such rebels are usually not as individualistic as they like to think. Very often they are merely conforming to the values of some other group, albeit a smaller, counter-culture group.

Examples of popular organizational values

Deal and Kennedy (1982) refer to a number of values held by firms such as Tandem Corporation, which they believe are associated with strong business performance. Such values can pertain to how employees are treated, how business will be done, how the environment will be respected, how customers are to be dealt with, what level of quality is important, how costs are to be contained, what ethics will be followed, among other things. The following list of organizational values is meant to be illustrative rather than exhaustive.

Relationships with employees

Respect – To the extent that people are respected, they will be given credit for being able to think for themselves and manage themselves.

Permanent jobs – Some companies believe in promising employees that there will be no compulsory redundancies.

Promotion from within – Many firms promise employees that all senior jobs will be filled from within so far as possible.

Selection and training – If these are strong values then a lot of effort goes into hiring the right people and developing them to their full potential.

Commitment/loyalty – In exchange for the above, employees are often expected to see their firm as a kind of family which has a right to expect unswerving loyalty, devotion and unquestioning commitment.

How business is done

Informality – An often lauded value is that all levels of managers are to treat everyone as equals, and junior employees can speak to any manager without going through formal channels. This value is often made visible by an open office environment.

Teamwork – Employees are encouraged to help each other out at all times rather than taking a 'That's not my job' attitude.

Hard work – In some cultures working long hours and even through the night is expected. This seems to be common among software companies. Other cultures insist on having fun at work; they infuse work with play.

Integrity – Some firms set great store by honesty and ethical dealings with customers, suppliers and employees. Lying or cheating are mortal sins.

Decision making – Some cultures delegate decisions extensively, others have convoluted group decision making processes that can be quite bureaucratic. IBM has been accused of the latter.

Functional focus – Some firms value sales and marketing. Others emphasize manufacturing or finance.

Product/service values

Quality – A high level of product quality is a nearly universal value by now – at least on an espoused level.

Customer service – As with quality, the customer service bandwagon of late has made sterling service one of the most important of all values.

Price – Many firms pride themselves on offering the cheapest products or, as they would say, the greatest value for money. Others take pride in offering the best product that can be built irrespective of price.

Cost – A similar value to price is evident in companies that are highly cost conscious. Such firms go to great lengths to eliminate waste and to re-engineer their processes to be the lowest cost producer in their market.

Innovation – Some companies strive to be the first to introduce novel products. They pride themselves on their rapid inventiveness. Heroes in such cultures tend to be renegades.

Consistency/tradition – Others offer consistency, tradition and reliability. Examples would be found in firms that make products such as soft drinks, toothpaste or chocolate bars which have been on the market in much the same form for decades. Recall how much flak Coca Cola got for trying to change the formula of this icon of pop culture.

Other non-business values

The environment – Some firms believe very strongly that harm to the environment (including or especially animals) must be minimized.

Public service – A common value is to make products that provide a useful benefit to society. This value often encourages executives to make time for charitable work as well.

HOW CULTURE INFLUENCES BEHAVIOUR

Culture consists of a distinct combination of values. There are a number of ways in which culture can influence employee behaviour. Most obvious is the strength of the culture, as Deal and Kennedy point out. Two organizations may espouse the same set of values, but one may treat them only to lip service while the other behaves as if it were a religious cult. The same values are treated with a degree of reverence in the latter firm, which makes behaving in accordance with them a virtual life and death matter. It is the hype surrounding a firm's values which supercharges the power of the sustaining reinforcement and punishment thereby minimizing deviance.

We have touched on the importance of employee needs in trying to understand the power of culture to influence behaviour. This area must be explored in more depth. Ultimately, we are interested in what employee needs you should consider if you are trying to create an entrepreneurial culture. This ties in with the question of what values are important in such a culture.

Using values to control behaviour

The use of the word 'control' is likely to be objectionable to some people. So it is important to make it clear that the word is used in a very general sense. If one of your organizational values says that employees should be empowered to make their own decisions and to take risks, you are likely to reinforce such behaviour to reassure employees that it is safe to take such risks. You could say that in so doing you are setting employees free, not controlling their behaviour. But your explicitly advocated value and the reinforcement you use will strongly influence the behaviour you want and this is a form of control in a broad, psychological sense. You may be freeing them from more punishing or directive controls, but you cannot free anyone from all of the external (and internalized) variables that influence their behaviour.

> As we noted earlier, employees will only be motivated to behave as you wish them to if your firm's values are in some sense motivational for them.

As we noted earlier, employees will only be motivated to behave as you wish them to if your firm's values are in some sense motivational for them. We discussed the importance of *acceptance* as one such motivational factor: many employees will be motivated to behave in accordance with your values if, in so doing, they are accepted as a member of a desirable group. There are, of course, several other motivational factors that may play a role in leading employees to 'buy in' to your organization's set of values. It is worth looking at them in some detail to see how they tie in with specific values and, more importantly, whether they are likely to motivate some sort of performance or whether they simply induce a desire to remain a member of the group. Finally, there is the question of what combination of values and motivational factors is most likely to facilitate the creation and maintenance of an entrepreneurial organization.

Common motivational factors

Acceptance – Most people want, in varying degrees, to see themselves as members of a group – it may be an arm's length relationship such as, say, being a member of the human race or of a professional body or it might be something quite intimate such as being a member of a close family. The desire to please others is closely related to the need to be accepted.

Affiliation – Here the motivation is generally to have a relatively intimate relationship with other people – such as in a close-knit work team.

Achievement – Many of us are motivated by getting challenging tasks done to our own satisfaction – we may not care who knows about it.

Recognition – In this case, we may not care how much of an achievement is involved, we simply want someone to notice that we are trying to contribute.

Independence – Those who are motivated by opportunities for independence want to do things their own way; complete task ownership turns them on.

Identification – Some people are motivated by values with which they can identify – such as environmental care; they may be independent otherwise.

Power – Many people are not satisfied unless they are able to influence others and have some say over how they behave. Managerial career progress is essential to them. Selling is also a form of power.

Responsibility – This is not the same as power or achievement. Some people can enjoy responsibility for a process that does not provide either an identifiable moment of achievement or power over others.

Self-development – For some people a chance to be continually learning something new is vital; they have an insatiable thirst for new knowledge.

Excitement – Many people are only really alive if they are doing something risky, novel and exciting.

Nurturing – What most pleases these people is helping others, whether it be to help them solve their problems or to simulate their personal growth.

Creativity – Creative people are only satisfied if they are using their imagination to create, preferably artistically, something new and unique.

Affection – Some people need spontaneous displays of affection from others. This is not the same as recognition which could be seen as not sufficiently genuine by people who want to be loved no matter what they do.

Justice – Those of us who are a bit concerned that others are getting a fairer shake than we are, will be motivated by perceived equity. It may not matter how such people are treated as long as everyone is seen to receive the same allotment.

Personal integrity – For some people it is of vital importance that the right thing be done, that the most ethical course of action is always pursued no matter what the cost. This means adherence to internal procedures as well as honest dealings with customers and colleagues.

Security – Many people want assurance that their world is not going to fall down around their ears, that they will not have to face loss or uncertainty.

Money – Last but not least, some people want all the money they can get their hands on. This is not the same as achievement because many of those who value money do not care how they come by it.

Motivating adherence to values

Some of the corporate values discussed above relate primarily to retaining employees and only indirectly to work performance. Having a permanent job may motivate me to stay with my employer because of my need for security, for example, but not to work any harder. Other values, such as hard work and quality are more performance related in that conforming to them will have a more direct impact on output.

Once we have isolated which values tie in with which motivators, we can more easily determine which values and motivators we should be paying attention to if we want to create an entrepreneurial culture. Strictly speaking, you could say that all of the values listed in Table 7.1 depend on the motivating power of acceptance because you would not be accepted if you did not adhere to them. However, in most cases, there are other motivators that seem intuitively to underlie more precisely many of the values listed.

Table 7.1 endeavours to match up values and likely prime motivators.

No value listed here seems to have much place for those who want affection. Those organizations that value respect for the individual could, however, show a much more warm and caring approach than is entailed by the definition of respect given here. In this case, spontaneous displays of affection would be encouraged and valued by all employees who are strongly motivated by affection. Similarly, if your employees know nothing about quality, then this value may appeal to their self-development motivation perhaps more strongly than the other motivators mentioned in the chart, at least until they have mastered quality disciplines. The point is that this list is not intended to be exhaustive. It is only meant to illustrate how a set of common motivators might link up with a set of typical organizational values. The actual link between corporate values and individual motivation will be much more personal and idiosyncratic than such a matching exercise might suggest.

Some interesting conclusions can be drawn from this exercise, however. First, many of the values Deal and Kennedy (1982) claim are associated with Tandem Corporation's strong performance may only function to encourage identification with the organization and a desire for acceptance by the company – leading to employee retention rather than improved performance. Second, values that do in fact relate more closely to performance may discourage innovation in favour of group solidarity.

Table 7.1

Values	Motivators
Retention	
Respect	Independence, acceptance
Permanent jobs	Acceptance, security, justice
Promotion from within	Achievement, recognition, power
Selection & training	Personal development, recognition, achievement
Informality	Acceptance, affiliation
Integrity	Personal integrity, identification
Functional focus	Identification, acceptance
The environment	Identification, integrity
Public service	Identification, integrity
Performance	
Teamwork	Affiliation, acceptance
Hard work	Recognition, money, achievement
Decision making	Independence, recognition, achievement
Quality	Achievement, responsibility, identification
Customer service	Integrity, nurturing, responsibility
Price	Achievement, responsibility, identification
Cost	Achievement, responsibility, identification
Innovation	Independence, creativity, self-development

Deal and Kennedy acknowledge that a potential pitfall of strong cultures is that they could lead to obsolescence or resistance to change. Individuals who identify with the value of innovation are likely, as suggested above, to be motivated by a desire for independence, creativity and self-development. Creative people are notoriously independent and rebellious with regard to the status quo. All they seem to care about is their own creative efforts and their own personal self-development. How can they possibly even survive, let alone flourish, in one of Deal and Kennedy's strong cultures? The stronger the culture the more pressure there is to conform.

A strong, uniform culture may well be a good idea in a single-minded sales organization such as Mary Kay, where, like religious conviction, a manic level of belief must be constantly fired up in people to get them to overcome any personal doubts they may be harbouring. In such a culture, the slightest doubt is seen as heresy and rejection is immediately threatened: you are labelled a sceptic, someone who is not a team player, a wet blanket or called all kinds of other punitive names.

> **An entrepreneurial culture is one in which the push for diversity and variation is paramount.**

But in an organization that depends on a high rate of innovation to keep ahead of a rapidly changing market, much more diversity must be fostered. And this is where a strong, uniform culture is most vulnerable.

VALUES FOR AN ENTREPRENEURIAL CULTURE

Of the values listed in Figure 7.1, the single most important one for facilitating an entrepreneurial culture is innovation. Respect for the individual and informality are likely to be critical as well. When it comes to employee motivating factors, the three most important ones are likely to be independence, creativity and self-development. Of slightly less importance may be achievement, recognition and excitement.

How the desire for independence clashes with other values

An entrepreneurial culture is one in which the push for diversity and variation is paramount. Innovative ideas may start out as distinct novelties, but if they must be subjected to the group-think pitfalls of too much central approval, they will likely be watered down to close versions of tried and true themes common to past successes. The only way to avoid this pressure towards conservatism and conformity is to allow leading-edge, innovative knowledge workers to take risks with a minimum of central control. This entails hiring and cultivating rebels – precisely those individuals who are not too strongly motivated by a desire for acceptance, affiliation or affection. This means that a strong culture may be totally self-defeating. Further, the implication of this conclusion is that the generally unquestioned value of commitment/loyalty may be just getting in the way.

> **An organization's demand for commitment and loyalty extends beyond the obvious wish to retain people who are highly motivated hard workers to a preference for excluding outside contributors to a large extent.**

An organization's demand for commitment and loyalty extends beyond the obvious wish to retain people who are highly motivated hard workers to a preference for excluding outside contributors to a large extent. It also includes subtle pressure to accept the views of senior management with little or no question. This common and otherwise understandable desire is a recipe for inbreeding and minimal innovation.

The clash between innovation (with its associated motivational desire for independence) and commitment/loyalty has profound implications for organizations. In these days of fast organizational decline and increased employee mobility, senior executives are naturally more insecure in their positions. Failure is always just around the next corner. They need more than ever to cultivate such a strong sense of family loyalty among all employees in order to share the strain. In a crisis, a group is often more united with a 'we're in this together' feeling. In these circumstances, nonconformers are even more strongly loathed. For example, being caught as a spy during a major war is much more seriously regarded than the same offence during peacetime.

This point may seem exaggerated, but think how important it is for an insecure chief executive to have everyone buy into his vision of what kinds of products the company will develop for the future. Anyone who suggests that the market is moving in a different direction may be just as loathed as a spy in wartime.

One way around this dilemma is to foster multiple visions of the future, all of which are developed bottom-up among different groups of product development leaders. So rather than share the stress of uncertainty by encouraging every employee to accept a single vision, it may be more effective to spread the risk by facilitating the formation of multiple visions. Of course, this diversity must result in the development of different products rather than different divisions offering virtually the same product on a competing basis. Little is gained by confusing one's customers.

Entrepreneurial values

Some of the values outlined below are taken from the list of general or typical organizational values listed above. However, other values are proposed which are likely to be especially conducive to the development of an entrepreneurial culture. (See also Psychological slant.)

Innovation – A high rate of innovation must be a paramount value. New products must regularly account for a high proportion of your profit.

Diversity – This must be such a strong value that managers must continuously be exhorted to seek out views contrary to their own and to publicly reward dissension. This also means vigilantly killing off the comfortable temptation to prefer a uniform or united culture.

Risk taking – Risks and entrepreneurial mistakes must be encouraged and rewarded assiduously.

Respect – Thoroughgoing respect for the individual's ability to engage in effective self-management must be cultivated – seeing each other as equals.

Decision making – Leading-edge knowledge workers must be empowered to make major decisions and coached on how to show technical/market leadership to the firm.

Learning – Individual self-development must be fostered fanatically at all levels – not just at the level of the organization as a whole.

Informality – Employees must be encouraged to see themselves as partners or preferred suppliers and not as 'subordinates' if they are to have the confidence to take risks.

Networking – This value is more important than teamwork; the creative individual must be encouraged to liaise widely within and outside the organization and not be restricted to a settled, conformity inducing team.

Partnership – Organizational relationships with a diversity of outside suppliers must be cultivated to open the organization to more outside influence and ideas rather than fostering a claustrophobic family feeling which can lead to the 'not invented here' syndrome.

Results – Many organizations are too enamoured of processes, procedures and religious adherence to cost and other creativity stifling values. What matters is results not due process.

Intuition – Intuition must be seen as a more acceptable basis for making product modifications. A one-sided concern for facts, evidence and proof is just too stifling to creative thinkers.

Disorganization – A certain amount of repetition, overlap, 'reinventing the wheel', inefficiency and confusion must be valued instead of castigated. Much sought after cross divisional synergy is no doubt valuable but must be encouraged as a networking process along with general external networking. Synergy should not be allowed to be imposed by efficiency fanatics.

NEW MOTIVATIONAL FACTORS TO CULTIVATE

We have identified three motivational factors as likely candidates to be of central importance to cultivate in employees who are to work in an entrepreneurial culture. These are independence, creativity and self-development. To round out this picture it will be useful to see if we can think of any other motivating factors that are likely to be conducive to fostering such a culture. It may also be useful to highlight motivational factors that may be counterproductive from an entrepreneurial point of view.

PSYCHOLOGICAL SLANT

It is a strange phenomenon when you think about it that we so strongly prefer a uniform culture. In an organization under pressure to produce in the short term (as all organizations are today), you can partially explain it by saying that senior executives need reassurance that their vision is correct, so they need to see widespread commitment to the total set of values adopted by the firm in addition to its current strategic objectives. But the issue is deeper than that. The fact that we feel varying degrees of hostility towards other cultures whether they are national, ethnic, religious or racially based, is a testament to the strength of our need to identify with some uniform culture. We seem to derive some sort of security from relating to others who are in many ways the same as us – a sort of safety in numbers feeling. Whatever the primitive psychological or evolutionary basis for this deep-set prejudice, it is surely counterproductive and self-defeating in today's world where learning depends on our ability to adapt rapidly to new ways of doing things and to leave behind us the comfort of sameness and familiarity.

A side effect of short-term pressure also has a part to play. When we are in a hurry it can be a considerable hassle to have to stop and listen to a lot of divergent views. Also, when we feel the anxiety caused by pressure to perform immediately, it does our self-esteem and confidence no good to have someone suggest that we may be pursuing the wrong track. Our immediate reaction is to take the defensive line of attacking back and labelling our critic as 'not being a team player' or worse.

The uncomfortable truth of the matter here is that the sooner we learn to value diversity of opinion, dissension and awkward cultural values, the sooner we will create an entrepreneurial culture – otherwise we risk staying in our familiar ruts.

Independence – The desire for independence does not have to be so strong that the individual prefers to be a recluse. It does have to be sufficiently strong, however, that he or she will be comfortable challenging the *status quo*. We like to think that we all have this much independence, but there is little doubt that most of us are often susceptible to the pressure to conform because of our stronger need for acceptance. We are so good at rationalizing away our conformity that we are generally not even aware of doing it. We all like to think of ourselves as individuals. Our self-esteem is based on our feeling that we can think and act for ourselves. Hence we have great difficulty in even recognizing, let alone admitting, that we may be conforming to group pressure.

Often such conformity will not take the form of explicit acquiescence in group values and practices, but the more subtle inability to even *see* how anything could be done differently. The products offered by the firm and the way they are produced and sold just seems so natural and correct that no alternatives occur to us. This is psychological conformity and it is much more debilitating than the sort of reluctant conformity to obviously restrictive bureaucratic procedures of which we are generally more aware.

Creativity – Independence without creativity merely yields stubborn rejection of existing practices. Individuals who are in fact creative in terms of ability and who are motivated by a need to be creative are often also independent in the sense described above. Such individuals have a natural and insatiable curiosity about how things work and why they have to be the way they are. They are like explorers in their constant quest to discover a better way. Despite the natural creativity of some individuals, everyone can be encouraged to think more creatively by a culture that explicitly and continuously challenges and rewards employees to come up with something new.

> **Despite the natural creativity of some individuals, everyone can be encouraged to think more creatively by a culture that explicitly and continuously challenges and rewards employees to come up with something new.**

This means a 180-degree shift for companies that suppress creativity unless it remains within subtly enforced conservative boundaries.

Self-development – Some people see self-development as a means rather than as an end in itself. As a means, personal development is seen as the way to get promoted. Some organizations only promote people to certain levels if they have an MBA for example. Others view self-development as an end in itself. They have a driving need to learn more. This need is really a corollary of the creative drive in that such people are simply driven to understand things in greater depth as an end in itself. Similarly, they are always concerned to be better and better in their chosen profession, not as a means to an end, but simply because they value knowledge and competence. These are the employees who feel such a strong need to know more that they are often too self-critical because they feel that they do not know enough. Further, they tend to respect only the authority of knowledge and competence in others and not the authority of position. As the work force generally become more knowledge orientated, many more employees will have this type of motivation.

All three of these fundamental motivating factors will contribute to the entrepreneurial values of innovation, diversity and risk taking. Such individuals are also keen on the values discussed above of learning, informality, networking, intuition and results. Because they tend to identify more with their profession than with any particular work team, they are more likely to network widely outside it. Their lack of respect for positional authority means that they will value a culture of informality. Their creativity necessarily requires them to pursue hunches based on a strongly felt intuition rather than pursuing only factual data. And their independence leads to a no nonsense focus on results rather than getting stuck in the tendency to be overly enamoured of processes.

Implementation – It is not enough to pursue creative ideas for their own sake. An entrepreneurial employee must be motivated to implement new ideas. There must be a desire to see one's ideas brought to practical fruition.

Perseverance – Similarly, the entrepreneur must be motivated to persist with a strongly felt intuition in the face of discouragement by colleagues and even sometimes by initial rejection by the market. This is where stories of heroes are helpful. Such tales abound of tenacious employees who would not give up on a new product idea and who eventually made a success of it. They often have to seek financing and other resources by quite unorthodox routes, but they become heroes when they succeed precisely because of the strength of their perseverance and because of the lengths they had to go to achieve their vision.

Individualism

The virtues of teamwork will be discussed in more detail later, but it is important to note briefly here that the value of individual effort should not be forgotten. Maximum variation is more likely to occur where several individuals are allowed to approach the same market issues separately. A similar high level of variation could, of course, be achieved by a large number of separate teams. Teamwork is most counterproductive when the entire organization is exhorted to see itself as a single team. The motivation to preserve individual effort is similar to independence, except that it more explicitly highlights the desire for individual responsibility, personal ownership and recognition. By contrast, independence is more to do with the confidence to challenge the *status quo*. You could have this form of mental self-sufficiency even if you worked in a close-knit team rather than as an individual.

Character traits or motivational factors?

You could say that such individuals are also comfortable with ambiguity and a lack of structure, but this gets into trying to characterize an ideal type of person who is most likely to succeed as an entrepreneurial employee or leader. Many of the above motivational factors are described in terms that make them sound as though they had to do with personal characteristics. However, by sticking with motivational factors rather than dealing with personality traits we can better emphasize the value of organizations striving to motivate all employees to develop such motivation.

The other critical point is that small teams could operate in accordance with these motivational factors just as well as individuals. A small team could be independent and have a creative synergy without any of the team members being particularly creative individually. As we concluded in an earlier chapter, quite different character types can be effective in an entrepreneurial capacity and teams of people with the right combination of traits working within an appropriately motivating environment can be equally effective as entrepreneurial units.

Developing an entrepreneurial culture, therefore, involves focusing on processes and values rather than directly on selecting, placing and otherwise controlling people. As we saw in discussing the applicability of evolutionary ideas to organizational dynamics, we should focus on the ecology and the underlying developmental processes rather than directly on non-existent clear objectives or directly on the selection and management of 'appropriate' people.

We also criticized the employee competency approach as being too structure orientated. It is reasonable to select employees with appropriate skills for the more structured jobs one needs to carry out: the efficient delivery of existing services or products. But entrepreneurial self-renewal depends on allowing people to find their own way, effectively treating them as if they were entrepreneurs already.

So the point of the above discussion is not to develop a person specification for organizations wishing to hire more entrepreneurial employees. The argument is that organizations that are interested in creating an entrepreneurial culture should cultivate the appropriate values and use motivational factors that will increase the likelihood of all employees behaving more entrepreneurially.

Motivational factors that inhibit an entrepreneurial culture

Just as certain personal motivational factors should be cultivated in order to create and sustain an entrepreneurial culture, so others should be either discouraged or channelled harmlessly in some other direction. Such factors would include:

> **Just as certain personal motivational factors should be cultivated in order to create and sustain an entrepreneurial culture, so others should be either discouraged or channelled harmlessly in some other direction.**

Security – The need for security should be channelled in the direction of individual competence and personal diversification so that employees develop their own security rather than relying on the organization to provide it. The need for security works with the need for acceptance to increase the tendency to conform.

Acceptance – There is no getting rid of this need. It must be rechannelled so that employees find acceptance in a large range of groups inside and outside the organization – such as with professional affiliations, so that they do not depend exclusively for acceptance on one group or on just their employer. An important objective of employee development should be to help them learn to balance the need for acceptance with a healthy degree of independence. Often we need acceptance to an excessive degree precisely because we have not developed a very strong degree of self-reliance.

Power – The need for power in small doses is necessary so that budding entrepreneurs can sell their ideas to those who have the resources they need to bring their ideas to fruition. Beyond this degree of power, the need to acquire authority for its own sake can very easily produce a high degree of tension between an entrepreneurial culture and an hierarchical one that may be constantly trying to reassert itself behind the scenes. Those with strong power needs should be encouraged to focus on managing large but short-term projects or to specialize in the delivery task where the creativity of the entrepreneurial culture is not important.

Where are we now?

We have explored what an entrepreneurial culture might look like in terms of a likely set of values and personal motivational factors. We still need to see what the implications of developing an entrepreneurial culture are for teamwork versus individual effort, how the relationships between employer and employee will become more like that between customer and supplier and how new career concepts must be developed.

All of these issues have to do with managing the transition to a more entrepreneurial culture. First it is important to look at some of the more psychological transitions involved – such as, for instance, what becomes of the managerial role and what forms of resistance we can expect.

PRACTICAL STEPS

- define what an entrepreneurial culture means in different parts of the organization and as appropriate for your industry

- conduct training for all employees on how to behave in accordance with entrepreneurial values and motivational factors

- visibly celebrate exemplary entrepreneurial actions

- focus strong subcultures on delivery, encourage cultural diversity for the sake of the self-renewal task

- provide training to encourage constructive diversity and dissension

- help employees find other avenues for needs that are either not conducive to, or are inhibiting to, entrepreneurial action

- encourage teams and individuals to develop their own brand of entrepreneurial culture.

"The usefulness of the distinction between delivery and self-renewal is that it reminds us that organizations do have two completely distinct tasks."

"To help the organization make the necessary transition to a more entrepreneurial culture, managers need to find new roles for themselves, to discover new sources of identity and motivation."

8

IS AN EFFICIENT ENTREPRENEURIAL CULTURE POSSIBLE?

Creating an entrepreneurial culture is vital for ongoing self-renewal. But it is not enough to ensure profitability. You still have to look after today's business as well and this requires efficiency above all else. We saw earlier that the reliable delivery of existing products and services cannot be forgotten in the rush to create the future. The usefulness of the distinction between delivery and self-renewal is that it reminds us that organizations do have two completely distinct tasks. Because the two tasks are so different, no single prescription is possible for the effective execution of both.

> **The usefulness of the distinction between delivery and self-renewal is that it reminds us that organizations do have two completely distinct tasks.**

In this chapter we need to look at how the cultures appropriate to such disparate tasks might live together and, second, how to manage the transition to a necessarily mixed culture. It is useful to treat these two seemingly different issues together because, for example, there is no doubt that some employees will prefer to work in one culture rather than the other. So this chapter will take us more into the implications of the preceding discussion for the work lives of employees who may, at the moment, not be sure where they fit in. Currently, most commentators on organizational issues are advising all organizations without exception to jump on the same bandwagon – whatever it is. If this unilateral and uniform prescription is leaving some firms and many employees confused and nervous, it is not surprising in view of the fact that most of these advisers ignore the existence of the two fundamentally different organizational tasks we have discussed here.

MIXED MARRIAGE – A UNION OF OPPOSING CULTURES

Earlier we explored new possible metaphors to help us picture what an organization might look like which is capable of evolving into the future with the old and the new living side by side. The most promising candidate for this role was the metaphor of the family dynasty where older family members run the existing, established business while younger members launch new ventures and run them quite independently. Later they repeat the same process with their own offspring. The metaphor of the family dynasty also captures some of the interpersonal and authority-related dynamics better than does the metaphor that has us envisaging the organization as just any social group. Succession battles exist in organizations, which are every bit as intense as they are in a family dynasty. Most importantly, this metaphor provides us with a model of sorts with which to visualize how the two tasks of delivery and self-renewal might be allocated.

> **Succession battles exist in organizations, which are every bit as intense as they are in a family dynasty.**

A very important and valuable feature of this metaphor is that a family dynasty is clearly made up of completely separate units.

A large extended family is composed of one set of oldest living parents with a family tree below it, perhaps branching out in several directions, and consisting of a number of individual children and offspring that have formed into new family units.

Although this metaphor has not been used on a wide basis, it is clearly implicit in the comments of other writers on organizational culture. For example, the Pinchots (1993), in their book on how intelligent organizations are replacing bureaucracies, refer to the big-name computer firms in Silicon Valley, such as Hewlett-Packard, Apple and Intel, as parents in just this sense: 'These "parent" organizations have given birth to thousands of companies launched by former employees.' Note the phrase 'former employees'. This spawning of new ventures has always been a common occurrence. Tomorrow's survival for large, established companies will depend on their ability to maintain a closer relationship with their 'children' than the reference to *former* employees implies.

Another useful feature of the family dynasty metaphor is that we can easily imagine how the older generation would be more conservative, more inclined to maintain their values and past interests while the younger generation would seek something new – perhaps rebelling to some extent if their elders tried too hard to impose their values and interests on them.

Our discussion of entrepreneurial culture and the important motivational value of personal independence comes to mind in this context. Part of what motivates the younger generation is a need to prove to their elders that they can make it on their own, that they can create a life for themselves, perhaps even outdoing their parents. Interestingly, it is the most rebellious children who are likely to be the most creative in their need to do something completely different and perhaps to upstage their parents who have possibly conveyed the message that these children were deviant and in need of stronger discipline and control.

The organizational implications of this metaphor are that established units should focus (albeit not exclusively) on the delivery of existing services or products while spinning off new units that have the promise of starting up successful ventures on an entrepreneurial basis. In practice this division of labour would not be quite so categorical. Units that specialize in the delivery of existing offerings still need to continually make incremental improvements to their services or products – improvements in quality, the addition of new features and the use of cost cutting new materials or processes. Wholly mature industries are likely to remain in this mode completely. Take the automobile industry, for example. Car manufacturers are unlikely to renew themselves by entering totally new markets with completely different products – they could do so – but their major focus for change and development is on incremental improvements to existing product lines.

There would only be a need for car makers to undertake renewal in the entrepreneurial sense described here if they needed to abandon car making at some point and dream up some entirely different product range. The most dynamic markets are those where a firm's whole product line could become obsolete suddenly and where managers cannot easily forecast what new products they could successfully launch.

How to change while remaining the same

Ironically, the family dynasty metaphor – despite its connotation of family feuds – should make for an easy transition to the mixed culture required for efficient delivery, on the one hand, and entrepreneurial self-renewal, on the other. This relative ease is possible, in principle, because there is no need for an entire organizational unit to simultaneously embrace both cultures. The two cultures will exist in different units under the same organizational umbrella. Many large organizations have already seen the merit of breaking themselves down into many discrete profit centres. The family dynasty metaphor suggests that it is quite legitimate to have some profit centres focus on established product lines that are likely only to develop incrementally, while other units enter more volatile markets where a more open-ended, exploratory, entrepreneurial, approach is more likely to be successful. The difference between the two types of units will, of course, be a matter of degree

> **The most dynamic markets are those where a firm's whole product line could become obsolete suddenly and where managers cannot easily forecast what new products they could successfully launch.**

A mixed marriage of two cultures will therefore allow some units to remain much the same over the medium term while others need to be more dynamic so they can change as fast as their market demands. Over time, units of each type could change places. An entrepreneurial unit that establishes a solid hold on a particular market, which matures and enters a reasonably steady state then needs to alter its culture so that it adopts aspects of the delivery culture. Otherwise there would be little effectiveness in terms of efficiently keeping quality up and costs down so as to make a profit over the longer term. This is especially true as new products enter the mature price war phase and need increasingly to be delivered more cost effectively.

Similarly, unexpected changes in the market for products offered by more delivery-orientated units could require them to become suddenly more entrepreneurial. The changes each type of unit would have to make would need to be made in different ways, however. When an entrepreneurial unit needs to become more delivery orientated, it will need to hire managers who are better at running efficient operations. This will entail a short-term clash of cultures as the delivery focus takes over from the entrepreneurial one. This transformation could lead to the departure of some entrepreneurial employees, or they could make the transition personally to be more concerned with efficient delivery.

A third possibility, provided they still have some creative ideas, would be to start a new entrepreneurial unit with a new product range. An example of an entrepreneur who could not seemingly make the transition to the delivery stage might be Steve Jobs, the co-founder of Apple Computer, Inc. He was pushed out and started a new venture called Next. In other organizations such entrepreneurs could just as well start a new unit rather than be forced out or depart willingly.

If a delivery unit suddenly feels pressure to be more entrepreneurial, it would be well advised to do so by hiving off new entrepreneurial sub-units. The point of this differentiation between how the two types of units would have to change is that, generally, it will be easier for some individuals to transform themselves from entrepreneurs to conventional business managers than it will be for conventional managers to become entrepreneurs. Again, however, the difference is slight. No doubt more entrepreneurs than not are unable to become managers and certainly a few managers could transform themselves into successful entrepreneurs. But, of course, a prime reason why so many entrepreneurial ventures fail is that their founders cannot become managers and they are unable to let go sufficiently in order to let effective business managers take over day-to-day delivery operations.

When a delivery-focused unit, which is staffed primarily by efficiency orientated managers, needs to become more entrepreneurial, those in charge can take lessons from the parental experience of letting one's children be themselves, learn to take care of themselves and establish their own independence. This means empowering budding entrepreneurs to take risks and launch their own new ventures with little or no interference from above. The potential culture clash in this case can only be avoided by those in power having the strength of character to let go, to avoid meddling in a future they may not like to admit they know little about.

The advantage of the parental metaphor in this context is that it is all too easy for enthusiastic senior executives to take too great an interest in new ventures. On the face of it, there would seem to be no reason why they should not take such an active interest, but the parental metaphor should serve as a warning that too much interference is likely to lead to rebellion and perhaps the loss of key entrepreneurial employees – just what you would expect with your own adolescent children.

Senior managers in large, delivery-orientated organizations should be appointed, in part, for their willingness to oversee the delivery function (rather than meddle in renewal ventures) and to perform other roles – ideal candidates are those who have made the transition to a mentoring phase in their lives and who are happy to offer coaching to budding entrepreneurs rather than expecting to be personally involved in new product decisions.

The cultural continuum

A large diversified enterprise should cultivate a continuum of cultures across the range of its various profit centres. Business units in the most mature industry sectors are likely to be the most efficient in delivering their mature products cost effectively and profitably. Their culture will have all of the positive features of the much castigated mechanistic organizational form. Structure will be important and designed to facilitate efficient co-ordination across departments. Empowerment in these units will not mean the freedom to take expensive risks or start entrepreneurial ventures. It will mean having the authority to solve local production or customer problems without consulting a superior. These units will still need a minimum of creativity to introduce minor modifications to their products even if it is only the packaging that changes.

At the other end of the spectrum will be the newest entrepreneurial units which are in the most volatile of markets and which need maximum variation across product models to ensure that some offering is always selected. However costly and wasteful might be the experimentation of such entrepreneurial businesses, these units will also need a minimum of managerial efficiency to ensure that what is offered has some chance of making a profit.

In neither unit will there likely be much in the way of a culture clash, because either the managerial or the entrepreneurial culture will be so dominant that the opposing subculture will inevitably be subservient.

Stuck in the middle?

If there is indeed a continuum of cultures across a range of units, then there will unavoidably be those with a more equal mixture of managerial and entrepreneurial subcultures. If a managerial type is appointed to head the group, he or she may be concerned with the next promotion. Regardless of the manager's personal motivation, however, the primary focus of the group could shift towards consolidation, cost cutting, more conservative risks, elimination of duplication and all those good disciplines that have the effect of increasing short-term profitability. This cultural shift entails a potentially serious clash with the more entrepreneurial subculture.

Interestingly, there are both managerial and entrepreneurial solutions to this dilemma. The managerial response might be to propose some formula, perhaps something structural, which would be expected to resolve such conflict normally if not universally. Perhaps some form of power sharing might work in some cases. The entrepreneurial approach is more about letting it happen. It recognizes that any resolution will come down to the particular personalities involved and how persuasive they are about what the future of the unit should be. The important matter, on this view, is that organizations should be prepared to support the entrepreneurial camp in departing the scene to set up a new venture under the same corporate umbrella, rather than allowing such conflict to lead to winners and losers with the losers then leaving the organization altogether. Similarly, the entrepreneurial employees themselves must be counselled to let go of products that are maturing. Employing the parental/family dynasty metaphor in this context, you could say that they need to turn their 'baby' over to 'nanny' for further nurturing while they go off and make more babies!

TRANSFORMING BUREAUCRACY

Organizations that are currently structured into numerous discrete units are already well along the road to having the right balance of the managerial and entrepreneurial cultures. What about organizations that are simply one large unified structure dominated by the managerial culture – one that also happens to be very strong, hence not much propensity to look very favourably on more than minimal diversity? Their transition will be unavoidably more painful.

The most difficult route to take – and one most often recommended by gurus is that the entire organization should transform itself, such as in turning an elephant into a rabbit – an impossible task. No wonder that most such change efforts peter out eventually through exhaustion due to the inevitable inertia and weight of the preponderant managerial culture. Part of the answer to this problem is easy: it is simply a matter of letting entrepreneurial employees start new ventures with a minimum of interference. Or they can be acquired and left to get on with it. AT&T's recent acquisition of MaCaw Cellular may be a case in point, although it is too soon to tell whether the parent will stifle its adopted child.

So long as new ventures are allowed to develop their own distinctive culture, they have as much chance of success under a corporate umbrella – perhaps more – than they would have independently. Often, however, corporate managers are bored and they want to get involved in new ventures. Not knowing much about the new ideas, they may be tempted to offer their skills at systematization and process efficiency. This 'assistance' generally means stifling bureaucracy to the fledgling entrepreneurial venture.

Corporate managers essentially need to learn to value entrepreneurial ventures more fully. This includes a better understanding of their need for independence and their own unique culture. The difficulty conventional managers face is finding a useful role for themselves in the new realities of life in organizations. Managers used to stable positions of authority find it difficult to adjust to the lower status existence of being roving project managers with no turf of their own. What happens to their territorial instincts?

Part of the adjustment larger unified cultures need to make is to find new roles for managers. At present many of them are either being made redundant, feeling displaced by increasingly powerful knowledge workers or simply left behind in the rapid pace of change. So what is to become of the managerial role? Before we explore the changing world of the manager it is important simply to list the several transition issues that need to be tackled in addition to the shift in managerial roles – however profound it will be on its own. So, here are some of the critical transition issues we need to take a look at in what follows:

- What becomes of the managerial role?
- Giving up a uniform culture – what does it offer? – why do you need it? – how to live without it, benefits of the mixed culture.
- How can managers get along with entrepreneurs without stifling them, i.e. before new ventures reach the stage of being hived off?
- Establishing and implementing complementary skills.
- Helping managers find and adjust to new roles.
- New career structures.

These critical transition issues will be discussed in turn, beginning with the transformation of the managerial role.

The end of management?

It is increasingly well documented that the managerial role is waning in importance – possibly to disappear altogether. This startling development will be explored in what follows. There is no doubt that organizations on the whole are becoming more entrepreneurial and less managerial in their orientation. The full implications of this trend have yet to be thought through clearly and are potentially astronomic in scope.

What we need to determine is, what are the implications of this trend for the bulk of workers who see themselves as managers or who aspire to this type of career? Second, how can organizations dominated by the managerial culture give up such a familiar way of existing, their comfortable and entrenched source of identity? It is

> **It is increasingly well documented that the managerial role is waning in importance – possibly to disappear altogether.**

interesting to note that no less an authority on the managerial role than Peter Drucker (1985) now says that he feels uncomfortable with the term 'manager'. He apparently prefers 'executive', now. Whatever the direction such a shift ultimately takes, it will have profound implications for the way organizations function.

First of all, what are the major trends that are pointing towards the decline in importance of the managerial role?

- Middle managers have borne the brunt of much recent staff cut-backs. They have been seen as adding little value – simply monitoring and checking the work of their subordinates. Using their authority primarily to prove they have it, more initiative is stifled than stimulated.
- Non-managers are increasingly encouraged to manage themselves, to make their own decisions and to see themselves as serving customers not as reporting to bosses. This ties in with the shift of performance appraisal away from the traditional top-down approach to 360-degree feedback.
- Sophisticated information technology has taken away the co-ordination and communication functions that managers once held (and companies want to retain only those who are doing *real* work).
- Customer service expectations now force organizations to let those who are closest to customers make decisions that used to be referred upwards to managers for adjudication.
- Rapid change at the firing-line now makes it very hard for the manager who is one or more steps removed from such reality to have anything useful to contribute. Such managers are often embarrassed by their ignorance and the greater knowledge of their subordinates, or they become so oppressively controlling in their desire to stay on top of the detail that they end up virtually doing their subordinates' jobs for them.
- Many managers are too strongly turf orientated – so they spend their time fighting with other managers over who has jurisdiction over what. This preoccupation contributes to political time wasting and generally too much internal focus on the part of the organization as a whole.
- Power is shifting from positional authority to knowledge. Employees who have become so-called knowledge workers are more up to date with fast changing developments in their fields, thereby acquiring more real power than their managers. From this perspective, empowerment is not delegation but the recognition of a natural and unstoppable shift in power.
- The trend towards projects and away from jobs as fixed positions means that, while project management skills are still valuable, there are no more management positions as such.

- To the extent that organizations see employees as self-employed suppliers of services rather than employees in the conventional sense, they expect them to add bottom-line value, not just manage.
- Increasing emphasis on the knowledge worker helps to make a career as a knowledge worker more desirable; people stay in touch with professions that often provide their strongest source of personal identity.
- According to a recent *Fortune* cover story, 'Kissing Off Corporate America' (1995), business school graduates in the United States are increasingly leaving university to become entrepreneurs rather than join large corporations to pursue the traditional managerial career. They now see large organizations as too slow and bureaucratic, offering boring and poorly rewarded jobs.

During any major transition, such as the one we are now experiencing, there is bound to be a great deal of upheaval – actual dislocation as well as psychological trauma. In the midst of such chaos, nothing seems clear or certain. Despite the fact that the managerial role is under attack as never even imaginable before, it is doubtless here to stay in one form or another. To help the organization make the necessary transition to a more entrepreneurial culture, managers need to find new roles for themselves, to discover new sources of identity and motivation.

> **To help the organization make the necessary transition to a more entrepreneurial culture, managers need to find new roles for themselves, to discover new sources of identity and motivation.**

Value-added managerial work

We touched on a few key emerging roles for managers when we discussed the transition from positional leadership to knowledge-based leadership, but now is the time to look at these new roles in more detail.

- **The delivery task** – First and foremost, all businesses will always have services or product lines which will be around for a while and which need managerial attention in order to wring maximum profit out of them. Computers can help to co-ordinate production, supply and sales, but managers will always be necessary in a trouble shoot-ing capacity to correct problems at the interface between employees, other people and machines. The slower moving the industry the more the emphasis will continue to be on managerial efficiency rather than entrepreneurial creativity.

- **Purchasers of services** – As employees increasingly become sup-pliers of services on a contractual or outsourced basis, managers will become customers who buy services and oversee their effective supply.
- **Coaches and mentors** – Even if employees are external suppliers they will often lack the experience of managers and could benefit from it.
- **Venture capitalists** – As with the purchasing of services, managers will always have the role of deciding which entrepreneurial ventures to invest in.
- **Strategists** – However much organizations move towards becoming venture capitalists rather than making things, there will always have to be decisions about what broad directions to pursue and this will call for strategic thinking managers.
- **Opportunity explorers** – Ideas for new ventures will increasingly emerge bottom-up from knowledge workers who are closest to changing technology, but astute managers can use a process recom-mended by Peter Drucker (1985) (in his book *Innovation and Entrepreneurship*) of systematically scanning niches for likely opportunities. They can then pull together the necessary technical experts to do a feasibility study.
- **Brokers** – Entrepreneurial insiders or outsiders may have ideas that require the bringing together of diverse internal groups and other external suppliers. The manager can serve in the role of broker to bring together disparate but potentially interested parties.
- **Project managers** – Some commentators see all management as becoming totally 'projectized'. This is perhaps going too far. Many delivery functions will always have a machine-like regularity to them which is not at all project-like. Nevertheless, much work will be of a project nature, especially in faster changing industries and many holders of formerly fixed managerial positions could have satisfying careers as roving project managers whose careers progress through ever more complex projects.

- **Mixed roles** – While there will be fewer 'pure' general managers, there will always be a place for functional, technical or industry specialists who also happen to have good managerial skills – who can interpret what 'pure' experts are saying and communicate that to more senior executives who need to decide what to invest in. This is a consulting role as much as a managerial one.

So managers do not have to worry about extinction – not yet anyway. Many will simply become entrepreneurs once their organization's culture is sufficiently conducive that they feel free to make this change in career direction.

Giving up the need for a uniform culture

Giving up the desire for a uniform culture involves several steps – becoming fully aware of the differences between a uniform and a mixed culture, understanding the disadvantages of the former and the benefits of the latter, coming to grips with why the strong, uniform culture has such a hold on us and learning how to release this grip in the interest of acquiring new values.

1. The major difference between a strong, uniform culture and one that is a mixture of managerial and entrepreneurial values is that diversity must be much more strongly promoted – not just encouraged – in the latter. The stronger the culture the more every employee is committed to a single vision of everything the business stands for and is trying to achieve. Diversity needs to be combined with the value and motivational power of independence – allowing those with divergent ideas to do their own thing. Otherwise diversity can simply mean more infighting with a thousand different visions all clamouring to be the one true faith. To keep it simple, there really is no other difference so critical as the need for diversity – this value is simply the statement that a uniform culture is counterproductive. It implies that diversity is necessary for the entrepreneurial spirit to flourish and that uniformity and diversity are diametrically opposing forces.

2. Advantages and disadvantages – The main advantage of a uniform culture, especially if it is also strongly uniform, is that extra effort can be focused on one single-minded objective. In a crisis or in an

industry such as cosmetics sales, inciting a single mindedness that nears religious fundamentalism in strength is no doubt useful for getting everyone to pull as hard as they can in the same direction. But, as with any such one true faith atmosphere, dissent is vehemently repulsed. There is just no time or room for doubt. The suggestion that the company should invest in quite different product lines can be seen as a fundamental challenge to those who have decided upon the firm's current direction and such dissension is rarely tolerated.

It is too simplistic to assert that all you need for the managerial culture to live with its entrepreneurial counterpart is unanimous agreement on the values of quality, customer service and the objective of making a profit. In reality most entrepreneurs are stifled by large businesses and either give up or leave precisely because they cannot cope with the imposition of excessively strong managerial values – specifically the demand that every decision be approved by the managerial hierarchy. Just as there will always be a degree of tension between enthusiastic property developers and environmentalists because of how profoundly their values diverge, so we will likely have to live with a similar stand-off between entrepreneurs and managers.

3. Releasing the comfortable grip of a uniform culture is not at all easy, especially if it is quite strong. The point of using the religious analogy is to underline the fact that organizations can be just as fanatical about their cultural values and just as loath to modify them. But why is uniformity so entrenched? It is so unquestioned that many commentators on the concept of organizational culture actually define culture as that which everyone shares – the values everyone believes in and which binds them together as a single entity.

Having clear values does help to raise one's level of self-esteem, confidence and personal identity. But this individual perception is not enough – we also need to be part of a group that shares our values. We define who we are by seeing ourselves as similar to one set of people in some respects and different from another group in other ways. The more we feel threatened by the existence of a group that calls into question our own values and hence identity, the more we bind ourselves to our own group and define the other group as an enemy to be repelled in some way or other. Such close binding to our own group leads us to expel any members who are not wholly on board with the group's values.

Fortunately, organizational values are not quite so central to one's core sense of personal identity as the religious analogy might suggest. The key is to recognize one's allegiance to managerial values and to sufficiently loosen their grip to enable greater appreciation of entrepreneurial values. The easy way to achieve this is through a form of group *segregation*, so that managers and entrepreneurs can sufficiently keep their distance in order that culture clashes are minimized. This idea fits naturally with the idea of setting up discrete profit centres.

At the same time, however, the 'mother ship' will often have budding entrepreneurs which need to be cultivated before they reach the level of separate profit centres. How can they be encouraged and developed in a culture that is predominantly managerial with a few separate and perhaps struggling entrepreneurial units? The entrepreneurial units you do have can be held up as role models for other employees to emulate. But more basically, managers need to be trained to value dissension – not just in the sense of inviting disagreement and challenges to the manager's ideas, but also in the sense of empowering employees to experiment with their own ideas, to take some resources and try 'off-the-wall' product initiatives.

The uniformity of the managerial culture needs to be relaxed precisely at this point – too much pressure to justify every use of resources by hard facts or to get approval from on high will certainly stifle entrepreneurial creativity. This is the specific form of diversity that managers need to value more highly. The manager must learn to value his or her strengths as being necessary for the present while seeing entrepreneurial activity as essential to create the future. This differentiation of focus can help to preserve identity and self-esteem. The point here is to encourage managers to distinguish between the fundamentally different tasks of ongoing delivery of existing offerings and entrepreneurial self-renewal. It is essential for proponents of both cultures not to downgrade either sets of values. Neither is more important than the other – both are necessary for the sustenance of a viable business.

Managing entrepreneurs without stifling them

Clearly there must be some parameters. Diversification that is too far from core competencies has too many well-established pitfalls to be ignored. The catch is to find the right balance of constraints and stimulating conditions. On the parameters side, an entrepreneurial proposal process should be developed to enable employees to bid for funds with guidelines on what form such proposals should take. Obviously, the key is to make such a process as minimally bureaucratic as possible. Whether a particular process is bureaucratic or just right will be largely in the eye of the beholder. If your firm is already quite entrepreneurial, then quite a minimal process would be all that would be acceptable to budding entrepreneurs. On the other hand, if your organization is quite bureaucratic at the moment, then any relaxation of controls will seem wonderfully liberal to your hitherto stifled entrepreneurs.

Much more needs to be done on the promotional side. A venture capital fund should be set up which makes funds no more difficult to obtain than they would be on the open market. We noted earlier that Xerox has just such a venture capital fund. In a sense an organization is competing for entrepreneurial start-up ideas with venture capitalists and you should treat your budding entrepreneurs as if they were clients – just as a venture capital firm would do. This in itself is a significant culture change – seeing prospective entrepreneurial employees as customers rather than as owned assets or human 'resources'. Actually you should see them as customers and prospective partners rather than as employees.

Taking this idea a step further, there is no reason why you cannot advertise your fund outside of the organization – not necessarily to attract entrepreneurial employees in the traditional recruitment mode, but to attract prospective partners who may set up a joint venture on some basis with you. There is no need these days for having new ventures either developed in-house or acquired and amalgamated into an in-house division.

Employees who know that such a fund is open to outsiders, not just to themselves, will be stimulated to undergo a culture shift of their own – that they do not have any exclusive right to such funds just because they are employees – the negative implications of felt ownership works both ways. Employees are constrained by being seen as owned resources but organizations are equally restricted by employees who think they have a monopoly on promotions and other benefits. Such mutual territoriality is born of overly closed cultures and is mutually stifling when what is needed is a more open market approach in both directions.

Based on success stories of other entrepreneurial ventures in your organization or within similar industries, you should develop your own blend of managerial and entrepreneurial values. This is not a rational, a priori process but one that should be guided by what works for you. Success stories have the value of being anecdotal rather than formulaic. They allow individual entrepreneurs to freely model their own approach after the success story that most inspires them and best suits their particular personalities. Some ventures will be a success with an almost equal blend of entrepreneurialism and attention to management disciplines. Others will be much more inefficient initially but will succeed precisely because of the chaos that sometimes leads to happy accidents.

> **Based on success stories of other entrepreneurial ventures in your organization or within similar industries, you should develop your own blend of managerial and entrepreneurial values.**

So there is no precise formula or recipe that will tell you that so much managerial discipline and so much entrepreneurial freedom will yield just the right outcome. To expect such precision is to be blinded by the rational managerial culture that most organizations live and breath all too exclusively and narrow mindedly.

Establishing complementary skills

In an organization dominated by the managerial culture, entrepreneurial employees will be seen as occupying a very subservient role. They will be viewed as providing a sort of fuel to propel the main engines of the business. On the other hand, in a more wholly entrepreneurial business, managers may have a status not unlike that of administrators in the offices of doctors, lawyers or other professionals. In this case, the manager provides a service to support the main thrust of the business which is to create the future through radically new products. As we noted above, there seems to be an irresolvable conflict between rampant property developers and fervent environmentalists. Yet such extremes clashes are necessary for genuine creativity. Similarly, there is often a difficult relationship between professionals such as doctors and hospital administrators. They are rarely more than uneasy bedfellows at best.

Business is moving inexorably in the same direction – so-called knowledge workers are increasingly seeing themselves as professionals in the first instance and they are coming to regard managers as providing a co-ordinating service – not as bosses or in any sense as their superiors. The upshot of this shift in perspective is a struggle for power. This conflict does not exist in a sole start-up launched by an independent entrepreneur. The problem occurs in a culture dominated by managers who are naturally loath to give up any power and have to swallow accepting a lower status position.

The reality is, however, that the market is forcing managers to make precisely this shift. Markets that are moving too fast to manage in the conventional manner are demanding faster innovation and this is pushing organizations to grasp at any means to become more entrepreneurial. Unfortunately, many managers see this need to share power with employees who have an entrepreneurial bent as being like having to hand over a spare key to their home to a family of homeless gypsies. Resentment and resistance are the standard and understandable responses.

Ultimately, the only possible amicable resolution to this conflict is for each side to see each other as partners, with neither subordinate to the other. The first step in this direction is to see that each side has complementary skills and that each side needs the other. The entrepreneurs need managerial disciplines to maximize profit and to keep customers happy with reliable, consistent and high quality service or products. The managers need entrepreneurs to create the future so as to ensure that they will have some prospect of ongoing future employment. This solution does not amount to some sort of negotiated stand-off. The reality is that their skills are indeed complementary. (See Psychological slant.)

PSYCHOLOGICAL SLANT

Individuals who are among the organization's best all round managers may see the transition to a more entrepreneurial culture as an opportunity for personal self-renewal. Often senior managers miss the excitement of the firing-line. They are bored by roles that force them to sit in meetings all day when they are dreaming of perhaps starting their own business or doing something else that they would find equally stimulating and challenging. It is only those managers who are excessively immersed in the managerial ethos of efficiency and control who will most resent this transition. A more entrepreneurial culture should encourage managers at all levels to get involved with new ventures – not as bosses in the conventional sense but as entrepreneurs with their own ideas to develop. While younger employees may generally have the fresher perspective necessary for maximum creativity, they do not have a monopoly on good ideas. So the transition to a more entrepreneurial culture is potentially an opportunity for all employees to unleash their entrepreneurial urges and renew themselves by starting a new career with their existing employer.

Helping managers adjust to new roles

Because managers in a culture dominated by rational managerial values are effectively losing a struggle for power, they have the most adjusting to do. As their skills are not obsolete, it is imperative for organizations to ensure that they are valued, not just chopped out or castigated for suppressing entrepreneurs. A step down in status inevitably entails a loss of self-esteem and this is generally accompanied by a range of defensively hostile reactions. Managers who take this line, however understandable it might be, are unavoidably seen as resistant to change – let's say by an incoming chief executive whose mandate is to make the organization more entrepreneurial overnight. Intense anger means a loss of objectivity and, for this reason, managers need coaching on how to adjust to new roles. Part of this process is to recognize that there are vital roles for them to play – as discussed above. A more important part of this adjustment assistance is for the organization to celebrate their contributions alongside those of the new entrepreneurial heroes.

We discussed in the last chapter how the extent to which an organization visibly values an outcome or behaviour pattern the greater will be the reinforcing power of engaging in that activity. So it is vital to place a balanced degree of value on both managerial and entrepreneurial practices. There is no other way for both sides to feel equally valued. One of the motivational factors we discussed in the last chapter was justice – the need to see that others are not treated better than we are. While some people are more concerned with justice than others, we all want it to some extent. It is especially important when people are adjusting to a lower status life and are prone to perceive injustice where none exists or is intended.

It has been convenient to portray managers and entrepreneurs as black and white categories. Clearly, however, people will lie along a continuum of these orientations. While some entrepreneurs are disasters at management, many are good managers. Similarly, some managers could not begin to launch a new product or business, but some could very well make the transition to being an entrepreneur and to use both skill sets.

Where are we now?

We have explored what a culture based on a mixture of managerial and entrepreneurial values would look like. Our discussion has focused on the psychological and cultural aspects of the transition to a more entrepreneurial culture. We need now to look in more detail at some aspects of how that would work in practice – not so much from an operational perspective but with regard to the people side. For example, what is the relative importance of teamwork and individual effort? Earlier in this chapter we noted the need to look at new career structures as part of managing the transition to a more entrepreneurial culture. These are topics for later chapters. The first priority, for the next chapter, is to explore in more detail how the employment relationship is changing beyond recognition and for good.

PRACTICAL STEPS

- work out for yourselves in teams what are the cultural blockages which could get in the way of becoming more entrepreneurial

- initiate an organization-wide change process to make room for more entrepreneurial values

- make specific plans to recognize and celebrate diversity

- plan how to value managerial and entrepreneurial skills equally

- get managers and leading-edge technical employees together to work out for themselves how their skills complement one another's

- have managers in teams identify new roles for themselves which add value to both the delivery and the self renewal tasks

- provide counselling services to managers to help them make the transition to a mixed culture.

"Because markets can shift so rapidly and with little warning, organizations can no longer offer permanent jobs and, more importantly, they need more creative people and fewer with settled work orientations."

"The economic insecurity and fierce competition behind the current wave of redundancies are motivating employers to look with greater favour on more flexible employment relationships."

9

LAST RITES FOR THE JOB

The transition to an entrepreneurial culture will not happen without developing new relationships between employees and employers. In previous chapters we noted that such a culture will flourish only to the extent that all employees take much more independent initiative in place of top-down control by managers.

It is not enough to empower people in the sense of simply giving them more authority. Employees need to feel free to think and act more creatively. The key is to remove the fear and tunnel vision caused by excessive dependency. This means helping employees to become more independent in the way they think and feel. How to instil this new mindset in employees is a topic we need to explore in this chapter. Part of the answer lies in helping employees to become more broadly employable or marketable. Developing greater marketability has a confidence building power not unlike diversification for a one product company. Another, associated, much needed transition is to encourage employees to see themselves as essentially running their own businesses.

Future employment relationships in a more entrepreneurial firm could range from the traditional to the radically different. For example, new ventures could be started *for* (not necessarily in) large organizations by a variety of sources:

- individuals who have a status like that of traditional employees
- those whose relationship to the organization is part time
- individuals who are external to the organization and who see it as a potential customer or strategic partner
- last but not least, teams of individuals who may have members from each of these categories plus from customers and suppliers.

The main question we need to address in this chapter is therefore: how will the relationship between employer and employee change as organizations become more entrepreneurial?

NEW EMPLOYMENT RELATIONSHIPS

William Bridges (1995) has forecast the end of the job in his new book, *Job Shift*. The central point Bridges makes is that the concept of the job has outlived its usefulness. He claims that jobs are essentially boxes in a structure that is no longer made up of fixed positions. Bridges does not see actual work disappearing. It is just that it will be done on a more flexible basis. The primary reason for this revolution in the way work will be done in the future is that organizations are increasingly needing greater flexibility. They see the need to match their internal

> **Because markets can shift so rapidly and with little warning, organizations can no longer offer permanent jobs and, more importantly, they need more creative people and fewer with settled work orientations.**

arrangements with the dynamism of their markets. Because markets can shift so rapidly and with little warning, organizations can no longer offer permanent jobs and, more importantly, they need more creative people and fewer with settled work orientations.

Although Bridges makes much of the fact that we have witnessed heavy job losses in recent years, the key issue is surely not job loss as such, but the fact that the *relationship* between those who do the work and those who pay for it is profoundly changing. That is, it is not that job losses are making the concept of the job less useful, it is rather that the business need for greater flexibility is causing *both* the high rate of job losses *and* the declining usefulness of the concept of the job. (Bridges seems to suggest that job loss is one of the many contributing causes to the decline in usefulness of the job concept, but this is clearly the wrong way round.) (See Figure 9.1.)

Competitive pressure has forced businesses to re-engineer their processes and this involves looking at every employee and asking 'Do we need this person (or this role)?' 'What actually do you do for us?' Businesses are essentially becoming much more sharply commercial and this leads them to rationalize everything. Further, the increased demand for better customer service is putting pressure on every single employee to think of all their relationships as revolving around providing a service to customers, whether they are external or internal.

Add these changes to the greater threat of redundancy and employees are compelled naturally to see themselves as self-employed – if only in the sense that they need to continually sell their services to their internal customers and improve them if they hope to retain their current employment status. The important point here is that this change is one of *relationships* and such change can occur irrespective of what industry you are in or how fixed, structured or long-term your job happens to be.

WHAT IS REALLY HAPPENING TO JOBS?

The essential causal force underlying the demise of the job is that increased competitive pressures on businesses now require all of us to justify our existence in terms of some closer profit-related contribution. This has the effect of creating an internal market and making all employees think of themselves as if they were in their own business.

Figure 9.1

Bridges focuses too exclusively on the concept of the job as a way of *structuring* work. While he alludes to the relationship aspect of jobs when he talks about how employees should see themselves as self-employed, his major emphasis is on the job as a structure for doing work. The problem with this focus is that it masks the fact that the revolutionary change will be in the relationship between employees and employers regardless of how structured and fixed the work happens to be in any given firm. As a result of emphasizing the structural aspect of the job, Bridges is forced into the somewhat absurd position of lumping all jobs into one category and claiming that they will all disappear. While this can be readily visualized in certain industries, such as movie making and computer software, where work is more project orientated, it is not so obvious in fixed roles in large, stable firms, such as the role of cost accountant, for example. Even if you continue to employ cost accountants in traditional jobs, you still want them to provide you with a service and to be continuously thinking creatively about how they can provide you with a better service – or the same service more efficiently. As a more commercially astute employer, you will demand the same competitive spirit from your 'permanent' employees as you expect from your external suppliers.

So the fundamental change in the notion of the job is not so much that the job is no longer a fixed box – it may remain so in some industries or functions – but that the relationship is altering for good between employee and employer. It is hard to see working as an airline pilot, a fire fighter, a waiter or as a dentist as being a contract or project worker in quite the same sense as people who make movies where the entire staff assemble from diverse sources purely for the one-off project of making a specific movie. That is, the role of such employees can still be seen as a job because it is fixed and well structured, but their more competitive and commercial position will still make them effectively self-employed.

The advantage of this distinction is that it makes it easier to see all employees as self-employed regardless of how traditional and structured their jobs might continue to be for the foreseeable future.

We need now to look in more detail at just how and why the employment relationship is changing beyond recognition.

Shifting employment trends

One of the most profound examples of changing employment relationships currently sweeping through organizations is contracting out: yesterday you were an employee, today you are an external supplier. In theory at least, you could now provide your services to other 'clients'. Your 'employer' no longer has nearly the same obligations to you – no promise of long-term loyalty to you, to look after your career, to train you or provide you with a pension. Your relationship to your 'client' is as transformed as it would be if you suddenly became a privatized industry.

The rise of knowledge workers and the empowerment theme are closely related to changes in employment relationships. Highly educated and technical workers naturally demand a greater say in their day-to-day work as well as in their careers. This close connection between education and the desire for greater independence coincides nicely with the greater need on the part of entrepreneurs for independence. Greater business complexity and the need for more responsiveness have necessitated handing over decision making to those with the power to make them properly. This is the power of knowledge and it comes from either being closer to the customer or from having specialist expertise. This change in the balance of power must lead employers to regard such employees as partners rather than 'resources'. Organizations are already referring to some of their key suppliers as 'strategic partners'.

As traditional employees become distanced from their employers through contracting out and those who are conventionally conceived as suppliers move closer to organizations, the line between being a member of the organization and being an outsider is blurred considerably if not completely erased. So far, popular thinking on contracting out is that core skills will be retained while only non-essential services will be contracted out. But current practice is surely just the thin end of the wedge. The door is now wide open for empowered and increasingly confident knowledge workers to supply their services on the same basis. Moreover, professionals often identify more strongly with their profession than they do with their employer. Many organizations, such as Dell Computer, contract out nearly everything – certainly all or most of their manufacturing. The existence of specialist research and development organizations also makes it possible to contract out even this allegedly core activity.

> **The economic insecurity and fierce competition behind the current wave of redundancies are motivating employers to look with greater favour on more flexible employment relationships.**

These trends are reinforced by continuing redundancies which inevitably discourage lifelong loyalty to one employer and facilitate, or rather force, the development of self-reliance and independence. The economic insecurity and fierce competition behind the current wave of redundancies are motivating employers to look with greater favour on more flexible employment relationships. Witness the booming growth in executive leasing services (interim management): engaging the services of an executive for a three- to six-month period. Short-term contracts and part-time arrangements will be increasingly easier to obtain across all levels and functions.

But if 'employees', especially highly skilled knowledge workers, become viewed as suppliers or strategic partners they will use their new-found empowerment to *sell* their services to prospective 'clients' (employers). Hiring such employees takes on a whole new meaning, becoming more akin to engaging a consultant or some other external supplier or partner than the conventional approach. Traditional hiring practices have a closer resemblance to marriage than to a contract to supply services. Although the employer drives the selection process today, the future may see these roles substantially reversed.

Employment relationships of old

To see how much employment relationships have already changed it is useful to contrast the scenario sketched above with how things were only a short time ago. When change was not so rampant, organizations were highly structured and stable with tightly defined job roles. They operated as machines needing only unthinking operatives to keep them running like clockwork. As we have seen, the major cultural value of these times was efficiency. Because rising costs were the main threat to profitability, efficiency was the best means of keeping them under control. This put a premium on cheap labour and the ability to mini-mize recruitment and employment costs. This in turn meant extremely unempowered workers, who, having no power, were naturally some-what desperate to get hired, hence needing to convince by any means the powers that be to take them on.

In addition, management attitudes were quite 'theory X', that is they regarded employees as lazy and unwilling to work unless they were closely supervised and controlled. As it was felt to be virtually impos-sible to change people or to motivate them once on the job, the burden fell on selection as the main point of leverage.

Part of the theory X attitude was the view that people were not to be trusted. This was a self-fulfilling prophecy to a great extent. Employ-ees knew they were not trusted so they responded by being less open on the job and more wary, thus proving their lack of trustworthiness. The effect on selection was similar. Because the employer did not trust job candidates, they in turn were less open thereby confirming the interviewer's presumption that they must be screened carefully. Selec-tion unavoidably became excessively adversarial.

In addition, because of the vast differences in power between the employer and the employee, the latter had far too much at stake in the recruitment process, no alternative means of proving himself and noth-ing to lose – hence a little necessary deception in order to get hired.

Getting a job was too all or nothing; there was too much emphasis on organizational *entry*. The power gap is now much reduced and knowledge workers are not quite so desperate.

Employment relationships were essentially and thoroughly paternalistic. Once in the door, the employee naturally saw it as the employer's responsibility to provide every form of direction and support – because it was difficult to get in and once in you expected to remain there for life. In addition, the significant power differential meant that you naturally saw your employer as a sort of super parent. This actually put too much of a burden on the employer's shoulders. So rather than have to fire, tolerate or hold the hands of less desirable employees, selection became the means of making life as easy and efficient as possible for organizations. The adversarial nature of the hiring process contributed to an employment relationship that was inescapably paternalistic – where employees could not avoid expecting to be told what to do rather than to think for themselves.

Entrepreneurial employment relationships

Knowledge workers will be the key employees of the future simply because business is becoming more knowledge intensive. As knowledge grows at an astronomic rate, we are forced to become more and more specialized and to rely on technical specialists for advice. Not so long ago it was still easy to be a 'general' manager by virtue of knowing a bit about every part of the business. Increasingly, only teams of specialists will have, among them, this level of general knowledge.

In a recent *Fortune* article entitled 'The new worker elite', Louis S Richman (1994) has underlined the shift in power to technical workers. Some startling US statistics are worth quoting: 'Since 1950 the number of technical workers has increased nearly 300 per cent – triple the growth rate for the work force as a whole.' This trend can only increase – it has to in order to keep pace with ever expanding technical knowledge. As knowledge expands, any given technical worker can only know an ever smaller portion of it.This increases the individual's power as well as making teamwork or some other means of pooling expertise all that much more essential.

Moreover, as we saw in discussing changes in the concept of leadership, it will be the technical expertise of knowledge workers that will figure most prominently in identifying the way forward in the entrepreneurial business. It will be up to them to show *content* leadership to their employers/clients. This entails less emphasis on the personnel specialist taking such a lead role in defining jobs in advance of recruitment. Knowledge workers who are not currently engaged by an employer that appeals to them, will take the initiative to sell their services to an organization by demonstrating how they might enhance the employer's business, much in the way consultants function at present. The resulting employment relationship could be anything from the conventional to a strategic partnership or joint venture.

So there will be a continuum of relationships from contracted-out suppliers and consultants at one extreme through those who are hired on something like the conventional basis. But the employment relationship will never be the same again even in the latter case. Those knowledge workers (and unskilled labourers) who are hired on a full-time basis by an employer will inevitably have a different relationship. They may become 'insiders', but they will identify more with their own career aspirations or their profession than with the company. 'So what happens to employee commitment and motivation?' you ask. This is a very important question. Fortunately, the answer does not seem so difficult.

The end of commitment and loyalty?

As an employer, you no longer want employees who virtually do nothing but put in their time. Sure, clock watchers may do a good job, exactly as they are told, but nothing more, no going beyond the confines of their role, no suggestions for improvement. While consistency will always be valued in delivery roles, you want highly independent, creative and challenging people focusing on new product development and taking entrepreneurial risks. You want people, in short, who are *as committed as they would be if they were in their own business*. And this is surely the solution to the problem! You may reply that you want people who are committed to *your* business success not to their own.

But is this not what you are already practising yourself in your business with respect to your own customers? Are you not also increasingly seeing your objective as helping your customers to be successful rather than just doing what suits you and offering products or services *you* happen to think are a good idea? Are you not more *committed* than ever to doing what is best for your customers? The really amazing fact here is that employers see a loss of commitment and motivation where there is every reason to see not a loss but a significant increase. How could employees be *less* committed and motivated than those who are treated as cogs in a machine and who are taken for granted as company 'resources'?

If this is as obvious as it seems to be, then the most interesting question is why do employers fear a loss of commitment in such radically empowered employees? It may be because they have a subconscious idea of what it means to be committed which goes beyond being treated to excellent customer service. And surely this is an artefact of the paternalistic mindset that infects the traditional employment relationship to the core. The best way to see this is to think of a firm that is literally paternal – one in which a father and his sons are running a family business. How does a father feel if one of his sons leaves the family business? Is he pacified by his son's promise to be an external supplier to his father's business and to provide him with service that is second to none compared to his other suppliers? No, unfortunately not, because father has a much deeper and more personal kind of commitment and loyalty in mind.

The same paternal anger and disappointment is observable in any organization when any employee quits. The reaction is stronger the closer the personal relationship between manager and employee but there is no question the anger can be quite intense. Actually this sense of betrayal is common to the severing of all close relationships, not just the paternal one. If you spring the idea of divorce on your spouse unexpectedly you will witness the same intensity of feeling. The employee who is unexpectedly made redundant feels the same sense of betrayal, anger and hurt that the employer feels when the employee suddenly resigns, so it works both ways. The double bind that employers are in is that they want their cake and to be able to eat it too. They want strong, empowered, psychologically independent employees who are also unswervingly loyal and committed to them exclusively. This is neither fair nor possible. It is as much a near contradiction in terms as the notion of a cost-effective state bureaucracy.

What is needed longer term is not the painful severance of existing relationships but the formation of quite different ones in the first place.

Forging new psychological contracts

The hard part is the *severing* of existing relationships. So far it is the employee who has suffered all the pain of rejection. This is not to say that it is now the employer's turn, but to suggest that it is time to begin searching for a more viable type of relationship. It is, after all, the violation of expectations that causes pain – it is not something inherent in relationships themselves. So the solution is to set up employment relationships on the basis of entirely new expectations.

> **What is needed longer term is not the painful severance of existing relationships but the formation of quite different ones in the first place.**

The notion of psychological contract deals precisely with generally unstated expectations. It is called 'psychological' because it pertains to how you expect to be treated on a personal level by someone else – generally the expectations employees have of their employer. The old-fashioned psychological contract was unhealthy because it reinforced excessive dependency. This was because it included too many expectations with regard to how the company was going to *take care* of the employee – to develop you, to promote you, to look after your welfare both on the job and after retirement, etc.

The customer–supplier relationship

A more effective model for future employment relationships is surely that between customer and supplier, ideally those that exist between businesses whose suppliers also supply their services to more than one customer. In reality, many employees will not have the option of working for two or more employers simultaneously, but we need to explore how even they can achieve a comparable relationship with their employer and a similar level of confidence which can only result from feeling that they have a *choice* of who you work for. Free markets are only free in relation to the amount of available choice for all parties.

Suppliers who supply their services or products to one customer exclusively are not in a stronger position than that of traditional employees. For example, large retailers who have the power to demand that their suppliers exclusively supply their products to them can too easily squeeze their suppliers to death. This short termism can often stifle the entrepreneurial vitality and innovation on the part of the supplier which is necessary for the long-term health of both

> **Initially the transition to new relationships will unavoidably mean some pain for employers used to a more possessive hold on employees.**

parties. Such a one-sided relationship is like a virus devouring a person's entire body thereby killing its host and dying off itself.

The pop psychology ideas of 'I'm OK, you're OK' and 'win-win' negotiation have as their core the important idea that the most healthy relationships are those between equals. So the goal in forming new employment relationships is to strive to see both sides as equals as much as possible.

This must be the goal despite the fact that it will be easier with scarce, highly skilled technical workers than it will with low skilled employees who are selling low-demand, high-supply services.

Assuming that we are talking about customer–supplier relationships between relative equals, what expectations do you have of your suppliers – other than the obvious contractual ones? You would primarily expect a degree of loyalty and trust beyond what you have in writing. This could include the expectation that the supplier would not disclose to competitors sensitive information which was casually passed on over lunch. Employees of each firm may expect some continuity of personal contact. But the essential core of the relationship is more arm's length than family or other personal relationships. You want to cultivate a balance between closeness and independence in order to reap the benefits of both types of relationship. What you want essentially from your supplier is provided by the motivating power of market competition and that is the dedication to doing everything possible and more to keep doing business with you. (See Psychological slant.)

Trading employees in for suppliers

Initially the transition to new relationships will unavoidably mean some pain for employers used to a more possessive hold on employees. But this can be viewed as a healthy growing pain – much like the one parents experience when their grown up children leave home for good. Such a change in your relationship to your children has nothing to do with disloyalty – although it may feel like desertion.

PSYCHOLOGICAL SLANT

Trust

How can you trust employees who do not fully depend on you? Can they not too easily desert you if they are not fully under your control? But this is like asking how we can keep our citizens from leaving our country without building a Berlin Wall around them. The concern over a lack of trust is clearly based on fear and insecurity. The national analogy is a useful one because it is so obvious that there is no need for a Berlin Wall in countries which are prosperous and where people are free to come and go as they please. But when the employer says 'I want you to work for me exclusively', he is putting a Berlin Wall around the employee which is the surest way to motivate disloyalty and a desire to depart. There is no substitute for trust based on complete freedom of choice. Employers who shout the loudest in favour of loyalty and commitment often do so precisely because they do not trust their employees. They fear that no one would want to work for them unless they were somehow bound to them. True commitment can only be freely given and is best obtained from suppliers keen to keep your business rather than conventional employees.

Personal loss always takes a major effort of adjustment, however. The best way to cope with such loss with regard to changing the status of employees is to focus on what is gained. And there are substantial benefits – the same gains we get when we expose protected state monopolies to market forces. Just as many state enterprises have a tough time adjusting, there is no doubt that many employees will find such a transition very difficult. A key responsibility of employers is to help employees manage this transition in their lives – especially older workers who have no experience of changing jobs over 20 or 30 years.

At present many employees are psychologically in transition already. They are demotivated by the loss of job security even though they personally may never be made redundant. Many of them are suffering a loss of commitment because they have not yet found a new source of identity, security and confidence. There is no going back to jobs-for-life security. And the only way ahead is to help employees begin to see themselves as being in their own businesses.

So just what are the advantages for you the 'employer' of shifting employees to supplier status?

- Greater self-reliance and initiative to sell their services to you on an ongoing basis rather than take their jobs for granted.
- Your needs will be treated as customer needs. The alternative is to treat you as impersonally as a state bureaucracy treats its 'clients'.
- Motivation to 're-engineer' their own services to ensure that you are getting maximum value for money.
- Similarly, more motivation to develop themselves, not for the old-fashioned, self-serving goal of getting promoted but in order to keep up with your changing needs.
- Flexibility to use a greater range of suppliers – taking full advantage of market forces. This may seem cold to existing employees but it is the only way to help them keep themselves sharp and up to date. The exclusive job-for-life relationship creates dependency that is as debilitating as putting animals in a zoo.
- Most importantly, increased creativity – self-employed suppliers have the greatest degree of motivation to create new work for themselves by anticipating your needs and preparing to meet them. This means exposure to as many different sources of new ideas as possible.

This last point deserves elaboration.

The incompatibility of creativity and permanent employment

Sustained creativity is more likely in an organization that continually looks for new perspectives. The longer anyone stays in the same environment working on the same problems the more likely that a narrowing of perspective will develop. Individuals are more likely to sustain their own creativity by moving around to quite different employment contexts with new colleagues and new challenges. Such vital stimulation can be achieved in a number of ways: changing jobs inside or outside the firm – sequential variation, serving different customers simultaneously – concurrent variation, or by getting involved in as many different cross functional projects for the same customer as possible.

A high level of variation in the stimulation that creative knowledge workers obtain can also be achieved by encouraging constant networking with customers and external specialists as well as through secondments. This tack can prolong creativity only so long as knowledge workers are exposed to widely differing perspectives from their own – otherwise the risk of staleness will be high. The point is that they need to seek regular variation in their sources of stimulation if they are to continue to produce variation in their own ideas.

The other negative aspect of long-term employment and relatively fixed jobs with one employer is that too much comfort and dependency will set in over an extended time period and this settling in process is not conducive to the degree of independence necessary for the development of new perspectives.

> **The more secure we become in the comfort of one employing firm, the less secure we become with the idea of making a significant move elsewhere.**

The more secure we become in the comfort of one employing firm, the less secure we become with the idea of making a significant move elsewhere. This security goes hand in hand with excessive dependency and the inevitable result is greater conformity lest you jeopardize your position. The more subtle form of conformity we discussed earlier also sets in – the inclination to see everything the way the organization sees it. This may be unintended brainwashing but the group-think outcome is every bit as powerful as it would be if such conformity were purposely induced.

So, a firm that wants to be more entrepreneurial needs to do just the opposite of what it is most inclined to do with regard to its most creative entrepreneurial stars. Sure, you want their dedicated output in the short term, but the longer you keep them focused on one narrow task, the greater the risk of a decline in creativity. What is needed is regular importing of new people and exporting of your best people – to partner firms, customers, new divisions or outside altogether for a secondment, assuming that you would want to bring them back later.

The need for creativity is paramount for the entrepreneurial task, less so for the delivery aspects of your business.

Employment for the delivery task

The delivery of ongoing products and services requires greater consistency and continuity than does the entrepreneurial self-renewal task. Moreover, there will always be organizational functions that are essentially delivery orientated – this includes production as well as more stable functions such as sales and finance. This functional focus does not preclude employees within these functions from taking entrepreneurial action either on their own or as cross functional team members.

> **The need for creativity is paramount for the entrepreneurial task, less so for the delivery aspects of your business.**

While employees within these functions will make incremental improvements to their work practices, processes or products, they will not necessarily be expected to launch whole new ventures based on completely new product ideas. Whether your accounting function is in-house or contracted out, most accountants could retain a form of permanent employment with some firm. Even working with one firm for an entire career in such a delivery capacity does not alter the fact that relationships with employers are now irrevocably changed.

HIRING EMPLOYEES AS SUPPLIERS

We do not choose suppliers or strategic partners by administering tests to them. That would be far too controlling, paternalistic and theory X, not to mention absurd and insulting. We ask them instead to reply to a tender, submit a proposal and make a presentation. The task of engaging suppliers is made easier by their having a very public reputation and the availability of legal recourse in case of poor performance.

This is straightforward for reputable suppliers, what about unknown quantities? The rise of contracting out will lead to a proliferation of suppliers and the bid process will have to be strengthened accordingly. But the increasing use of sophisticated customer satisfaction surveys will help relatively unknown suppliers to document a track record. In the end, it comes down to the supplier's ability to make a convincing case that he has something unique to offer.

In choosing a supplier, we do not normally endeavour to assess individual competencies or personalities. Our main concern is with the commercial value of their proposal, track record, various contract terms, cost and whether we think we can work with them. The anticipated working relationship is not so crucial because it will be more distant and transient than that of a conventional employee, hence there should be less anxiety about how well the supplier (individual) would fit in. Consultants, like other kinds of suppliers, are taken on now with no tests of their personality or competence. Other than track record, what counts is having good ideas, the ability to sell them and a reasonable degree of chemistry with the client.

How will this apply to the individual employee who perhaps wants a conventional job? An approach to assessment and selection that approximates the process of engaging a supplier would be to invite the prospective employee into the organization to diagnose possible needs by interviewing key people in his or her area of specialization. The 'candidate' could then go away and develop a proposal on how he or she could add value to the organization. Because of the ambiguity inherent in the self-renewal task, this 'hiring' process would not often involve the prior advertisement of a job – because the organization would often be unaware of what value it needed adding. Empowered knowledge workers would approach the organization on speculation just as consultants and some job seekers do now.

> **Other than track record, what counts is having good ideas, the ability to sell them and a reasonable degree of chemistry with the client.**

To further reduce any concern of being stuck with a lemon, 'employees' can readily be taken on for a short-term period, perhaps to do a specific project or a feasibility study on some aspect of what they are proposing – and on terms similar to those used for any supplier (not unlike interim management). This approach reduces the need for obtaining airtight proof in advance of a candidate's abilities.

The emphasis on selection criteria will switch from specific role competencies and personality to commercial factors and technical expertise for at least three reasons:

● the more distant nature of the envisaged employment relationship

- the unavoidable ambiguity inherent in leading-edge jobs
- the increasing need for diversity instead of uniformity, which will lead us away from selecting people in terms of fixed organizational competency profiles.

More general competencies will always be vital, such as adaptability, creativity and the ability to learn quickly, as well as interpersonal skills, but employees considered as suppliers are nonetheless likely to be hired on the basis of their track record to a greater extent than on their personal (non-technical) strengths – again just as consultants are engaged at present.

The role of assessment and selection professionals

Current trends suggest at least three distinct categories of employment relationship emerging: one will be conventional, another will include those who would be better classed as suppliers. The third group will be slightly more transient, involving an associate/contract arrangement on a short- or long-term basis.

For employees classed as suppliers, the role of assessment and selection professionals will not be to profile jobs and administer tests but to help in designing and facilitating the bid process, including thorough checking of prior customer satisfaction in the case of unknown candidates. They could also help to empower employees so they are better able to understand and market themselves. Such an initiative should have the same advantages as industrial privatisation has over excessive dependency. The most promising approach to assessment for this

> **The employee should own the results as their prime use would be to identify development needs, with appointment based fundamentally on demonstrable results and track record.**

purpose would be structured self-assessment which could include self- and peer-assessed career development workshops based on Assessment Centre techniques. Also of great value would be questionnaires designed to gather feedback from internal and external customers. The employee should own the results as their prime use would be to identify development needs, with appointment based fundamentally on demonstrable results and track record.

The formal recruitment and assessment process so common today would still be useful for stable, well-defined jobs, but leading-edge 'jobs' will be increasingly filled (created) informally as knowledge workers become sufficiently empowered to take full control of their careers. But much formal recruitment as it is currently practised could well be replaced, even for many stable, structured positions by the use of short initial contracts and employee services at all organizational levels.

Impact on recruitment consultants

Possible changes in recruitment consulting practices may include:

- more employee leasing across a broader range of functions and levels
- serving as a broker to bring employers and potential suppliers together
- providing advice on the employment relationship/contract that is most likely to benefit the client.

There should be no less need for recruitment services, but the recruitment process and resulting supplier–client relationship will be markedly different.

As employment relationships and organizational needs become more flexible and varied, and organizations need increasingly to look to knowledge workers for leadership, it will be hard to resist the temptation to short-circuit conventional forms of assessment in favour of simply trying people out on the job on short projects. This conclusion will, of course, apply much less to highly structured and stable jobs – if there are any left.

'HUMAN RESOURCES' STRATEGY FOR ENTREPRENEURS

The entrepreneurial firm is committed to creating a future for itself by continually surprising its customers with new products. The only way to be this prophetic is to cultivate a high level of diversity of new initiatives. The best means of ensuring a suitable level of diversity is to create a free market for new ideas, one that has no organizational or functional boundaries or monopolies. This means external sources competing with internal sources, traditional R&D types competing with accounting staff or secretaries – whoever has the entrepreneurial spirit and the burning ideas.

Another more basic implication of this fundamental attitude shift is to start thinking of 'employees' as suppliers of services and to drop terms such as 'employees' and 'human resources'.

What do the following statements all have in common?

- 'We treat our people with the utmost respect.'
- 'Our employees receive training that is world class.'
- 'The career opportunities we provide our people are second to none.'

No, it's not that all of these statements reflect a dedication to world-class human resource management. What they all have in common is the use of the insidious word 'our'. In future, the sense of ownership of people implied by the term 'human *resources*' must disappear. You may counter this point by arguing that you also say *'our* customers' and *'our* suppliers'. But you don't feel the same sense of ownership of your customers and suppliers. You also say *'our* competition' and while you may wish to acquire them, you certainly do not (yet) own them. This implicit owning of employees is symptomatic of the stultifying dependency that keeps would-be entrepreneurial firms chained to a bureaucratic past.

However, you still need to think strategically about how you are going to deal with the people whom you *used to call* employees if you are to get maximum value for money out of them. There is no relenting on this goal.

The appropriate 'human resource' strategy in this context consists in taking action on a number of fronts. The practical steps at the end of the chapter pertain primarily to changing the relationship you have with your employees.

An important part of such a strategy involves action on careers, training and rewards. This subject goes beyond the nature of the employment relationship and will be explored in the next chapter. These issues need to be resolved if organizations are to help employees make the transition from their current feeling of cynicism, dread and helplessness as they await the next round of redundancies or bail out before it is their turn.

Where are we now?

We have moved from discussing the cultural environment you need to consider if you are serious about unleashing your budding entrepreneurs to an exploration of how the status of the new knowledge workers is changing. While you may rue the ensuing loss of control, the payback in creativity will be more than ample compensation for your loss. Managing these new relationships will call for entrepreneurial human resource practices because there will be a greater range of unique arrangements and less of uniform policies and common, organization-wide practices. One important area of great traditional interest to both human resource specialists and employees is the notion of career and it is to that topic we now turn. How we think of careers will have to change as fundamentally as how we think of employees.

PRACTICAL STEPS

- create a stimulating culture as we discussed earlier

- empower employees to a deeper level so their relationship to you is as free and independent as that of your most confident suppliers

- take entrepreneurial risks by investing in employees who appear to show the most entrepreneurial promise

- encourage ideas from all other employees, external suppliers, customers, consultants and the world at large

- foster a free market for ideas and an associated competitive spirit

- allow your most enterprising employees to serve other customers so as to diversify and develop new ideas

- develop new forms of trust and loyalty based on mutual respect among equals.

"One of the most incredibly destructive features of hierarchy is, therefore, that it monopolizes the concept of career success by restricting it to climbing the managerial ladder."

"Specifically, a successful career can be one that is simply enjoyed for its own sake in an organization that does not define career success so narrowly as managerial advancement."

10

CAREERS – LEAVING BEHIND THE DARK AGES

If there will be no more *jobs* in the future do we need to think about careers at all any more? If everyone becomes, in some sense, a self-employed supplier of services, then what does it mean to have a career?

WHY BOTHER?

We have suggested that organizations have two fundamental but distinct tasks: delivery of today's offerings and self-renewal to create the future. The emerging trend towards new employment relationships, based on everyone becoming a supplier of services, will affect equally these two central organizational tasks. However much the lathe operator, the personnel clerk or the cost accountant may have relatively stable, fairly traditional jobs, they will nonetheless have a

> **Organizations should soon be embarrassed to find themselves still using the term 'human resources'.**

new status as suppliers of services rather than as employees. Still, today, in most organizations employees are seen as company *resources*, where this word is used in the same sense as it is to refer to machinery, buildings and finances. Tomorrow, all 'human resources' will all be seen as suppliers of services. Organizations should soon be embarrassed to find themselves still using the term 'human resources'.

The other extreme is not an option either – to say you need not take *any* interest in how your suppliers manage their careers: 'If they are no longer our employees, then surely it is up to them to manage their own careers.' But this is to operate with the old dichotomies in mind: either they are in the organization or they are outsiders, either they are with us or they are against us.

Ford Motor Co. and many other firms do take a very active interest in how their suppliers manage themselves and keep up to date. They often provide extensive training for their suppliers on quality standards, for example. You can just as easily take, as a strategic course of action, the decision to invest in key employees-as-suppliers as you now do with conventionally conceived external suppliers. So the organization still has an interest in some form of career management, but what about the employee perspective? Does it make sense to say that a supplier of services – a business in effect – can have a career? Or like other institutions, do they merely have a *history*?

What difference does this make to the organization that might be inclined to take the easy way out? It can surely say: 'We can now simply regard all of you as suppliers of services and now that you have empowered yourselves to look after your own careers, get on with it. We don't need our customers looking out for our careers so why should you need your customers (us) helping you to manage your careers?'

The short answer to this question is that the increasing balance of power that we see developing between organizations and ever more empowered knowledge workers entails more power for the 'employee' and less for the company. This is because power is shifting to knowledge creating ability and hence those who have it.

This shift in turn means *less dependency* for service-providing 'employees' but *more* dependency for organizations or those suppliers of services who hold the key to the self-renewing future of their employers-turned-customers. The organization is more dependent by definition because this is what is meant by a levelling out in the balance of power. But, more specifically, the organization is more dependent because business is becoming more knowledge driven and this gives knowledge workers more power. This is not a loss to rue because it will have all of the benefits of the break up of any monopoly hold on power in favour of free-market mechanisms. But as your key knowledge workers are increasingly mobile and free to offer their services elsewhere (and more motivated to do so for the sake of their own personal self-renewal), you will simply have to work that much harder to keep them interested.

So why should organizations be interested in career management? Because in the old days they could see career management as a sort of paternalistic benefit which they doled out primarily to keep people pacified. Now an interest in careers is essential for long-term survival – as a form of competing with other firms to hold the interest of the best talent.

A particularly important and immediate reason for taking an interest in careers is to help cynical and confused, but highly valued, employees develop new sources of identity, confidence and security. Too many of them at the moment do not know whether they have a future in your firm or whether they are next on the redundancy list and this state of mind is hardly conducive to creative thinking.

In what follows, we will see that careers will still be more or less of the traditional variety for employees who spend their lives specializing in delivery-related functions. Careers will take a different tack, however, for the more entrepreneurial types who are so essential for organizational renewal. Career management will therefore mean different things for these two separate career streams. First of all, we cannot say anything about how the notion of career might change without getting a bit clearer about what we mean by 'career' in the first place.

WHO HAS A CAREER?

The most significant shift in our thinking about careers is well under way and this is the declining relevance of conceiving careers in terms of a person's work life within large organizations. Writers on careers in the seventies and eighties confined their interest to large firms – as if it made no sense to have a career outside of them.

So what is a career, anyway?

If entrepreneurial knowledge workers are going to be suppliers of services who can move around regularly or never be quite inside any organization in the traditional sense, we need to develop a conception of career that encompasses their more transient and ambiguous work lives.

The place to begin is surely to examine the concept of career that is implicit in large organizations. In this regard it is interesting to note that most career theorists of the 1970s and 80s were one-sidedly concerned with careers in big businesses. They virtually defined career as a form of long-term relationship within an organization – typically within one firm.

But this blinkered view of careers excludes having a career as an artist. Those who try to define career in organizational terms suggest that all lone operators such as artists belong to *some* organization, association or society at least in the sense that some organized society must exist to define what is acceptable and what will be valued. But this is not the same as having a career *in* an organization. An artist is not *employed* by an organization.

Those who want to define careers in organizational terms also argue that *most* people work in organizations, hence for all practical purposes we can ignore fringe cases. But this overlooks the contemporary and growing trend towards contracting out of services whether to other organizations or lone operators. It is therefore increasingly necessary to be able to think sensibly about careers outside of organizations. Early career theorists seemed to need to distort the meaning of career in order to justify their exclusive preoccupation with career progression as hierarchical advancement.

Careers in the good old days

The most (perhaps only) significant feature of how careers used to look in big organizations was indeed just this intimate relationship with progression up the managerial hierarchy. You *advanced* your career by getting promoted. The implication here is that your career stagnated in some retarded state if you did not advance up the promotion ladder. The intense preoccupation in most organizations with managerial advancement is abundant testimony to this obsession. But why is it that sole entrepreneurs are more interested in new products and new business while their large organizational cousins are clamouring for advancement? This dichotomy suggests quite disparate notions of what it means to achieve career success.

Successful careers do not always mean more power

Those in power tend to define what is important and what key concepts mean. Senior executives in organizations strongly need to view careers in terms of striving to reach the top. Otherwise what have *they* striven for? 'What, not interested in promotion?' Such *rebellion* is as shocking in large organizations as it is to the army general whose son wants to be a ballet dancer rather than enter the army. Or the entrepreneur who built up a big business only to see his son become a rock musician. Senior executives *need* to see their juniors following in their foot-steps both to take over from them eventually and to admire their achievements. Who would be their admiring audience if they had no one clamouring to imitate

> **One of the most incredibly destructive features of hierarchy is, therefore, that it monopolizes the concept of career success by restricting it to climbing the managerial ladder.**

them? Admiring someone often includes or implies wanting to be like them. If no one wanted to succeed the top manager, no one could be properly said to fully admire or value the role (or its current occupant). Anyone who is not seen to exemplify the up-or-out policy risks being seen as a dissident and potential detractor. Someone who does not aspire to follow in the boss's footsteps could be seen as implicitly devaluing his or her achievements.

We all instinctively admire heroes and dream about emulating them. No doubt the best people, generally, do in fact succeed to top positions in most companies and they are only too naturally admired. But this channelling of the best talent into a competitive scramble for the top must be seen as a colossal waste of human creativity and energy given the far greater importance of entrepreneurial knowledge workers to the future success of organizations. (See Figure 10.1.)

One of the most incredibly destructive features of hierarchy is, there-fore, that it monopolizes the concept of career success by restricting it to climbing the managerial ladder. Just as 3M is notable for its reliance on technical knowledge workers for new product innovation, it is not surprising that they have dual career systems so that employees have a choice of whether they want to advance via the managerial route or to continue their development in their preferred technical direction.

Many individuals naturally desire power over others, however. There are very primitive benefits – speaking in evolutionary terms – of being head of the pack. But the value of being in power is surely much inflated by the cultural pressure of hierarchy and this gives it a disproportionate power to motivate every employee to define career success in terms of advancement. Hierarchy is a powerfully self-serving and self-sustaining system, as we have seen.

The case for a dual career system is easily made as well. It is widely recognized, if little admitted, that many employees would actually prefer to stay closer to the application of their technical expertise but they need the money associated with managerial advancement so they give up what they do best and most enjoy doing, simply because there is no other way to earn more money and more status. Many such reluctant managers end up becoming ineffective as well as unhappy managers in the process. Sounds a bit like the world's oldest profession.

TIME FOR NEW HEROES

The upshot of the foregoing is that we need to start admiring new heroes, as they now do in entrepreneurial firms. We don't hear stories about the heroics of senior executives at 3M – instead the heroes are the lowly types who invent successful new products such as their Post-it notes. Such people have to be seen as failures in conventional career terms if they never rise above churning out new products in spite of their importance in continually renewing the company's fortunes.

Figure 10.1

New careers based on knowledge as power

If non-managerial knowledge workers are critical for organizational renewal then the non-managerial career stream must become more respectable and more associated with financial success. To have a full, lifetime career as a professional – much as doctors, lawyers and other professionals do now is becoming increasingly desirable anyway. Young technical workers are finding themselves feeling more and more reluctant to give up the closeness they have and enjoy with the leading edge of their field for the sake of a managerial career which is seen to be of increasingly dubious value. This means undoing much of the conventional wisdom of the past 30 years on the essence of careers and career management.

Writers on the subject of careers have overly limited the concept of career to life in large organizations precisely because they have also been blinded by the idea that career success is equivalent to managerial advancement. People working outside of big companies cannot after all be promoted in quite the same sense. How many books on career management have you read that are not primarily about management development?

So just what is a career then if not a succession of bigger managerial jobs? What does it mean for a professional to have a successful career? Surely there will still be some residual managerial careers in big companies, however irrevocably and unrecognizably altered.

The emerging proliferation of the professional career

If you are a doctor or a lawyer, your career success consists in a growing reputation as someone who can handle ever more difficult cases. Those who are most clever in their profession often develop breakthroughs of one sort or another which leads to prospective clients hearing of them and thinking of them as minor miracle workers. Supply and demand principles go into action and they can command ever higher fees. They then acquire status in their profession which is based partly on what they have achieved thus far and on the level of earnings they are able to command. To take an example closer to business life, top-name consultants can command exorbitantly higher fees, for the same reasons, in comparison with junior consultants in a big six firm who are totally unknown outside of their personal friends.

A pecking order is hence still involved in the professional career world. But there is no hierarchy or pyramid. There can never be only one kingpin at the top of a pile. There is room for as many at the top as can establish a sterling reputation for themselves. Further, any top professional can suddenly be displaced by a young upstart who shows that a new procedure makes the big-name professional's bag of tricks obsolete. The beauty of the professional career market, such as in management consulting for instance, is precisely that it is in fact an open *market*. What distinguishes the managerial career, in contrast, is that it is much more monopolistic – at least within any one organization. Once the key slots at the top of the pyramid are filled, it's just a matter of holding on to your seat. There is no room for a larger number of slots – especially in today's flattened – or better still, crushed – pyramids. Of course, you can compete to displace a slot holder, but it is much harder to push a monopoly power holder aside than it is to move to the top in a free and open market.

If you are an independent professional you can say what you like about a competitor's approach or methodology as a self-promotional ploy, but try saying something similar about your betters in a large organization and you will discover that jokes about 'career limiting' moves are not jokes at all.

Competition among independent professionals for career advancement is identical to competition between businesses selling the same product and therefore much more in the entrepreneurial spirit. As an entrepreneur you have to produce and keep producing if you are to continue to compete successfully. There is very little room for resting on laurels. In large organizations, by contrast, it is notorious that shrewd political skills are often more valuable for success than providing services that are in such demand that internal customers will fall over themselves to buy them. No wonder so many observant junior employees view this form of career advancement with a mixture of yearning and resigned cynicism.

> **Specifically, a successful career can be one that is simply enjoyed for its own sake in an organization that does not define career success so narrowly as managerial advancement.**

Your career as a supplier of services

The fact that the term 'professional' is, for the most part, restricted to those with certain educational qualifications is irrelevant. Any person who identifies with the supply of whatever services can have a career with success defined in similar terms: advancement in status and financial reward. Even better, an organization that places a higher value on career patterns other than climbing the ladder opens the door to other ways of having a successful career. Specifically, a successful career can be one that is simply enjoyed for its own sake in an organization that does not define career success so narrowly as managerial advancement.

If a career is the history of one's experience in the supply of some service, then it is immediately apparent that such a career can occur inside or outside of organizations, big or small, and you can transport it anywhere. Often we see ourselves as having failed if we move to a new employer because we were blocked from advancement with our old employer. As a supplier of services you can see yourself as moving or as supplying your services wherever the demand is such that you will gain the most compensation, the most personal development or the most of whatever rewards attract you. This is just your own business development – it is not akin to having failed in one market, hence having to try another.

CAREERS IN *EFFICIENT* ENTREPRENEURIAL FIRMS

Referring to careers 'in' organizations has to be taken as transitional talk until better terminology is developed. Regardless of how much of an insider you may be in any organization at a specific point in time, your relationship to your employer can no longer be the same. As we saw in the last chapter, you are now effectively self-employed. This is because you have to continually prove your worth in a more hardnosed commercial sense than ever before. No company has space for free riders in today's hyper competitive arena. You have to establish and maintain some form of commercial added value for your internal customers or your services will no longer be required. What is the difference between your status and that of the self-employed person who supplies your product packaging or your company stationery? Virtually none – only no one seems yet to have noticed. All that is left is a remnant of the psychological binding that used to ensure you of a job for life – a sort of familiarity that will allow you a temporary breathing space before contempt sets in and until the next round of re-engineering asks questions about your usefulness.

The immediate implication of this transition is that you need to take more initiative to manage your own career. Career management will be explored in some detail later, but at the moment it is essential to look at what different types of career streams there will be in efficient entrepreneurial businesses.

Entrepreneurial careers

Your most entrepreneurial employees will be so called because they have an insight into how you could capitalize on some new market opportunity or develop a novel product. They will be knowledge workers at least in this sense – they will use their intelligence and understanding of your market to help you create new offerings. Some of your most creative employees will make invaluable contributions to your bottom line by identifying ways to cut costs – but that is not entrepreneurial behaviour and hence not the subject we are discussing here.

Entrepreneurial knowledge workers, then, are any employees who can use their intelligence to contribute to developing new products for your business. They will often have specialized technical knowledge as well, but such knowledge by itself is useless if it is not combined with insight into what might sell in your market. So the distinguishing feature of entrepreneurial knowledge workers is their ability to take your existing offerings into the future – either individually or in teams.

> **Like many doctors and lawyers, technical specialists often make bad managers and they often look down on the managerial role as if it were nothing more than an overblown clerical job.**

Such knowledge workers, much in demand, will be in the vanguard of new career streams and, strategically, it is primarily their career development you need to invest in for the benefit of your future business prosperity.

A successful career for a entrepreneurial knowledge worker could involve promotion to a management position at some point but, increasingly, it will not. Like many doctors and lawyers, technical specialists often make bad managers and they often look down on the managerial role as if it were nothing more than an overblown clerical job. In fact, managers often have a lower status in professional firms such as large doctors' offices, clinics, hospitals or in firms of lawyers. In a large clinic, for example, the term 'manager' is often not used – instead these functionaries are labelled administrators. Clearly, these days, managers in medical establishments are gaining a higher status due to the need to run such institutions more profitably. But just as managers are gaining clout in these professional environments, it is professionals or technical workers whose profile is on the rise at the expense of managers in knowledge intensive businesses.

The growing importance of technical knowledge in business will inevitably lead to more friction with managers. As innovation gains an increasingly prominent profile, it will be easier to be a hero simply as a product innovator. Knowledge workers who love their technical profession will find it easier to gain status and remuneration by acquiring a reputation of creating best-selling new products. They could then have a more satisfying career by working on increasingly complex projects and continually upgrading their expertise and knowledge. This is how scientists and other professionals find career satisfaction.

As being an innovative knowledge worker becomes increasingly valued by organizations, relative to being a manager, it will be easier to avoid feeling a failure for not becoming a manager.

At the same time, the managerial role in knowledge intensive businesses will decline in importance as knowledge workers become more self-managing and as the manager's contribution moves from one of providing direction to one of providing no more than co-ordination and administration. Many knowledge-based businesses could end up looking like health centres with yesterday's managers enduring the lower grade status of current health centre administrators.

As being an innovative knowledge worker becomes increasingly valued by organizations, relative to being a manager, it will be easier to avoid feeling a failure for not becoming a manager. There will be less pressure to climb the managerial hierarchy. The faster that knowledge advances, the greater are the challenges in pulling together complex disciplines and turning them into strong selling products. (This sounds like a job for a team of knowledge workers rather than an individual technical guru, if not for a manager, but the relative roles of individuals and teams will be discussed in the next chapter.)

The pursuit of new knowledge and its conversion to sellable products will provide more than enough career satisfaction for those knowledge workers who are not specifically motivated by a desire to have authority over others. As the cultural value of climbing the managerial pyramid loses its attraction, there will be fewer people clamouring to climb it.

Many knowledge workers in entrepreneurial organizations will lead projects on which they are the main technical authority, but this is not the same as having a fixed managerial position or pursuing a managerial career. In fact, the term 'project leadership' is appropriate because the actual management functions on a project could be distributed across all of the project team with an administrative assistant thrown in to mop up the normal managerial co-ordination and monitoring duties – those not handled by computers. Project leadership is not management, but technical direction.

Careers devoted to delivering today's business profits

It has been convenient to think of the delivery and self-renewal tasks as totally separate functions, but in practice all employees will be engaged to some degree in both parts of a business and they will often move back and forth between majoring on the two tasks throughout their careers.

Nevertheless, it is possible, at least in principle, to distinguish a quite separate type of career stream for employees whose major orientation is towards keeping today's business offerings on the rails profitably. Career salespeople, accountants, personnel professionals and even production workers may spend most of their careers in delivery functions. They will still have to see themselves as self-employed and they will have to be entrepreneurial in terms of thinking creatively about how they can offer better services to their internal customers. But this is not the same as directly altering the products on which your business depends to make money.

A career in a delivery role will inevitably be more conventional – managerial advancement will still be a more important career prospect than it will be for the manager's entrepreneurial colleagues. At the same time, the growing complexity of such disciplines as personnel and finance are leading these professionals to see themselves as internal consultants and to identify more strongly in many cases with the role of consultant than that of manager. Similarly, as they increasingly work on cross functional teams with colleagues who are more directly concerned with product development, they too will identify more closely with their specialist expertise and the professional identity that such work can provide rather than exclusively with the idea of being a manager.

Further, as all such team members become more self-managing and the role of manager becomes less glorified, even those who specialize in delivery type work will aspire less longingly to a managerial career. There will simply be fewer managers as everyone becomes more self-managing or relies on either networking or computers for co-ordination. As internal consultants they can become brokers and catalysts who can help technical colleagues who are too narrowly specialized to pool their expertise to create new offerings. In this way, a personnel or finance professional could show more entrepreneurial insight and initiative than someone who actually works in a product development function.

Still, there will be some finance, sales and personnel professionals who are happy to stick to the technicalities of their own area of expertise. Their career aspirations may be very similar to that of a doctor or lawyer – to be increasingly sought as an expert in their field whose advice is ever more widely valued and in demand. Again, this career aspiration is decidedly outside the managerial career stream.

The end of the management career?

All of the evidence points towards a decline in importance of the managerial career. Given the omnipresence of this career path and the vested interests in preserving it, there is good reason simply to list the trends that are pushing the managerial vocation into the shade:

- flattening hierarchies – vanishing pyramids to climb
- large-scale redundancies of middle managers
- rising importance of knowledge-driven innovation and the resulting shift in power and status to knowledge workers
- increasing complexity and rapidity of change has led to greater empowerment so those on the firing-line can share more of the decision making load to solve urgent problems
- demands for faster customer service also means more power for those close to customers to make decisions once made by managers
- greater importance of entrepreneurial action means spreading initia-

tive across a greater number of minds – less feasible to provide direction on a top-down basis
- trend towards contracting out leads to fewer people to manage
- pressure to justify your existence means more self-management for all
- new emphasis on organizational learning – another activity that has to be released, stimulated and encouraged, so that it evolves of its own accord – it cannot be channelled on a top-down basis.

The distinction made by William Bridges (1995) between jobs and work is useful in this context. There may be fewer managerial *jobs* or positions around in the future, but there will still be a lot of managerial work and great need for managerial skills. The main difference is that managerial work will be done by a combination of computers and those who were once managed – as they learn to manage themselves. Those who specifically aspire to a managerial role are likely to have greater professional expertise or specialization to offer as well and they will ply their managerial skills mainly on an internal consulting basis. They will hence serve as project 'advisers' or co-ordinators, pursuing a career across a range of widely differing and increasingly complex projects. Again, their career, too, will be more like that of the doctor or lawyer, enjoying rising credibility and status through their performance on specific projects, but in many cases never really having a fixed managerial position to call their own for very long.

Nevertheless, a good number of such semi-permanent positions will remain. The more delivery orientated the function, the more scope there is for a conventional managerial career. Similarly, the more delivery orientated the industry, the more there will be the possibility of climbing a managerial hierarchy. Sales organizations in the financial services sector provide as good an example as any. They will have a need for an hierarchy of regional managers for a good while. The same is true of chains of retail outlets or restaurants.

So the managerial career is not extinct – not in the foreseeable future anyway. Organizations, especially those in the fastest evolving, knowledge-driven industries, should not be advised to forget the managerial career, but to think strategically about how best to invest in both types of career development if they are to get maximum value from *all* of their 'suppliers'.

NEW-WAVE CAREER MANAGEMENT

The greatest change in career management practices will occur in dealing with entrepreneurial knowledge workers, but this is not to suggest ignoring managerial aspirants altogether. Career management for delivery-orientated staff will change little in the future except that they will increasingly take this initiative for themselves as they become more used to the idea of being self-employed and as they learn to manage all aspects of work and career. More needs to be said, however, about emerging trends in career management for innovative, highly self-reliant knowledge workers. (See Psychological slant.)

> **Career management for delivery-orientated staff will change little in the future except that they will increasingly take this initiative for themselves as they become more used to the idea of being self-employed and as they learn to manage all aspects of work and career.**

'Managing' the careers of entrepreneurs

Managing the careers of knowledge workers is not quite the right term, but it will have to do as long as it is understood in a transitional sense. Again, the best analogy for exploring the new meaning of career management is the way in which many firms are already investing in the development of their suppliers. This interest in the skill or competence of your suppliers cannot really be called managing them in the sense of managing conventional employees.

So what are you actually doing when you develop suppliers? First, you are making a strategic guess about which suppliers are likely to be most important to the future success of your business. Then you are working with them to identify and address their development needs. Clearly, the only difference between this activity and what you are now doing with employees is that suppliers are not conventional employees. You will likely have a range of employees/suppliers, just as you have of conventional employees who differ in terms of how much 'managing' they need. Some you will reject altogether, just as you now reject suppliers whose quality or price are too unacceptable to you. Others will need a bit of development. Still others will provide *you* with leadership and development. They will be showing *you* how you could use what they supply to enhance what you offer. The latter type of employees/suppliers will clearly be quite capably in charge of their own careers.

PSYCHOLOGICAL SLANT

'Gung ho' knowledge workers will need little encouragement to manage their own careers. Managers who need to get used to a diminished status in life are most in need of help. Significant loss is difficult to come to terms with, especially when it is a major source of personal identity and self-esteem. Providing conventional outplacement counselling is not enough if it merely focuses on skills to find a new job, when what is needed is a whole new way of seeing one's relationship to work. The managers who survive re-engineering cutbacks need coaching if they are not to be left in an unproductive state of demoralization. What can be their source of motivation if the pyramid they aspired to climb disappears? Something must be put in its place if you expect to obtain committed effort from them rather than merely resigned acquiescence. This is no easy task as it may mean finding whole new roles and sources of identity for many. The strategic investment for them must be in some form of role transition counselling – preferably externally provided to ensure maximum openness and confidentiality.

The intermediate group, however, you may have to worry about a little bit – speaking here of individual employees who you now consider as suppliers of services. Are they getting enough exposure to new ideas? What effort are they making to keep up to date? Despite the fact that their greater empowerment will lead many of them to take more initiative to manage their own careers, your strategic goals depend on them too heavily to leave this to chance. Hence you need to think creatively about how you can help them to continually enhance their skill base.

Such new-wave career management ideas will encourage you to:

- Share employees with strategic partner organizations (your customers or suppliers) in lieu of internal moves.
- Encourage independence: employees to go elsewhere for career development, possibly to return in a few years.
- Fund groups of employees to set up as suppliers outside the organization. Think of the motivational advantages of privatization versus state (corporate) ownership.
- Encourage employees to think of themselves as businesses and of the organization's various departments as their customers.
- Encourage employees to develop customers outside your organization.
- Help employees develop self-marketing, networking and consultancy skills to enable them to search out, recognize or create new opportunities for both themselves and for you.
- Identify skilled individuals in other organizations who can contribute on a temporary/project basis or part time.
- Regularly expose employees to new people and new ideas to stimulate innovation.
- Foster more cross-functional teamwork for self-development.

Such 'management' of your entrepreneurial employees will be a strategic investment, not a matter of *responsibility*. It is not the individual's responsibility either. This is outdated paternalistic language. No one has a responsibility to manage their own career or that of anyone else – any more than you have a *responsibility* to follow a sensible diet in order to live longer. It is simply a matter of personal choice. Organizations have a responsibility to those whose *expectations they have violated* but none on an ongoing basis for those who are effectively contracted to you on some sort of self-employed basis. Your responsibility is to employees who have worked only for you for 20–30 years and who you suddenly find you no longer need. This is an important distinction, because it is essential to stop viewing career management so paternalistically as to have to see it as someone's responsibility. With regard to new employees seen as suppliers, you have a responsibility to honour contractual agreements with them but this should not include helping them with their career management. If you do help them, you will be doing so as a strategic choice not as a responsibility.

Career self-management

Organizations and educational institutions do have responsibilities to help people during any period of major transition. Such help should steer away from teaching people how to find jobs, as William Bridges (1995) rightly points out. What is required is the teaching of entrepreneurial skills, self-management and how to *create* work in an entrepreneurial sense, rather than just seek it out as most people are still doing.

Employees within organizations need to manage their own careers primarily by copying what any good entrepreneur would do – by being alert to emerging opportunities and sniffing them out before anyone else does. Essentially this entails very active and continuous networking both inside and outside the organization in order to stay on top of developing market trends. It also includes regular attempts to diversify so as to acquire new skills – those that, strategically, the individual guesses will be most in demand tomorrow.

Career self-management means creating your own sense of security, which you can do in two ways: by diversifying, keeping yourself as up to date with current needs as possible and, second, by keeping in touch with as many potential customers as possible. Most current job seekers only approach other such 'customers' when they are out of work or dissatisfied and then only once. If they are rejected by company X, they assume this means for life. Yet any good salesperson would keep in regular touch with all possible and desirable prospects in the hope of an eventual breakthrough. Those who want to manage their own careers effectively need to learn such disciplined sales skills – specifically how to manage a potentially big account.

Where are we now?

We have seen how to think differently about the 'management' of careers so as to ensure ongoing entrepreneurial vitality. So far the focus has been primarily on individuals, but what about teamwork? Are teams more important in the ongoing delivery of existing offerings or are they more critical to the renewal task? Does teamwork take different forms in carrying out these two tasks? This is the subject of the next chapter.

PRACTICAL STEPS

- identify which 'supplier' roles are strategically most central for your organization's future success and focus investment on them

- be a catalyst to get your core employees to brainstorm career paths for themselves which help them enhance their technical edge

- begin to unravel the culture of aspiring primarily to managerial careers

- identify and celebrate your innovation heroes, elevate their status and pay them more to make it more attractive to emulate them

- start rewarding and investing more in the development of core competency skills and less in skills for purely management positions

- provide transition counselling to managers to help them redefine their place in the future scheme of things

"Fear of change and uncertainty, so rife in organizations today, increases the pressure for excessive teamwork which can cause dysfunctional conformity and stifling of creativity."

"If task requirements are our guide to what sort of teamwork is needed, it is equally easy to ask whether teams or individuals are likely to be better at some tasks than others."

11

TEAMS OR INDIVIDUALS – WHICH ARE BEST?

So far we have not looked at the place of teamwork in achieving either efficient delivery of today's business or entrepreneurial self-renewal. However odd this may be in light of the prominence of teams today, individuals are still the prime focus of much organizational thinking. After all, you hire, fire, pay and promote individuals. Only individuals have careers. It is individuals you want to motivate. When we think of entrepreneurs we think first of rebellious but creative individuals, not teams. No doubt, however, an exclusive concern with individuals paints a biased and inaccurate picture.

Teamwork is increasingly vital simply because of the sheer complexity of most business activities. There is less and less that one person can accomplish alone, so much so that we are at risk of seeing teamwork as another panacea. The danger of the teamwork bandwagon is that we may overlook its pitfalls and forget the value of individual initiative. We need a more balanced view that helps us to put the right emphasis on the respective contributions of both teams and individuals.

So, in this chapter, we need to take a look at just what teamwork means and, specifically, whether it is equally critical for both of our key organizational tasks: delivering today's offerings and renewing your business for the future.

WHAT IS TEAMWORK?

Teamwork or herd instinct?

Greater teamwork will solve all your problems, you are told. If only you could stop interdepartmental feuding and all pull together you could really leave your competition behind. If we are all specialists and have limited knowledge, so the argument goes, how can we expect to get anywhere without the help of others? But are there no pitfalls to watch out for in teamwork? Does teamwork have no dysfunctional aspects at all? Fortunately, we can reap greater productivity benefits from teamwork, but only if we understand its limitations and actively strive to avoid them.

Every so often, a bit of research pops up that points out the dangers of teamwork. But we tend to ignore anything that contradicts whatever we are fervently excited about at the moment – which is precisely the major pitfall of teamwork. In every team there is incredible pressure to conform and if we do nothing to minimize the downside of such conformity we end up having not a team but a *herd*!

> **In every team there is incredible pressure to conform and if we do nothing to minimize the downside of such conformity we end up having not a team but a *herd*!**

One recent research paper by an American economist develops a theory of 'yes men' based on an analysis of the impact of economic incentives on the relationship between boss and subordinate. Canice Prendergast (1993) of the University of Chicago argues that all employees have an unavoidable incentive to agree with their boss. He points out that the same pressure exists in teams, although the incentive here may be more psychological than economic. 'What nonsense', you object, 'our organization is riven with conflict. A little conformity would be an immense relief and a great boost to productivity!' Certainly there is cross-functional friction but that is only because most organizations are groups within groups and it is sub-group conformity that provides the foundation for cross-group rivalry. Also, we all have difficult colleagues who stubbornly refuse to conform. But we can so easily think of who they are precisely because they are such an exception.

The fact is that, however much we all want to stand out, most of us want even more to be accepted by an attractive group. And this desire for security, both economic and psychological, underlies our disposition to agree with our colleagues. Prendergast shows how even such an essential feature of everyday organizational life as the sharing of information breeds conformity. We share and receive information most willingly wherever there is mutual liking and respect. Clearly, we also tend to agree with those whom we most admire. Organizations with so-called 'strong' cultures are most at risk of tripping over the pitfalls of excessive teamwork.

What is the worst criticism that could be levelled at you in your organization? That you are not a *team player*? Is this not pressure to conform? Rapid change in organizations today puts everyone under greater pressure and this induces fear. It is well known that even sworn enemies will pull together if their group is threatened by an external enemy. Fear of change and uncertainty, so rife in organizations today, increases the pressure for excessive teamwork which can cause dysfunctional conformity and stifling of creativity.

> **Organizations with so-called 'strong' cultures are most at risk of tripping over the pitfalls of excessive teamwork.**

Prendergast agrees with research that suggests that individuals are generally more creative than teams. But this claim flies in the face of our everyday experience that a lone product developer working in isolation from marketing, production and customers can develop bad products. All of the more entrepreneurial businesses place great store by the innovative power of cross-functional teamwork. So who is right? The key is surely to strike a balance between teamwork and individuality. Too much of either will lead to problems. But in order to develop a clear view of the respective contributions of teams and individuals we need to figure out what teamwork is all about.

How many kinds of teamwork?

This question can be approached from quite different angles and you will be led to very different answers depending on your starting point. Here are a few typical ways of beginning to think about teamwork:

- *Team as structure* – if you begin with the question of what *is* a team you will be led to focus on team composition and the roles of team members – implicitly, such teams are relatively long-term entities.
- *Teamwork as process* – if you see teamwork as a process by which diverse individuals pool their efforts, you might major on the best ways to facilitate this process – here there is no implication that teams are necessarily more than transient units.

- *Teams as groups* – if you see a team as a relatively long-term, settled group, you will be led to bring in all of the research into the social functions and dynamics of groups – teams are a bit like families.
- *Teamwork as shared culture* – when a whole organization or the smallest unit is described as a team, the idea is that everyone shares the same values, so you would be inclined to focus on what binds the team together.
- *Teamwork as information sharing* – if you see teamwork as having mainly to do with communication between individuals, you could focus on networking between people who otherwise do not work together at all – they need have no common culture.
- *Teamwork as consensus* – for many people, teamwork *means* that every member is in agreement – this is the point of participative decision making, to achieve as much consensus as possible – on this view, mild conflict can be constructive, but disagreement is primarily something to be *resolved* in favour of consensus.
- *Teamwork as orchestrated conflict* – if your major concern is creativity, you might see teamwork as a means of providing loosely associated 'members' with the constant stimulation of challenge, disagreement and dissension – on this view, settled teams and consensus would spell the death of creativity. For example, any specialized area of the scientific community could be seen as a team in this sense – even if none of them actually work together. Their creativity is generated by conflicting opinions.

The suggestion that there are several ways of thinking about teams leads naturally to the idea that maybe we need to think about varying kinds of teamwork for different tasks or purposes. As obvious as this implication may seem, it will be upsetting to those who want the elegant simplicity of one best way for all things – one best way of organizing, one best way to manage and, in this case, one best way to think about teamwork. If you are prepared to consider a plurality of approaches, you will nonetheless want a reasonable basis for accepting any proposed differentiation.

To establish a rationale for just such a pluralistic outlook, the best place to begin is with the traditional way of thinking about teams – the idea that teams are structured units with specific roles. We need to address the question of why it has seemed appropriate as a way of viewing teamwork, what are its limitations and what organizational

purpose might such teams serve. While much of what follows is negative, a necessary first step in adapting to new ways of looking at issues
is to fully rid ourselves of older, firmly entrenched viewpoints.

Teams made of boxes

Those who focus on the team as a particular kind of unit within organizations seem inevitably drawn to the question of how best to orga-
nize a team. This line of thinking arose out of seeing organizations as
structures designed primarily for co-ordinated task achievement. This
orientation in turn presupposes that tasks are easily broken down into
clear goals, resources, processes and definitive time frames – in short
– boxes.

Once you envision a team as a discrete unit of performance, your
next question might be about what variables affect the performance of
teams. These will include matters external to the team, such as broader
organizational support, cultural attitudes and corporate politics as well
as the internal dynamics that depend on the particular personalities in
a team.

While there are numerous factors that can have an impact on team
effectiveness, the major concern of many writers on this subject seems
to have been team *composition* – not in the sense of *who* you put on a
team but what *roles* a team must be composed of in order to work
effectively. You are naturally led to look at team composition if you
see organizations as structures made up of specific functions to be fulfilled by discrete roles. A team therefore becomes a miniature organization, with its own peculiar functions which are seen as best carried
out by allocating members to suitable *team roles*.

The basic idea of team-role theories is both simple and appealing. It
is intuitively obvious that a team must do several things well in order
to be effective, such as, for example, propose ideas, critically evaluate
them and implement them, while co-ordinating and preserving harmony among team members. The simple observation that different
people are better than others at some of these tasks leads to the idea that
there are various team roles that complement one another to make up
an effective team. Unfortunately, mixing together the obvious fact of
individual differences with the concept of *role* leads to problems.

As most of the team-role theories on the market are broadly similar it will be convenient to look at one that is fairly popular and widespread, in the UK at least: that of British expert on teamwork, Meredith Belbin (1981; 1993). Careful study of teams working on management problems during management courses led Belbin to the very persuasive theory that there are nine distinct team roles:

- **Shaper** – aggressive achiever to help drive a team into action.
- **Plant** – thoughtful innovator to provide creative, new ideas.
- **Monitor Evaluator** – critical thinker to challenge suspect ideas.
- **Implementer** – hard worker to take practical, efficient action.
- **Team Worker** – socially-skilled harmonizer to defuse conflict.
- **Co-ordinator** – facilitator to organize the efforts of others.
- **Completer-Finisher** – detailed follower-through to tie up loose ends.
- **Resource Investigator** – outgoing explorer to liaise outside the team.
- **Specialist** – technical expert to supply specialized knowledge.

No doubt many teams do get more done if all of these roles are covered and if each member fulfils his or her specific role competently. But is such a highly structured approach to thinking about teamwork really practical in today's dynamic and loosely organized businesses?

Problems with roles

- *Facts vs norms* – assigning people to a role based on factual personal differences leads not only to an expectation that they will behave accordingly at all times, but a restrictive obligation to do so.
- *Rigidity* – having a well-defined role does not preclude flexibility or personal development, but it does not immediately suggest it either.
- *Territoriality* – reluctance to contribute from the point of view of someone else's role lest they feel usurped.
- *Abdication* – avoiding contributing within another's role because that is someone else's responsibility.
- *Human nature* – the annoying habit of being unpredictable, straying from the expected role.

As an illustration of such problems, suppose your strongest team role is that of Co-ordinator, but on a certain subject you happen to have a lot of knowledge and some good ideas. You could make some Plant-type contributions to the team, but your inclination to contribute and even your actual ability to think creatively could be inhibited by: a) the knowledge that this is not your role, b) fear of stepping on the 'official' Plant's toes, and c) fear that you will be violating the expectations of the other team members who expect you to stick to your knitting and co-ordinate rather than make substantive contributions. (See Figure 11.1.)

Look! I'm the Plant
in this team!!! It's
MY job to come up
with good ideas!!!

Figure 11.1

You could water down the theory by saying that every team member should try to play as many roles as possible, but this would be a poor defence of the theory. Why bother to talk about roles at all in this case? Better to go one step further and substitute a list of team *processes* in place of team roles. This approach would avoid the absurdity that a team meeting should be cancelled because the Monitor Evaluator could not make it that day.

Oddly, Belbin (1993) seems to prefer just the opposite course. While he admits that an individual might have more than one prominent team role, he advocates, in his latest book, that you should 'Outlaw those team roles foreign to the self . . . the avoidance of unsuitable team roles needs to be actively, and even energetically pursued. Failure to do so means that the self will be poorly placed and in a weak position.' Surely this is very bad advice for the majority of managers.

It may be appropriate guidance for those who are extreme in their team roles and hence rather one sided, but surely the majority of managers will be somewhere in the middle range of scores on many of these team roles and therefore quite able to adjust their contribution to teams as needed. Role theorists are irritated by these adaptable middle-of-the-road types, because, disliking ambiguity, they want to be able to pigeon-hole everyone. This is not to suggest, at the other extreme, that everyone can be all things to all people: those with more extreme profiles will, as Belbin indicates, have difficulty 'wearing other hats'.

In light of Belbin's stern warning, one imagines the archetypal Completer-Finisher cowering under his mass of detail as if it were a sort of security blanket from which he dare not venture forth. The role preferences of managers with such extreme scores are as much weaknesses as strengths and they are of limited use in organizations that need more adaptable people. Unfortunately, role theories do not tell us much about managers who do not have extreme role preferences.

Further, Belbin's team-role theory is based on work within a college environment with 'captive' teams. Not many real-life organizations could afford the luxury of calling a meeting on some issue without giving prime consideration to including those who could make a substantive contribution. All of the members of a cross-functional team may need to be Specialists, for example, while many of Belbin's team roles have a bit too much of a purely *process* leaning, i.e. Team Worker, Monitor Evaluator, Co-ordinator. Teams will no doubt need to use such processes, but they will inevitably all be *content* 'Specialists' of one sort or another.

Applying team-role theory

If these concerns with the theory are set aside for a moment, there is still the question of how to apply the idea of team roles. Belbin's teams work on problem solving tasks in order to make a decision of some sort. But much real-life organizational teamwork is about the *implementation* of decisions, the co-ordination of ongoing activity across numerous and disparate disciplines. Teamwork in this context is a matter of *co-ordination*. Belbin focuses mainly on problem solving teams whereas the most commonly felt need in organizations for improved teamwork is for better co-ordination across functional disciplines such as Sales, Production and Purchasing.

To implement complex decisions in a co-ordinated fashion, Shapers, Implementers and Completer Finishers would come in handy, but Monitor Evaluators and Plants would just slow things up (unless the team got stuck and needed to solve a problem). In any case, ongoing co-ordination mainly calls for every functional representative to do his or her part. They may only rarely sit down to solve problems together.

Belbin's roles are also too internally focused (as you would expect if you studied teams in a classroom). Their foremost concern is what is going on within the group. But in these days of intense external pressures, only the lowliest project teams far removed from commercial realities could be satisfied to rely on only one person (the Resource Investigator) to maintain contact with external reality. Just as every member of the organization must be more customer orientated these days, every significant decision maker needs to network actively and widely both inside and outside the organization. Even relatively stable decision-making teams (to which Belbin's theory best applies) will pick up as many ideas outside the team (Plant territory) and have them critically evaluated by outsiders (Monitor Evaluator territory) as they will by these role occupants within the team.

In addition, the Shaper is likely to be most effective when a clear objective is in sight or when the task or problem has some definition. *This is characteristic of closed systems.*

Leadership has a more open-ended, outward looking perspective, accompanied by a vision of a better scheme of things. The Shaper is firstly a driver, the Co-ordinator just co-ordinates and the Plant is a thinker not a leader. There does not appear to be any role for a leader as conceived in more open-ended, visionary and change-orientated terms. Good leaders are likely to have a mixture of the attributes of several of Belbin's roles, among others, but once you opt for a theory based on roles, you tend to want everyone to fit categorically into one role.

What is wrong with team roles?

Most team-role theories were developed at a time when organizations were relatively static. The major managerial task was to achieve incremental growth and to keep everything on the rails. Managers could spend much more time solving closed-system problems, simply fixing whatever broke. The problem with any team *role* theory is that very little of organizational life is like this any more.

> **Empowerment means multi-skilling people – everyone is expected to contribute to everything, within reason. It is old fashioned now to say: 'This is my job. That is your job.'**

Empowerment means multi-skilling people – everyone is expected to contribute to everything, within reason. It is old fashioned now to say: 'This is my job. That is your job.' Customer service is a prime example of a crucial task that is no longer role-related. Every employee must now strive to serve customers better. It is irrelevant that some are better at it than others. A high premium is now placed on adaptability and quick learning. The need for adaptability cannot simply be labelled 'role flexibility'. The concept of role just gets in the way. It would be more effective to use a concept such as *fluid skill sets* or any terminology that is more dynamic than 'role'.

Teamwork as process

Structures are fast being replaced by processes. Instead of seeing a team as a discrete unit made up of roles, you would now look at the processes a team needs to use to be effective. The more transient nature of teams is partly responsible for the downfall of the role approach. The impossibility of assigning people on a long-term basis to a team in accordance with their preferred roles leads to the only alternative, which is to focus on processes all teams can use. This approach allows for greater flexibility so that no matter what the duration of the team's existence or what style the transient members have, who need to come together for a brief purpose, they can still be effective.

Typical processes might deal with how problems are solved, how conflict is handled, how leadership is shared and how communication is achieved. There are several benefits to be gained by a switch to process talk:

- it applies to transient groups of people who would not work together long enough to be seen as a team in the structural sense
- it is consistent with empowerment because every member is expected to contribute to the use of all appropriate team processes
- process talk is flexible and pluralistic – there is no need to settle on one universal set of processes for all contexts where some form of teamwork might be useful
- despite individual strengths and weaknesses, effective processes can be learned – no one is boxed into a discrete role

Some processes will be clearly more appropriate in a strategic planning context than they will be in a product assembly situation. The former will have processes for gathering data outside the organization while the latter will rely more on processes for pooling past experience of solving immediate production problems. The production team will have to employ processes to maximize quality and cost effectiveness whereas the strategy team will need to major on obtaining diversity of input.

Further, some time-driven tasks will benefit from processes that encourage a sense of urgency. This might lead to a team agreeing a process for rewarding themselves as they achieve each milestone. Empowered knowledge

> **Empowered knowledge workers are likely to be demotivated by a whip-cracking Shaper standing over them rather than inclined to work faster through such pushing.**

workers are likely to be demotivated by a whip-cracking Shaper standing over them rather than inclined to work faster through such pushing.

Are not some processes universal? What about the need to produce harmonious relationships in a team? Do not all teams need harmony so they can focus on the task instead of being distracted by infighting? The first point to make in response to these questions is that harmony is mainly important in teams that work closely together on a more or less continuous basis – such as in a hospital operating room. It is also important wherever task goals are clear, and efficient co-ordination is required in order to meet deadlines and cost objectives. In this context, disharmony slows down work and can lead to missed targets or cost over-runs. Harmony is important in any crisis where pulling together to achieve an immediate result outweighs individual differences about the best way to proceed. In these situations action is necessary rather than debate.

> If task requirements are our guide to what sort of teamwork is needed, it is equally easy to ask whether teams or individuals are likely to be better at some tasks than others.

Where innovation is the focus, you may not want outright war, but you certainly want active debate and the expression of viewpoints that are diametrically opposed to each other. A strong harmonizing influence in such a team could be very counter productive by virtue of shutting down debate too prematurely.

Most importantly, seeing teamwork as a set of adaptable processes makes it easier to see how different types of teamwork are appropriate for different tasks. If task requirements are our guide to what sort of teamwork is needed, it is equally easy to ask whether teams or individuals are likely to be better at some tasks than others.

INDIVIDUALS VERSUS TEAMS

The major division of labour which organizations need to attend to is how to be effective at delivering today's products as profitably as possible while at the same time throwing everything in the air for the sake of creative renewal. Before we look at the relative value of individual versus team effort, it will be useful to explore just how teamwork might differ with respect to these fundamental tasks.

Teamwork for the efficient delivery of today's offerings

Teamwork for delivery is above all else a matter of *co-ordination*. It involves the efficient production and sales of often very complex products. And it is specifically their complexity that makes teamwork most essential. Better co-ordination of purchasing, production and sales leads to a just-in-time process which minimizes the cost of having unused stock or unsold product sitting around losing money. Good co-ordination between marketing, engineering, R&D and production creates an efficient product design process. Product design here means all of the steps involved from initial idea through design and manufacturing of a finished product. The innovative idea stage is something else again and will be discussed as part of the renewal task.

There is no question that teamwork is more valuable than individual effort alone. Further, the whole idea of team *roles* is more appropriate in the structured delivery of ongoing services. While you want each team member in a manufacturing facility to be as multi-skilled as possible, efficiency – which is the primary value in the delivery function – demands a high level of individual accountability. This is because the delivery function is necessarily a structured activity made up of discrete sub-tasks. In an automobile manufacturing plant, for example, teams or individual members might build whole cars rather than just fasten doors onto vehicles along an assembly line, but they will not generally also do the purchasing of parts or the selling of completed cars.

Specialization is still a good idea if you want to achieve the maximum efficiency possible. As the Pinchots (1993) rightly point out, you would lose money if you allowed every team to be a completely separate business with no broader organizational integration with other functions. The point is that however much you push the concept of empowered multi-skilling, efficiency demands some specialization. This is easier to see in simpler service firms such as a fast-food restaurant. Consider McDonald's – again. Maximum efficiency and prompt attention to customers is best achieved by having some employees cooking the food and others serving it. Some multi-skilling has been implemented in such businesses by giving each server his or her own till rather than customers being served and then having to go to another counter to pay for the food.

Again, it is clear that teamwork comes down to good *co-ordination* in a fast-food restaurant – or any other type of eating establishment for that matter. The point of focusing solely on co-ordination as a distinguishing feature of this type of teamwork is because co-ordination is characteristic of complex tasks, which have a clearly defined output that can be specified in full detail in advance of starting.

The same type of teamwork is crucial in any major project, such as movie making, for example. Some commentators on management practices would have us believe that all organizational work is becoming 'projectized', but there is a world of difference between making a movie and operating a fast-food restaurant profitably. In making a movie, you are organizing a one-off team to produce a unique product – perhaps never to work together again. In contrast, a fast-food restaurant is essentially a machine which, so far, requires human interaction. But there is no getting away from the fact that people in restaurants are performing mechanical tasks. Obviously this does not mean waitresses who just go through the motions, it means simply repetitive, regular and efficient attendance to a precisely definable task – with no project-like outcome of any sort involved.

This is essentially what organizational delivery is all about. Teamwork is simply the flip side of the coin where one side is specialization of labour and the other side is its co-ordination into a definable whole. You really cannot have one without the other. Some degree of specialization is demanded by efficiency, but inevitably, the specialized parts need to be put together in a usable, whole output. Otherwise the efficiency gains of specialization are lost when the parts are brought together. (See Psychological slant.)

Teamwork for organizational renewal

Teamwork as co-ordination is most valuable for the implementation of decisions once they are made. Brainstorming is a form of teamwork that can be useful for making those decisions in the first place and this form of teamwork gets us closer to the renewal task. But entrepreneurial decision making in the most volatile industries will more often take the form of trial and error action. This is also a *form* of brainstorming, one where you interact with your market – with your customers making responses and suggestions to improve the products you have on offer. Your ideas thrown on the table for debate in this case are the product iterations you are actually asking customers to try out. Their ideas offered in return are their views of what it is like to use your product. This form of brainstorming is not so much a matter of sitting in a meeting room sharing ideas with colleagues prior to taking any action – although you would do some of that as well.

So what exactly is the task that teams are tackling for the sake of renewal? The essence of renewal is entrepreneurial action on as broad a front as possible. And the key to such action is being willing to introduce products quickly in spite of not having had the time to gather all of your facts in advance to define exactly what form the product should take. Not that you should skimp on market research or talking directly to customers. But you must also allow independent initiatives as well which may often have no more than some fanatic's hunch to back them up.

The role of teamwork in this context is to stimulate rather than suppress off-the-wall thinking. This requires a team culture of one-up-manship in a sense, where the objective is to see who can come up with the most original – however implausible – ideas. This is not teamwork as co-ordination of effort but as a catalyst for stimulating and rewarding diversity.

PSYCHOLOGICAL SLANT

The prime danger in teamwork is when it is equated with the notion of a strong culture. In this sense, teamwork is used as a very oppressive form of control. When teamwork is used to enforce adherence to the vision of the chief executive or to compel acceptance of company values, then you are telling people that they must either agree or be rejected. Why is teamwork abused in this way? It comes down to fear and short-term thinking. The short-term goal is to raise sales of profits immediately no matter what the longer-term cost in terms of failing to invest in renewal. The fear factor stems from senior executives feeling that they need to act fast to justify their existence. Either way, a crisis mentality is operating and, as in any crisis, it is seen as legitimate to quash dissension. Organizations that deliberately foster a state of permanent crisis are least likely to survive in the long term because they have no time and no tolerance for diversity of opinion. Despite the lip service they may pay to individual initiative, their crisis mentality necessitates implicitly and most insidiously that everyone pull together.

Despite the obvious association of entrepreneurship with an almost excessive individualism, there are clear uses for teams on the self-renewal front.

Where entrepreneurial teamwork wins

- Brainstorming among diverse employees in a context where dissension and off-the-wall ideas are of premium value.
- Pooling of specialist expertise – again not for co-ordination but to discuss the technical feasibility of complex product ideas.
- Product development efforts that bring together suppliers, customers, employees and other 'outsiders' such as consultants.

The objective of teamwork in tackling the delivery function is co-ordination to produce a defined target. On the renewal side, the objective is idea generation and feasibility testing.

Networking as teamwork

Many entrepreneurial individuals will drive new venture creation more through their own effort than via teamwork. They may need assistance on the implementation front but getting the initial idea accepted and off the ground may be 80 per cent due to one individual's commitment. Teamwork of a different sort may, however, be essential. This is networking and it takes the form of liaising with diverse specialists inside or outside the organization. While everyone you consult on your network may make an invaluable contribution to your project, the network as a whole is not a team in the conventional sense because they may not even share a common purpose let alone common values. Yet it is nonetheless a form of sharing, a pooling of ideas – in short, co-operation. It has the value of resolving the problem that complex tasks cannot really be achieved by one person who cannot conceivably know enough – without at the same time being as claustrophobic to a stubbornly independent mind as more closely knit teams can become. Networking is also a mixture of individual and group effort where the balance between the two could be quite variable from one group of people to another.

> Despite the obvious association of entrepreneurship with an almost excessive individualism, there are clear uses for teams on the self-renewal front.

Individuals and (not or) teams

A fully entrepreneurial organization will keep rules and absolutes to a minimum and this includes prescriptions about who (and how many) can legitimately take entrepreneurial initiative. So there can be no exclusion of individual action. Some employees thrive in a team atmosphere. Others are fiercely independent. The goal of fostering maximum diversity can only be served by letting both approaches flourish. Individuals help to ensure *creative diversity* while teams produce *creative synergy* – both are vital.

> **Networking is also a mixture of individual and group effort where the balance between the two could be quite variable from one group of people to another.**

Often, an individual initiative will still amount to a form of teamwork in that the individual entrepreneur will network with a wide range of people to get information and ideas. This is very loosely structured teamwork indeed, but it may often be the best kind simply because the individual can pick and choose what he or she will act on. There is no risk of a watering down to the lowest common denominator that you risk when such a 'group' of people actually get into the same room together.

Team leadership

While all teams will be increasingly self-managing, there will still be a role for team leaders – primarily in the delivery of existing offerings. Again, the job of team leader is to facilitate co-ordination and to stimulate employee motivation. Often the team leader will simply be the person who has most experience in the jobs performed by the team.

In the entrepreneurial team, direction is less experience driven than it is knowledge dependent. In teams of diverse specialists, there may be no appointed leader, but each member will exhibit leadership acts in accordance with the specialist issue under discussion at any given moment. This is where bottom-up leadership comes in.

Where are we now?

We have looked at new employment relationships, motivational factors for entrepreneurial employees and how to think creatively about their careers. In this chapter we have discussed the need to take an eclectic and a very entrepreneurial approach to the place of teams and individuals in fostering organizational renewal. Chapter 4, on bottom-up leadership, alluded to what remains of the leadership function at senior executive level.

Now that we have a better idea of how an entrepreneurial, self-renewing business might operate, it is time to take a final look at what sort of leadership would be most conducive to transforming your organization along these lines so that you can fully 'unleash the entrepreneur within'.

PRACTICAL STEPS

- provide teams with training on how to disagree constructively

- train managers to solicit honest feedback (anonymously if necessary)

- reward healthy dissension and celebrate individual initiative

- get rid of the pejorative label 'not a team player' and take a close look at how such diversity of opinion may be used productively

- face the mutual fear of change and uncertainty with a full awareness of the pitfalls of an excessive 'we're-in-this-together' herd instinct

- balance the need for autonomy (individual or departmental) against the drive for a total 'one organization' philosophy

- experiment open mindedly with different types of teamwork for different contexts – avoid 'one best way' thinking

- stop using a crisis mentality as an excuse to defend against criticism.

"The power to make decisions must be replaced by the power and motivation to mould the broader environment."

"So the balance that needs to be struck involves upgrading the status of entrepreneurs, but salvaging the esteem of conventional managers so that a true balance of power is achieved."

12

AFTERWORD

WANTED: LEADERS WHO CAN UNLEASH ENTREPRENEURS

Earlier we looked at the shift in leadership power away from hierarchical position in the direction of knowledge to create bottom-up leadership. Leaders at the bottom of your organization will be those employees who have the vision and the drive to initiate new entrepreneurial ventures – like the employee who created 3M's Post-it note business. They will not necessarily manage other people. If they do have a team of people working with them on a project to launch a new business, it may be a self-managed team of peers – a mixture of technical and marketing specialists plus perhaps some customers and suppliers. Each team member will supply a share of leadership input based on his or her area of expertise.

> **Each team member will supply a share of leadership input based on his or her area of expertise.**

We also touched on new roles for executives. They will become customers for employees or contract workers, all of whom, whatever their employment status, will be suppliers of services. As powerful customers, executives could wield quite a lot of power, still too much in many cases with those suppliers that are too dependent on one customer. Executives will also increasingly assume the role of venture capitalists who fund entrepreneurial start-ups within their firms. A third role we alluded to was that of broker, helping in the very difficult task of bringing diverse customers and talented technical suppliers together – often to form joint ventures or other types of alliance

The question to address here, however, is: How can senior executives make the transition from autocratic power, calling all the shots, to a role where little direction can be given from the top, one of facilitating the efforts of others? There are two major personal transitions to negotiate. One is the *loss* of power entailed by the new ways of working. The second is how to cultivate leadership in others – often technical employees/suppliers who otherwise may have no personal influence skills with which to lead people in the conventional sense.

Losing power without losing face

The best way to cope with losing anything is to find something else to take its place – preferably something even better than what was lost. Clearly, if the replacement is indeed something better, then you can preserve your self-esteem and save face by demonstrating to the world that your life is still progressing rather than degenerating. If you are already operating in a facilitative mode and have been delegating substantive directional decisions to subordinates for years, then your transition will be relatively less traumatic.

Leaders who identify too closely with their technical or functional background will have the biggest challenge on their hands. They are used to providing *content* leadership rather than focusing on process. The engineer at the top still wants to have a say in product development. The chief executive with a marketing background still likes to have a hand in how the firm's products are marketed. Giving up this source of identity at a later stage in one's career is much harder than earlier in the ascent up the managerial ladder. The greater the disparity between your current source of identity and that required of new leadership roles, the more you will need mentoring yourself. It is a rare but vital form of leadership to recognize and admit when you need help.

New leadership challenges

In the old days when everything was much simpler, the top executive's job was much more straightforward. You could sit atop an hierarchy as if you were the head of an army. You could see the objectives to head for and it was your job to decide what direction to take. Then it was just a matter of getting everyone committed and enthused about your decision.

Today you are trying to control a fire that is spreading in all directions and threatening to burn out of control. The best you can do is to contain it and steer it away from areas where it will do too much damage. This is a crude analogy, but it highlights the multi-directional speed at which your organization needs to develop as well as the sense of losing control over its development. It also underlines your role in steering from the sidelines. Such nudging of a self-generating mass with a dynamism of its own contrasts starkly with the image of leading at the head of a cavalry charge where you and only you are in charge of its direction.

> **For the sake of preserving self-esteem and developing a new identity it is essential to find new and, for some people, bigger challenges.**

Essentially your new role is to create the *conditions* for your organization to succeed rather than to create that success directly yourself. Seen this way, you have not only a much bigger job on your hands, you also have a more difficult one. For the sake of preserving self-esteem and developing a new identity it is essential to find new and, for some people, bigger challenges. The new role for executives is bigger and more difficult for a number of reasons:

- A culture based on top-down positional authority is very hard to alter and will take much more work than merely empowering employees.
- You have to bear the burden and responsibility of taking more risks entailed by empowering a greater range and diversity of new ventures.
- Everyone will need help to cope with the greater ambiguity caused by market uncertainty as well as greater cultural diversity.
- The absence of bureaucratic integration across profit centres means more networking and bottom-up, self-generated relationships. Someone at the top needs to foster continual networking and relationship building if the organization is not to disintegrate altogether into totally separate businesses.
- It is much harder to steer a volatile, less integrated mass, threatening to fall apart, than to drive a uniform culture in a single direction.
- Someone has to find new ways of attracting and holding the brightest entrepreneurial prospects, often forging new relationships.
- Each such venture could be a unique relationship depending on the amount of equity the entrepreneur has in his or her venture. The idea is to prevent completely losing such opportunities as many organi-

zations do when such entrepreneurs totally leave the firm to start up completely independent new businesses. Such people are often hard to manage – which is why they depart – so this calls for special leadership skills, both to induce the entrepreneur to stay and to convince the rest of the organization to accept his or her terms – which might upset someone else's sense of equity (or 'justice' to use the term we used when discussing motivation).

- Mentoring skills are going to be at a premium to help displaced managers cope with these changes but also to help budding entrepreneurs feel fully empowered and confident to show the technical leadership of which you feel they are capable.

Unleashing entrepreneurs

The leader of today will succeed by unleashing entrepreneurial talent and energy. This will be achieved by creating and fostering the conditions in which they are likely to flourish. An example would be 3M's LD DeSimone, Chief Executive since 1991. When he took over as Chief Executive, he found 3M slipping in the entrepreneurial race. This realization underlines the point made earlier that no one firm has all the answers and that the effort to be more entrepreneurial is a continuous journey rather than a formulaic end state. Some of the conditions DeSimone focused on to increase 3M's rate of productive innovation were as follows:

- setting a target to reduce product development time by half
- moving R&D closer to practical product development
- encouraging closer liaison with customers
- fostering more cross-functional teamwork
- encouraging teams to look for new applications of existing technology.

The key to this revitalization of what was already a renowned force in the innovation game is the word *encouragement*. Multi-disciplined teams are empowered to develop their own products, to liaise directly with customers and to scour both the market and 3M's existing knowledge base for new ideas. The role of senior management is to analyse and adjust the conditions under which the entrepreneurial spirit will flourish.

Other leaders set targets for the number of new products they expect to see released on to the market in a given time period or the percentage of revenue they expect each year from new offerings. As noted earlier, DeSimone upped the rate for 3M from 25 per cent of sales on new products introduced in the past five years to 30 per cent from products over the past four years.

The courage to transform yourself and your business

If your organization still has a very bureaucratic culture, then setting product development targets will not be enough. Much has been written about the streamlining process that allows large organizations to become sufficiently lean but not a lot has been said about the twin leadership challenges of facing up to a diminished level of authority and at the same time finding the courage to show leadership in new ways. There are clearly many organizations in a state of transition with much more room for improvement than the likes of 3M. Specifically, they may take many of the steps along the road to empowering knowledge workers to act more entrepreneurially, but they may still require them to endure a bureaucratic project approval process that gives top management a feeling that they are still running things much as they were in the good old days. Hoechst Celanese has been criticized for not removing enough of just this sort of outdated bureaucracy.

The courageous behaviour of leaders in the throes of transition is to put junior technical workers in the spotlight and get out of it themselves. This means helping junior employees to see themselves as having freshness of perspective to offer – and to help them recognize that they are not inferior simply because they lack the years of experience of their older colleagues. This means taking the lead in raising the value – for the sake of innovation – of naïvety, inexperience, greenness and making dumb suggestions. The flip-side of this valuing of freshness is to help more experienced employees to preserve their self-esteem in a culture where they may now feel that they have slipped backwards by virtue of having lost this valuable freshness. They need to be helped to find ways of refreshening their perspective – of being made to feel that what they have to offer is a combination of experience and a refreshed perspective, perhaps acquired by a lateral move or more exposure to different colleagues and more outsiders.

Years of experience can contribute to the efficient delivery of existing offerings but it can create a mental block when it comes to creating something entirely new. This is not such a problem where you are simply making incremental improvements to existing products. But you cannot rely on this 'safe' form of innovation. Hence the need to celebrate the totally novel ideas of the more naïve, younger and newer employees.

Mentoring

A good mentor will help people be the best they can be at whatever they are interested in doing. If you are trying to turn a top-down power culture upside down, the difficult bit is to help junior employees learn to be less deferential, less afraid of appearing foolish, and to feel less inferior because they do not know the ropes. This is a tall order. It means truly valuing *new* knowledge and a new perspective above years of experience and this requires a fundamental attitude change from top to bottom. Every longer-term employee will need to go through a similar transition to that of senior executives as the business increases the value it places on newness. For longer-term employees it also means finding new roles: moving into the delivery side of things, teaming up with younger, naïve employees, or focusing on incremental improvements to existing lines. It will always be next to impossible for many experienced employees to avoid laughing at the mistakes and naïvety of junior colleagues. But the greatest leaders will find a way.

> **Years of experience can contribute to the efficient delivery of existing offerings but it can create a mental block when it comes to creating something entirely new.**

All managers will need to give up the power, and the need, to prove themselves by making substantive decisions. Despite all the talk of increasing empowerment, it is not easy for anyone – especially if they obtain all of their job satisfaction from a more 'hands on' style of management. Empowerment means less power for managers – inevitably because two people cannot make the same decision. The power to make decisions must be replaced by the power and motivation to mould the broader environment. This means learning new influencing skills and adjusting to less tangible or direct feedback. The organization's best leaders will serve as role models and coaches to help others make this fundamental personal transition.

On not being a role model

While the best leaders will always want to be excellent role models for other aspiring leaders, they need to create entrepreneurial role models and elevate their status so that they are seen as heroes on a level that is at least the equivalent of the organization's greatest senior executives. This means viewing the brightest entrepreneurs within your organization as you might think of great lawyers, world renowned doctors or famous scientists.

> **The power to make decisions must be replaced by the power and motivation to mould the broader environment.**

The leadership challenge is to identify such role models, coach them on how best to play this role and ensure that they are accorded the status they deserve.

Moulding the broader environment

Much of this book has been about moulding the broader environment to produce conditions in which entrepreneurial employees will flourish rather than seeing them leave the company in frustration only to start a highly successful business independently.

In summary, the cultural environment should be moulded by taking steps such as these:

- create an entrepreneurial culture that allows independent risk taking and mistakes to live side by side with efficient delivery of today's offerings
- create a learning organization that emphasizes organizational adaptability first and foremost, but including employee development
- capitalize on the metaphor of organizational evolution to ensure that

your business understands and makes use of the forces of variation and selection

- develop entrepreneurial leadership at the bottom of the firm so that young employees can see themselves as having real power to do great things
- encourage more self-confidence in employees by helping them to see themselves as valued suppliers of services or strategic partners instead of obedient, conforming subordinates
- help all employees to see themselves as being in their own business and to begin to see their own career management as a form of personal business development and diversification
- stimulate networking, teamwork and individual effort as all equally viable means for the development of entrepreneurial ventures
- cultivate a 'no one best way' mentality to foster open-ended, entrepreneurial learning

The balancing act

Despite the need to lead your organization towards a more entrepreneurial future, you still have to show leadership to the delivery side of the business. In part, this means not letting the culture become so one-sidedly entrepreneurial that other functions are derided by hot-shot entrepreneurs who think they own the world. Little is gained if you create a culture of risk takers who destroy the business through risks that are based on some technical wizard's delusions of grandeur. This would be to lose all of the gains made over recent years in cost reduction, efficiency and quality .

> **So the balance that needs to be struck involves upgrading the status of entrepreneurs, but salvaging the esteem of conventional managers so that a true balance of power is achieved.**

So the balance that needs to be struck involves upgrading the status of entrepreneurs, but salvaging the esteem of conventional managers so that a true balance of power is achieved. Recall the point that the healthiest of relationships will be those between relative equals.

The even more difficult balancing act is to create and maintain the right degree of variation and entrepreneurial freedom, on the one hand, and integration, on the other. Integration can no longer be forced by bureaucratic organization structures or policies that coerce business units to work closely with other parts of the organization. The leadership task here is to create a free-market atmosphere in which every player sees clearly the personal benefits of sharing expertise across divisional boundaries.

The real leadership challenge in this respect is to determine why cross-corporate integration is important in the more loosely connected enterprises which are now emerging and just what level of integration is necessary. The answer to this question will have to be to develop entrepreneurially on a trial and error basis. This ambiguity is in itself a major leadership challenge.

BIBLIOGRAPHY

Belbin, R Meredith (1981) *Management Teams: Why They Suceed or Fail*, Heinemann.

Belbin, R Meredith (1993) *Team Roles at Work*, Butterworth-Heinemann.

Bridges, William (1995) *Job Shift*, Nicholas Brealey Publishers.

Carroll, Paul (1994) *Big Blues: The Unmaking of IBM*, Weidenfeld & Nicholson.

'Corporate reputations' (1995) in *Fortune*, March 6.

Deal, Terrence and Kennedy, Allen (1982) *Corporate Cultures*, Addison-Wesley.

'The drought is over at 3M' (1994) in *Business Week*, November 7.

Drucker, Peter (1985) *Innovation and Entrepreneurship*, Harper & Row.

Garvin, David, (1993) 'Building a Learning Organization', *Harvard Business Review*, July-August 1993.

Hamel, Gary and Prahalad, C K (1994) *Competing for the Future*, Harvard Business School Press.

Kiely, Tom (1994) 'Innovation congregations', in *Technology Review*, April.

'Kissing off corporate America' (1995) in *Fortune*, February 20.

Miller, Danny (1990) *The Icarus Paradox*, HarperCollins.

Mitsch, Ronald A (1990) 'Three roads to innovation', in *The Journal of Business Strategy*, September/October.

Moss Kanter, Rosabeth (1989) *When Giants Learn to Dance*, Simon & Schuster, p. 32.

Peters, Tom (1987) *Thriving on Chaos*, Alfred A Knopf.

Pinchot, Gifford and Elizabeth (19XX) Intrapreneuring.

Pinchot, Gifford and Elizabeth (1993) *The End of Bureaucracy and the Rise of the Intelligent Organization*, Barrett-Koehler Publishers.

Prendergast, Candice (1993) 'A theory of "yes men" ', in *American Economic Review*, September.

Richman, Louis S (1994) 'The new worker elite', in *Fortune*, August 22.

Senge, Peter (1994) *The Fifth Discipline Fieldbook*, p. 48, Nicholas Brealey Publishing.

Stares, Mike (1993) 'Empowered freedom', in *Total Quality Management*, October, pp. 27–9.

Zaleznik, Abraham (1989) *The Managerial Mystique*, Harper & Row.

INDEX

"Management was by the rules, and by the numbers. That was then, this is now. The boundaries have gone. The game has changed. The old rule book is out of date. This is a handbook of answers for management."

– *Gary Hamel, Financial Times Handbook of Management*

the state of the art

1000 pages   1000 ideas

£50.00
Hardback

Dear Pitman Publishing Customer

IMPORTANT – Please Read This Now!

We are delighted to announce a special free service for all of our customers.

Simply complete this form and return it to the FREEPOST address overleaf to receive:

A Free Customer Newsletter

B Free Information Service

C Exclusive Customer Offers – which have included free software, videos and relevant products

D Opportunity to take part in product development sessions

E The chance for you to write about your own business experience and become one of our respected authors

Fill this in now and return it to us (no stamp needed in the UK) to join our customer information service.

Name: Position:

Company/Organisation:

Address (including postcode):

                                                Country:

Telephone: Fax:

Nature of business:

Title of book purchased:

ISBN (printed on back cover): $\boxed{0}$ $\boxed{2}$ $\boxed{7}$ $\boxed{3}$ $\boxed{\ }\boxed{\ }\boxed{\ }\boxed{\ }$ $\boxed{\ }$

Comments:

- |Fold Here Then Staple Once| -

We would be very grateful if you could answer these questions to help us with market research.

1 Where/How did you hear of this book?

☐ in a bookshop

☐ in a magazine/newspaper
(please state which):

☐ information through the post

☐ recommendation from a colleague

☐ other (please state which):

2 Where did you buy this book

☐ Direct from Pitman Publishing

☐ From a bookclub

☐ From a bookshop (state which)

3 Which newspaper(s)/magazine(s) do you read regularly?:

4 When buying a business book which factors influence you most?
(Please rank in order)

☐ recommendation from a colleague

☐ price

☐ content

☐ recommendation in a bookshop

☐ author

☐ publisher

☐ title

☐ other(s):

5 Is this book a

☐ personal purchase?

☐ company purchase?

6 Would you be prepared to spend a few minutes talking to our customer services staff to help with product development? YES/NO

The Business Publisher

Written for managers competing in today's tough business world, our books will give you a competitive edge by showing you how to:

● increase quality, efficiency and productivity throughout your organisation
● use both proven and innovative management techniques
● improve your management skills and those of your staff
● implement winning customer strategies

In short they provide concise, practical information that you can use every